At the Crossroads
of Fear and Freedom

This book is dedicated to my parents, *Thomas J. and Alberta Green*, who raised their five boys and four girls during a period of American history when racism was inflicted on blacks on a daily basis. Thanks and praise is due to them for pushing all nine of us to obtain an education so that their sons and daughters could give back to the less fortunate in our society.

Contents

Foreword

George White

Through our scientific and technological genius, we have made of this world—a neighborhood. Now, through our moral and ethical commitment, we must make of it—a brotherhood. We must all learn to live together as brothers or we will all perish together as fools.

—Martin Luther King Jr., February 11, 1965, at Michigan State University

W hen he arrived on the campus of Michigan State University (MSU) in 1965, Martin Luther King Jr. had two objectives. The primary objective was to give a speech to help MSU kick off a fundraising drive for an initiative called the Student Educational Project (STEP). He knew STEP would be significant because it would fund the first student-administered Civil Rights educational outreach program of its kind in the country. Dr. King realized that the funding for STEP would enable MSU students and faculty to go to Holly Springs, Mississippi, later that year to help provide instruction in the area's segregated schools and tutoring services to students at Rust College, a historically black school in that community.

However, Dr. King also had an unannounced objective. It was a goal that he had in mind when he visited college campuses previously—to find a scholar-activist who could help him build bridges to university communities.

MSU was already engaged. Faculty, staff, students, and residents from East Lansing and Lansing filled MSU Auditorium, and an overflow crowd packed into Fairchild Theater to hear an audio feed of the speech. Dr. King knew that Michigan State could be a platform for such activism because it was a globally conscious, solutions-oriented institution with visionary leadership. Dr. King made reference to that leadership during one portion of his speech, a segment on the need for voting rights for African Americans.

> We need new federal legislation that will bring into being federal registrars. This is asking for nothing new. The great president of this university who has served in such a magnificent manner with the Civil Rights Commission, joined with that commission in making a recommendation—years ago—that there should be federal registrars after studying patterns of discrimination all over the South.

He was referring to MSU president John Hannah, who had become the first chairman of the United States Commission on Civil Rights under President Dwight Eisenhower in 1958 and was serving in the same capacity in 1965 under President Lyndon Johnson.

President Hannah was in attendance. However, after spending time on MSU's campus with the organizer of his visit, Dr. King decided he had found the person who could help him achieve that second objective. He decided he wanted to recruit a specific member of President Hannah's faculty, a professor who could become the symbolic activist-scholar that he had sought.

Robert Lee Green, an educational psychology professor at Michigan State, had organized King's visit with the assistance of the Reverend John Duley, a campus pastor. King had first met Green immediately after he had given a speech in 1956 at a National Association for the Advancement of Colored People convention in San Francisco. Green had been working part time as a cab driver as he pursued a BA degree at what was then San Francisco State College.

Green, a native of Detroit, had kept in touch with Dr. King and his organization, the Southern Christian Leadership Conference (SCLC), as he obtained a BA and MA at San Francisco State and—later—his PhD, which he earned at Michigan State in 1963. Now, nine years after he had initially met King, Green was first in the receiving line after the Civil Rights leader completed his landmark address at MSU. Dr. King was receiving a standing ovation when he turned to the young MSU professor and said quietly, "Brother Green, you ought to join us in the struggle." Green told him that he was interested.

As they rode to the airport together, Dr. King told Green, "You ought to consider working with us in the South." Again, Green affirmed his interest. He decided to request a one-year leave of absence to help Dr. King and the SCLC. Subsequently, he made the request during a meeting with President Hannah, who approved the leave. At that point, Green, one of nine children raised by parents who had migrated to Detroit from Georgia to escape poverty and racial oppression, had embarked on a remarkable journey.

From grueling but successful fights for open housing and voting rights, to campaigns that desegregated America's schools and challenged South African apartheid, to his current role as a scholar in the battle for educational equity, Green has been an agent of change and an eyewitness to history.

There have been hundreds of books, movies, and theater productions on the Civil Rights movement, stories of brave activists who—on behalf of beleaguered African Americans—blazed a path to legal equality that also paved the way for social justice movements for women and Latinos. But none of these treatments have the remarkable perspective of Robert L. Green, a friend and colleague of Dr. King. Green served as education director for King's SCLC during a crucial period in Civil Rights history. Today, as a consultant for many of the nation's largest school districts, he continues to fight for social justice and educational equity. Those objectives motivate him now as he serves as an advisor to school districts in some of America's poorest communities, and the same goals prompted him to help lead the historic 1966 March against Fear that—despite attacks by southern state troopers and Ku Klux Klan threats—reached its destination and advanced the prospect of Civil Rights legislation.

It's a quest that began in 1963 when Green helped the Kennedy administration resolve a catastrophic education-related impasse in Virginia, and it has continued—nearly fifty years later—when he served in 2012 as one of the participants at an Obama administration summit on a current academic crisis.

It is commonly said that education is the new Civil Rights. However, *At the Crossroads of Fear and Freedom*—Green's story—helps us understand that educational equity has always been a central objective of the Civil Rights and human rights movement.

Working with Green, I was able to help craft the narrative for *At the Crossroads* because I have known him since my days as a freshman at Michigan State. As a journalist, historian, and education policy analyst, I have kept in touch with Green. I know his history, and I have had the privilege of working with him on education consulting projects in recent years.

At the Crossroads includes accounts of his current activism and untold stories of critical episodes in the fight for Civil Rights and educational equity. Consider these milestones.

Successful Challenges: Exclusion in Publishing and Housing

Shortly before forming a strategic partnership with a book publisher dedicated to including black characters in elementary schoolbooks in 1964, Green began his successful campaign to end housing discrimination in his university community of East Lansing.

The housing fight would engage Michigan governor George Romney, legendary MSU president John Hannah, a future U.S. senator named Carl Levin, and a Lansing native known as Malcolm X. It would generate intense news coverage, prompt hundreds of MSU students to protest on his behalf, and prompt others to make death threats that would eventually reach his five-year-old son, Vince. In 1964, Green and his wife, Lettie, would win this fight by becoming East Lansing home owners.

Battling Apartheid Abroad and at Home

Buoyed by his successful fight against housing discrimination, Green launched a campaign against discrimination in college athletics. He led an MSU research team that produced a 1972 report that documented the exploitation of black athletes and discrimination against African Americans seeking opportunities as game referees and coaches. The report generated hate mail from sports fans, criticism by sports reporters, and praise in a book by James Michener. The Big Ten athletic conference responded by agreeing to hire blacks to officiate all games in major sports and mandated the adoption of other recommendations made by the MSU team.

One year later, in 1973, Green became dean of MSU's newly formed College of Urban Development. (He is now an MSU dean and professor emeritus and a distinguished MSU alumnus.) The young Green developed a close friendship with tennis great Arthur Ashe, a man motivated by the same *global* sense of justice encouraged by Dr. King and Mohandas Gandhi—as an immigrant lawyer-activist in South Africa—developed the concept of nonviolent resistance before moving back to his native India.

Ashe would do anything he could to help end apartheid in South Africa. Realizing the power of the media and its interest in sports heroes, Ashe decided to play at a 1974 tennis tournament in South Africa. He would use the tournament as a platform to call for an end to apartheid and for the release of Nelson Mandela. Green and Andrew Jackson Young, tennis buffs who were also key players in a budding antiapartheid movement, decided to attend the tournament in support of those objectives.

Ashe, Young, and Green began to agitate against apartheid before they departed for the tournament. They told the white minority government's ministers that Ashe would not play in the tournament unless the stadium was integrated. The South African government agreed, setting the stage for the first integrated seating at a sporting event under apartheid.

When they arrived in South Africa, Young tried to see the jailed Nelson Mandela, but the government denied him access. During that momentous 1974 visit in South Africa, Green also visited the impoverished black township of Soweto and saw the seeds of rebellion among the country's black youth. (As a journalist, I closely covered the South African divestment movement that Green and others would help lead. I began to cover this campaign in the mid-1980s for the *Detroit Free Press* and subsequently followed the impact as a *Los Angeles Times* reporter until this economic pressure helped bring an end to apartheid in that country in 1994.)

A Key Role in School Desegregation

The 1975 Delaware school desegregation court case *Evans v. Buchanan* set a precedent. A group called the Positive Action Committee engaged in fearmongering to reverse the court desegregation ruling. However, the Supreme Court declined to hear the case, allowing the ruling to stand. Green was the court-ordered expert assigned to develop curricula and training to help the newly integrated schools. In September 1978, busing commenced. It was the first sustained, court-ordered desegregation across school district lines.

Creating Solutions on Education Policy Issues

The organizers of a 2012 national summit convened by the U.S. Department of Education and the Council of the Great City Schools, a coalition of the nation's largest public school districts, welcomed the "solutions brief" that Green, his son, education software engineer Kevin Green, and I created on how to help raise the academic achievement of black male students. That solutions brief and the briefs submitted by others at the summit are chapters in a 2012 Houghton Mifflin Harcourt anthology titled *A Call for Change.*

In *Expect the Most—Provide the Best* (Green et al. 2014)—a book produced by Robert Green, Kevin Green, University of Wisconsin professor Bradley Carl, and me—we advanced Green's research on the power of expectations in academic achievement. Again, he documents how expectations are a factor in effort and outcomes. If a teacher holds high expectations, that teacher will seek to have students achieve those standards. If students have high expectations, they will make an effort to meet those standards. Conversely, low expectations discourage effort and achievement.

In the final chapter of this book, on the future of education, he also makes the following recommendations:

- Many teachers and administrators must receive diversity training to overcome their fear or ignorance of black and Latino culture if they are to engage them and raise their expectations of students of color.
- Also, as schools work to improve the math and reading scores of students, they should eschew back-to-basics purity and also provide the arts education and culturally relevant studies that help many students achieve in all subjects.
- In addition, the U.S. Department of Education should follow up on its plans to encourage schools to adopt digital technology that will promote the kind of "personalized learning" that will produce graduates who can help America remain competitive in a rapidly changing global economy.

The Power of Connections and Convictions

Green has been successful partly because of friendships, partnerships, and associations with high-powered people who share his convictions. For example, he met long-time friend William vanden Heuvel, a former assistant to U.S. attorney general Robert F. Kennedy, when the two of them worked on a 1963 project designed to reopen a Virginia county's public schools, which local politicians closed to avoid compliance with a desegregation order. Later, Bill vanden Heuvel, a prominent lawyer and businessman, would serve as U.S. deputy ambassador to the United Nations and is now chairman emeritus of the Council of American Ambassadors.

In 1964, Green also met Dwight Follett and his son Robert Follett shortly after he learned that their company, Follett Corporation, had published the first elementary schoolbook that included black characters. Working with Follett, Green encouraged school districts to acquire integrated readers for primary school students. Later, Follett Corporation would publish two of Green's books—among them, the 1977 landmark *The Urban Challenge: Poverty and Race*. Green and Robert Follett, chairman of the company from 1979 to 1994, are still close friends.

In 1967, Green struck up another decades-long friendship when he met Allen Calvin, founder of the Behavioral Research Laboratories in Palo Alto. He also founded Pacific Graduate School of Psychology, now known as Palo Alto University. Calvin recruited Green to join the governing board of the Behavioral Research Laboratories, which produced research on programs to enhance classroom instruction in reading. As a result, Green became close associates of wealthy investors on that board—among them, investors William Hambrecht, Albie Wells, and the late Peter Bronfman, nephew of the founder of the Seagram Company, a Montreal-based giant that was, for many years, the largest distiller of alcoholic beverages in the world.

To be sure, Green has been one of the few black activists to have access to political leaders and captains of commerce as well as Civil Rights giants. The most prominent of the surviving King-era leaders, Andrew Jackson Young, is Green's best friend. I have the honor of knowing them both.

Green forges ahead as he enters his eighth decade of life. Now, he has left us a book that chronicles his life and legacy. When it comes to a crossroads of fear and freedom, the correct path should now be clearer because much of that trail has been blazed by Robert L. Green.

Acknowledgments

We are all indebted to countless individuals—including many students—who have struggled for social, educational, and political justice in the United States of America over generations. Some of these individuals gave their lives or put themselves in jeopardy for the right to vote, to desegregate public facilities, and to fight for equity in education. Many blacks suffered and died simply for refusing to bow to the tyranny of racism. This is a debt that is not yet fully paid. Some of their stories are told in this book.

We all need to continue working hard to make sure that this debt is fully repaid. As Martin Luther King Jr. said years ago, "I want young men and young women who are not alive today but who will come into this world with new privileges and new opportunities . . . to know and see that these new privileges and opportunities did not come without somebody suffering and sacrificing for them."

On a personal level, I have to give thanks for the sacrifices of my parents, Thomas and Alberta Green. They left a segregated, oppressive, and violent South to settle in Detroit, Michigan, providing my siblings and me a better opportunity to achieve. They overcame poverty, raising five boys and four girls during the Great Depression. Their influence has had a positive, profound, and lasting impact on my life. They taught me and my siblings the importance of high expectations and the need to keep education and spirituality foremost in our lives.

I also want to thank Lettie C. Green, my wife, a registered nurse and mother of our three sons, Vince, Kurt, and Kevin. She has always been a special team player. She supported me while I pursued my advanced degrees and helped tutor and mentor our sons while also helping members of our extended families. Her strong and unrelenting support brought joy to both sides of our families. I am very grateful for her support.

Support was also provided by Lettie's parents, especially her mother, Inez Clemons Cornelious, the best mother-in-law ever. She was always available to us during the one hundred years of her life. Lettie's dad, Willie Goree Clemons, and her stepfather, Fred Cornelious, were also supportive of our family.

To the members of my personal family—my sons Vince, Kurt, and Kevin—you have been all that a dad could expect. You are smart, educated, loyal, and care for "the least of these."

I am especially thankful for Martin Luther King Jr. He changed my life when in 1965, after giving a dramatic speech on the voting rights campaign and southern police brutality at Michigan State University (MSU), he asked me to work with him in the Civil Rights struggle. From Dr. King, I learned to eschew fear and to press for paths to freedom. He provided the opportunities and encouragement I needed to become a scholar-activist. My work with Dr. King also provided an opportunity for me to engage and work with Civil Rights icons such as Fannie Lou Hamer, Septima Clark, Hosea Williams, C. T. Vivian, James Bevel, John Lewis, Stanley Levinson, Harry Wachtel, and Andrew Young.

My relationship with him also enabled me to know and value his family. His wife, Coretta, was a close friend who inspired me with her grace and her dedication to social justice. I was happy to be "Uncle Bob" to the four children of Martin and Coretta—Martin, Dexter, Bernice, and the late Yolanda King.

Andrew Jackson Young has been more than a friend to me; he is a beloved brother. He helped usher me onto national and international stages and was a friend and colleague as we tried to—as Dr. King wanted—engage the world and make a difference.

MSU has a tradition of engaging the world to help create positive outcomes, and I want to acknowledge its leadership. I honor the legacy of John Hannah, who was president of MSU from 1941 to 1969. Under President Hannah, Michigan State became a global outreach leader in international development in Asia, Latin

America, and Africa. At home, he was committed to social justice and served as the first chairman of the U.S. Commission on Civil Rights under Presidents Eisenhower, Kennedy, and Johnson. He understood why I had to be an activist-scholar.

I want to thank Clifton R. Wharton Jr., president of MSU from 1970 to 1978, the first African American to lead a major predominantly white university. With the support of President Wharton and his wife, Dolores, I was able to create MSU's College of Urban Development, which sent scholars and student researchers into cities to identify ways to address educational inequities and poverty. Under his watch, Michigan State also dramatically diversified its student population.

MSU president Lou Anna Simon, elected by the university's trustees in 2004, has extended this legacy of leadership by overseeing a system that has further diversified senior management at the university. Under her stewardship, MSU has also begun to tell its story more effectively by, for example, creating a multimedia Spartans Will. 360 campaign that highlights the achievements of faculty and students at home and abroad. These experiences, President Simon has noted, involve "sharing knowledge, finding solutions that increase prosperity, and creating circumstances that enhance and protect the quality of life." President Simon has always been supportive of me and my work.

On a personal level, many friends have played a significant and positive role in my life. Joseph White, a scholar and colleague who encouraged me to pursue my doctorate in psychology. A leader as far back as our student days at San Francisco State College, Willie Brown is a great friend and sounding board. One of my former students at MSU, Bishop Ira Combs, is nationally known as a religious leader who serves the poor and provides support for my continuing struggle for social justice. Clark County School District board member Linda Young, who has supported me academically and professionally and has been a champion of my work on high expectations. In the greater Las Vegas community, Ken and Sarah Harris have been special friends and supporters. Our many Las Vegas friends, especially Charles and Chris Moody—a couple from my native Michigan who welcomed us to Las Vegas—and Michael and Deborah Walker, have been supportive personally and professionally. I also want to acknowledge Myrtle Davis and her husband, the late Louis Davis—my roommate in the military and civilian life before we served as best man at each other's weddings—for their friendship. In addition, I want to express my appreciation for the work of former U.S. representative Steven Horsford and his wife, Sonya, an educator and author. The Horsfords have been dedicated to helping those who cannot help themselves.

I am extremely grateful to members of both sides of our family. I take special note of my sister, Lethia, who gave me books to read early in my life. I learned about racism and segregation by reading the works of Langston Hughes and Richard Wright. The books she encouraged me to read exposed me to social injustice long before I traveled to the South or experienced racism as a youngster in the North. Lethia helped instill a love of reading that put me on a path to teaching others.

Also, the late Havious V. Green, my eldest brother, helped me more fully appreciate the value of hard work and educational excellence. In addition, I received unconditional support from my other deceased brothers and sisters—Evelyn, Thomas, John—and from my surviving siblings, Naomi, Bertha, and Richard.

I also want to thank relatives and in-laws of my wife, Lettie, the following among them: Lettie's sister Catherine and her husband, the late Luther Elarms, were very special to us in our early lives, caring for our sons and providing me employment in Luther's janitorial business. Denise Elarms is a caring person who has been like a daughter to Lettie and me. Willie Mae Hewitt, Lettie's sister, and her late husband, Amos, were very supportive and sent their two sons—Amos and Tony—to MSU. Amos Lathan Hewitt and Keith Way, nephews who are like sons to me, have helped both sides of the families remain cohesive and close. My scholarly and spiritual nieces, June Green Rivers and LaClaire Green Bouknight, helped me obtain important facts and details on Green family history.

Moreover, I want to acknowledge the support and assistance of many educators, scholars, and administrators who have worked with me on reports, books, or efforts to improve public schools or the prospects of university job candidates. The following are among them: MSU professor John Schweitzer and his wife, Elizabeth; Mary Ellen Furseth, my former administrative assistant; MSU professor Ron Hall; MSU administrator Theodore (Terry) Curry II; MSU research specialist Ted Ransaw; Bradley Carl at the University of Wisconsin; education consultant Caesar Mickens; former Memphis mayor Willie W. Herenton, who has been there for me since his days as a school district superintendent; and Dr. Brenda White, an outstanding graduate student of mine who later became an associate dean of students at Harvard University and who admitted and mentored many African American and other minority students.

In addition, I want to thank those who helped me with this book and with previous publications.

The work of the late Eugenia Zerbinos must be acknowledged. She was my editor and researcher for more than twenty-five years. She helped me and my MSU research teams document racial and gender inequities in numerous books, monographs, and articles. Her work was highly respected by all of my team members.

I am also grateful to Yvonne Morris, who has worked for me as a researcher and computer specialist. She spent many hours working with me during the preparation of this manuscript. Her master's degree in multicultural education was an asset to me in reflecting on equity issues in education.

A special thanks to my editor, George White, whom I have known since he was a freshman student at MSU. I've watched over the years as he used his education to become a prize-winning journalist, author, editor, and education policy analyst. In recent years, he has worked with me as an education consultant for school districts. George helped me develop the manuscript's narrative, a framing that makes *At the Crossroads* relevant nationally and internationally. Unlike other editors of memoirs, George not only knows me and my history, he has also been a participant in some of the important events in this story. Thanks George!

CHAPTER ONE

Legacy and Leadership

was transfixed by the photos on my personal computer, images that were being assembled for an update to my website. Each image was a window to a different point in the past—fifty-five years of strife, danger, disappointments, and successes. There they were in front of me: images of more than five decades of events that helped change America.

There has been positive change in this nation—the enactment of Civil Rights laws, for example—because America has, at times, chosen the correct path. However, the country has regressed in some ways by taking bad paths, choices that could lead to disaster if not addressed.

Fear can prompt individuals or societies to make bad choices such as limiting the liberties of racial and ethnic minorities. It requires courage to overcome injustices. For example, Martin Luther King Jr. helped this country take a path that ended statutory racism because he was fearless.

I looked at my computer. There was the photo of me with Dr. King, firebrand activist Stokely Carmichael, and Civil Rights leader Floyd McKissick with our arms linked to each other at the elbows in a nonviolent resistance circle as Mississippi State troopers tried to push us off the highway during a protest walk called the March against Fear. There was also the photo of young Civil Rights activist Willie

Ricks, a white conductor, and me on a runaway train. Willie and I had jumped on the moving train to stop it because it was headed for hundreds of Civil Rights protestors crossing the railroad track.

Some of the images were letters, among them a 1966 letter from a top executive at the Texaco oil company responding to my letter about an aborted assassination attempt against one of the most important men in America. I actually witnessed this incident, which has never before been disclosed to the public.

Some of the images do not provide the context of relationships. For example, there's an image of me with my close friend Andrew Young and the late tennis great Arthur Ashe dressed for a match on a court. The three of us would go to South Africa in 1974, successfully challenge one apartheid rule, and also witness a budding black student rebellion that would help end that insidious system. Also, there were photos of Joseph McMillan and Thomas Gunnings, two of my fellow faculty members at Michigan State University (MSU). However, those images could not display work the three of us did to help end racial bias in college sports.

Moreover, there were photos of me with icons such as Coretta Scott King and Robert F. Kennedy and images of the covers of some of my books. Some of the books explore the impact of racism and poverty on African Americans, and others document the connection between high expectations and academic achievement.

In addition, there was the 2012 photo of basketball champion and entrepreneur Earvin "Magic" Johnson, one of my former students, discussing education issues with me at a Las Vegas fundraiser.

Finally, there was the photo of me, my wife Lettie, my son Kevin, and my former student and current consulting associate George White standing in front of the impressive Martin Luther King, Jr. Memorial in Washington, DC. Those images from the King Memorial triggered a stream of memories.

It had taken us one year to make the trip from Las Vegas to Washington, DC. When my wife, Lettie, and I landed at Dulles Airport on a bright, clear morning on Sunday, August 26, 2012, we had an official greeting party of two—my adult son Kevin Green, a brilliant computer vision engineer who had won awards as an educator, and George White, a prize-winning journalist and education policy analyst. If we had made the trip one year earlier, as originally scheduled, the greeting party would have been a *bit* larger and would have included old friends and colleagues such as Ambassador Andrew Young, Congressman John Lewis, and a man and woman who knew me as "Uncle Bob"—Martin Luther King III and Bernice King, one son and one daughter of Dr. Martin Luther King Jr. and Coretta Scott King.

At a 1967 press conference in Chicago, Martin Luther King Jr., Bernard Lee, and Robert L. Green announce the SCLC's Summer Reading Project.

We were all scheduled to meet for the official dedication of the King Memorial on August 28, 2011. The organizers of the event had expected two hundred fifty thousand people. They had set out thirty thousand folding chairs for dignitaries, and President Barack Obama was planning to attend and speak. However, when Hurricane Irene threatened to bear down on the nation's capital, she blew away plans for a massive celebration. Prudently, the organizers cancelled the August 28 event, fearing that the site of a joyous dedication would be destroyed. That dedication was rescheduled and downsized, and we could not attend.

Ironically, I was now in the District of Columbia for another late August event— an August 27, 2012, national summit on black male academic achievement. At the behest of President Obama, the forum was to be convened by the U.S. Department of Education and the Council of the Great City Schools (CGCS), a coalition of the nation's largest public school districts. The council had asked a dozen scholars, including me, to produce "solutions briefs" to the academic challenges facing black males. George and Kevin had helped me prepare a report, dubbed "The Expectations Factor in Black Male Achievement: A Foundation for Educational Equity." I would be among the scholars serving as panel speakers at the event.

Like the King Memorial dedication, the summit had also been scheduled and postponed. It was set for early summer but was rescheduled for August 27 despite the protests of some invited scholars who wanted yet another postponement for a date after the November election. They were concerned about Hurricane Political Winds. Specifically, they feared that some conservative Republicans, in a bid to help blow away Obama's reelection plans, might attack his administration for launching an education initiative to help African American youth.

The organizers did *not* postpone this gathering because they were concerned that if they didn't do more to narrow the historic academic achievement gap between blacks and whites—a divide linked to a legacy of slavery, racism, and failed education policies—there would be fewer opportunities for many members of a new generation of African Americans.

I supported the decision to proceed with the August 27 summit. After all, as Dr. King's education director at the Southern Christian Leadership Conference (SCLC), I had learned that it was necessary to push ahead for social justice and educational equity when standing at the crossroads of fear and freedom. After all, Dr. King did not act as an apologist or guardian for well-meaning liberal politicians; he organized grassroots movements that pushed the powerful for change.

Lettie and I were tired after the red-eye flight from Las Vegas to DC, but my son Kevin and my associate George White were fresh and energetic. Kevin and George urged us to go directly to the King Memorial, which we had not seen, instead of our hotel. They mentioned the rain of the previous day and possibility of rain on that Sunday, the day before the summit. We relented and agreed to proceed to the memorial.

My immediate reaction to our decision was relief. As we neared the memorial, I felt a surge of energy and anticipation. Kevin, who was driving, dropped us off at the entrance to the memorial and parked his car. Walking through the entrance of the memorial, Lettie, George, and I could see the massive, flat back of the monument. As we moved toward the granite structure to circumnavigate it on the right, I stopped to inspect the inscription near the base on that side. It read: "Out of the Mountain of Despair, A Stone of Hope." I could feel adrenaline rising from my stomach through my chest to my head as we rounded to view the front of the monument. Rising thirty feet above us was an image of Martin Luther King Jr.—a

At the SCLC's staff dinner meeting in Miami, Florida at Eden Roc Hotel (1966): (*front row*) Hosea and Juanita Williams, Bob and Lettie Green, Otis and Edwina Moss; (*back row*) Lillie Hunter, Coretta Scott King, Martin Luther King Jr., Fred Shuttlesworth, Juanita and Ralph Abernathy, Clarence Jones, Bernard Lee, Andrew Young, and Dora McDonald.

man I knew and had worked for—in white granite emerging from a stone facade, arms crossed, looking forward with a resolute expression.

I glanced to my right and left and could see the slate-colored walls behind the statue angling right and left with inscriptions of Dr. King's quotes. I considered the irony that a man who had drawn so much criticism during his last year of life was now an officially recognized giant with a memorial comparable to those devoted to Jefferson, Washington, and Lincoln. "This is first class," I said to myself, realizing—moments later—that I had made that comment out loud.

It was 8:30 A.M., and there were only about a dozen tourists at the site, which enabled us to view the full scene of the memorial setting as it might have looked at an exclusive private unveiling. Behind us was a glistening Potomac, which separated the King Memorial site from the distant but visible dome of the Jefferson Memorial. Facing King's statue, I could see the imposing obelisk known as the Washington Monument hovering from a shorter distance to the right. "First class," I thought. "America has finally valued one of its greatest heroes."

My next thought related to what America had not yet recognized about the legacy of Martin Luther King Jr.—the end of America's Jim Crow education system. King had created an education director post for SCLC and had asked me to serve in that position because he understood the power of education. He knew that it could be harnessed to empower a traumatized black population and inform and liberate whites who were either burdened by guilt or burning with hate and resentment born of ignorance.

Many things flashed in my mind. I knew and understood what most Americans still don't know: that the earliest and the most prominent of Civil Rights martyrs died for equal education opportunities—King and earlier activists among them. "Yes," I thought, "here I am in Washington, DC, for a national conference on education, and many people still don't understand that Dr. King believed that education was a major key to social justice."

I recalled when I met Dr. King. A native of Detroit, I had been drafted and began to serve in January 1954 as a corpsman assigned to a psychiatric ward at the army hospital at the Presidio in San Francisco. I worked nights and pursued my undergraduate studies at San Francisco State College during the day. I completed my two-year army commitment in January 1956 and eventually took a part-time job as a guard at the San Quentin State Prison and later as a Yellow Cab driver on the night shift as I continued my education.

My first application cabbie position was rejected—as were the applications of my schoolmate friends. We filed a complaint with the local National Association for the Advancement of Colored People (NAACP) chapter. Realizing that we were top-notch college students, the chapter launched a successful job discrimination boycott. Subsequently, my two friends and I became the first blacks hired as drivers by Yellow Cab in San Francisco. (The other two are Willie Brown, who later became speaker of the California House of Representatives and mayor of San Francisco, and Louis Davis, my college and army roommate, who later became a widely respected physician.)

On June 27, 1956, I learned that Dr. King would be speaking that night at the NAACP national convention at the San Francisco Civic Auditorium. King had generated national and international attention for his leadership of the Montgomery Bus Boycott, which had ended successfully earlier that year. I was an admirer. I drove the cab to the conference site and worked my way in to hear him speak. When he completed his address, I waited patiently among the throng of other admirers, drew up close to him, and extended my hand. "I'm Robert L. Green," I said. "I want to get to know you." His face—then a bit thinner than the 1960s dauber immortalized in the statue—rounded into a smile. "Pleased to meet you, Brother Green," he said.

At that time, there was skepticism about whether a young, unheralded southern minister could lead a national movement for Civil Rights. During that convention, then NAACP counsel Thurgood Marshall called King "a boy on a man's errand." The great African American leader and scholar W. E. B. Du Bois questioned the efficacy of nonviolent resistance. He said, "If passive resistance could conquer racial hatred . . . Gandhi and Negroes like King would have shown the world how to conquer war itself."

However, I was a true believer in Dr. King. Two months later, I learned that he would be speaking in Berkeley at a brunch gathering of Alpha Phi Alpha, a black fraternity. (We were both members of that fraternity.) I attended and reintroduced myself. He remembered me. "Good to see you again," he said, beaming.

I continued to follow King—now from a distance—by reading newspaper accounts about his efforts to end discrimination. During my undergraduate and MA studies at San Francisco State and later, during my PhD studies at MSU, I was among thousands who sent checks to support the SCLC.

These were formative but life-affirming years. I had met my future wife, Lettie Clement, a nursing student, in the fall of 1954. She was smart, petite, and attractive. She was the only woman I ever dated. We were married August 10, 1956. Eleven months later, we had our first child, Vince, who is now an attorney in Lansing, Michigan.

I also met people who would become lifelong friends during this period—among them, Willie Brown, who was also a San Francisco State student. At that time, Willie was a gregarious man who seemed to know everyone. The same can be said of Mayor Brown today.

I obtained a BA in psychology in 1958. My second son, Kurt, was born in 1959 as I was completing my MA studies in school psychology at San Francisco State College. After completing my MA in 1960, I applied for psychologist positions at the Oakland, San Francisco, Los Angeles, and San Diego public school districts. In Los Angeles and San Diego, the human resources department representatives, impressed with my credentials, expressed great interest in my candidacy during telephone conversations. However, when I arrived in person for an interview for both district jobs, I was told that the supervisor who was to interview me was not available.

When I applied for the school psychologist position in San Francisco, I was told that the job was filled, though the position was still posted. The most disappointing was my experience as an applicant for the position in Oakland. I had served as an education psychologist intern in the Oakland School District during my MA studies and was given a good rating by my supervisor. For that reason, I thought the Oakland School District would give me serious consideration. However, my former supervisor told me that the position was filled. I knew it wasn't true because the district later offered the job to someone I knew, and she did not take the job. In addition, a district employee later told me that my former supervisor had been overheard saying that it "wasn't time" for a black school psychologist, contending that white parents would object.

Many blacks who had also been victims of discrimination lowered their sights and settled for jobs for which they were overqualified. However, I had been inspired by Dr. King and did not lower my goals. I was determined to overcome the impact of discrimination on me and my family. I decided to pursue a PhD and was accepted as a doctoral student in educational psychology at Michigan State. With my wife and two sons in a car—and a trailer in tow—I drove from California toward Michigan. Although there was no official segregation in the plains and mountain states, we had trouble getting motel rooms. Exhausted, we stopped at a motel in Montana one night. When I asked the manager for a room, he said, "No." He then looked at my family. "Where you going?" he asked. "I'm driving back to Michigan to go to school," I said, hoping he would at least respect my dedication to education. He said, "You're going to school, and you're a colored boy with two kids. . . . I'll give you a room."

I pursued my PhD studies diligently, but I kept contact with Dr. King and his team advisors by writing letters. I obtained my doctorate in educational psychology in December 1962, and Michigan State hired me in January 1963 as an assistant professor in the College of Education.

At that time, whites in the South tried to deny all blacks the right to vote regardless of their education level; but officially, whites claimed they were disqualifying only those who could not read and write. I didn't know it at the time, but King was beginning to realize that he needed a scholar to provide instruction in reading and writing to semiliterate blacks to enable them to pass prevoting literacy tests. He also wanted a professor who could help him build bridges to other scholars who might be able to help the Civil Rights campaign.

Meanwhile, I was thinking about ways I could help Dr. King. The Student Nonviolent Coordinating Committee had been formed in 1960 with support from

The Green family, photographed in Detroit in 1942: (*front row*) Bertha, Grandma Emma, Alberta, Thomas, Evelyn, Richard, and Robert Lee; (*back row*) Naomi, Lethia, Havious, Thomas Jr., and John.

the SCLC, and I wanted to help the SCLC recruit more college student volunteers for the Civil Rights crusade. To generate interest, I asked Dr. King to deliver an address at MSU. He accepted.

On February 11, 1965, more than 4,500 MSU students and community residents attended a lecture by Dr. King. It was standing room only in the auditorium, with an overflow crowd packed into another site with an audio feed. King's appearance kicked off fundraising for the Student Educational Project (STEP), the first student-managed educational outreach program of its kind in the country. Under STEP, student and faculty volunteers went to Mississippi and helped expand education programs at Rust College, a historically black institution in Holly Springs. STEP was organized by students and the Reverend John Duley, a campus minister.

After the speech, I went on stage to join Dr. King. He was receiving a standing ovation, when he said to me, "Brother Green, you ought to join us in the struggle." I told him I was interested.

As I rode with Dr. King to the airport, he said, "You ought to consider working with us in the South."

I immediately developed a plan. I would request a one-year leave of absence to help him and the SCLC. Subsequently, I met with MSU president John Hannah and requested a one-year leave, to which President Hannah agreed. This did not surprise me because Hannah was president of the U.S. Commission on Civil Rights at the time, and he had received a written request from Dr. King.

However, a short time after he granted the leave, Hannah and I were both in attendance at a campus speech delivered by Roy Wilkins, national chairman of the NAACP. Hannah and Wilkins were on stage, and I sat in the front row. When Wilkins completed his address, President Hannah leaned over and asked me to join them on stage. Hannah introduced us, telling Wilkins that I was a young professor at MSU who would be taking a leave to work for Dr. King.

Wilkins gave me a serious but friendly look. He said, "You need to stay here—not work for Dr. King. Whites and blacks need role models like you." I listened politely, but I had made up my mind. I would join Dr. King and help him encourage blacks in the South to resist their fears and challenge an oppressive system.

I joined the SCLC in September 1965. Dr. King was very proud to have me on his team. When introducing me to friends, associates, and supporters, he would say, "Robert L. Green is the only PhD who has left a university to come to work for me."

King understood the power of education and knew that it could be harnessed to empower a population traumatized by racism. "Activism must be combined with education," Dr. King said, signaling the importance of my involvement. It was a phrase he would frequently invoke.

I did much more than help the SCLC develop initiatives to improve education. I helped the organization seek redress for attacks and discrimination. During my year with the SCLC, I would counsel terrified blacks who were forced off of their property by armed whites. Once a month, I would go to the Penn Community in Frogmore, South Carolina—with a small staff that included SCLC veterans Septima Clark, Dorothy Cotton, James Orange, Bernice Robinson, and Ben Mack—to encourage fearful African Americans to register to vote.

As a staff, we also had to remain undaunted despite intensive monitoring activities by the U.S. Justice Department and the Federal Bureau of Investigation (FBI). On one occasion, my secretary, Marilyn Hayes, called the SCLC office from her rented room. When the line connected, she could hear the faint voices of men on a crossed line discussing SCLC phone conversations.

Our government monitors certainly knew that many blacks came to our Atlanta office to see Dr. King about incidents of discrimination because the senior staff would refer them to me, and I would encourage them to file complaints with U.S. Justice Department. When Dr. King was traveling or unavailable, I also helped black farmers in Alabama and Mississippi who had their land illegally seized under schemes by southern tax assessors who would redraw property lines.

However, Dr. King, a taskmaster, also pushed me to help educators at poor black rural schools and to work on proposals for federal support for education initiatives for underfinanced African American institutions in the South's segregated school systems.

As an educator, I knew about his focus on the value of learning. I knew that he had written passionately about education as early as his teenage years and wrote and spoke about the lack of educational equity for blacks throughout his life. For example, as a young student at Morehouse College in 1947, King made it clear that education was the key to creating a wiser, more compassionate society. In "The Purpose of Education," a column in the student newspaper, he wrote:

> At this point, I often wonder whether or not education is fulfilling its purpose. A great majority of the so-called educated people do not think logically and scientifically. Even the press, the classroom, the platform, and the pulpit in many instances do not give us objective and unbiased truths. To save man from the morass of propaganda, in my opinion, is one of the chief aims of education. Education must enable one to sift and weigh evidence, to discern the true from the false, the real from the unreal, and the facts from the fiction.

As a Civil Rights leader, he demonstrated his devotion to learning by creating the Citizenship Education Program (CEP), and he later appointed me to head the CEP in September 1965. The CEP newsletter edition that announced my appointment noted that I had traveled the South as a consultant for President Johnson's Task Force on the War on Poverty in 1964 and included a quote from me:

> I became convinced after what I saw ... that the Southern educational system was systematically and deliberately set up to ensure that Negroes would be forever relegated to second [class] citizenship. By working with the Citizenship Education

Program, we can . . . alert Negroes to what is available—then to what they don't
have and to what they should have. (Green 1965)

Dr. King had expressed similar sentiments the previous year on March 14,
1964, when he accepted the John Dewey Award from the United Federation of
Teachers:

> The walling off of Negroes from equal education is part of the historical design to
> submerge him in second-class status. Therefore as Negroes have struggled to be
> free they have had to fight for the opportunity for a decent education. . . .
>
> The richest nation on Earth has never allocated enough resources to build
> sufficient schools, to compensate adequately its teachers, and to surround them
> with the prestige our work justifies. We squander funds . . . on the overabundance
> of overkill armament, but we pauperize education.

Dr. King believed blacks and whites could address inequities if they could overcome
fear. He said, "People fail to get along because they fear each other; they fear each
other because they don't know each other; they don't know each other because
they have not communicated with each other."

He frequently encouraged African Americans by calling for courage in the face
of violence. From the pulpit of Ebenezer Baptist Church in Atlanta, I heard him
tell the congregation, "Do not be afraid." In one famous speech, he said, "We must
build dikes of courage to hold back the flood of fear" (King 2003, 118).

Dr. King also demonstrated political courage. I was reminded of that when I
walked toward one of the slate-colored panels of the wall of quotations behind the
statue. I recognized it as a statement he made on Christmas Eve in Atlanta in 1967.

> If we are to have peace on earth, our loyalties must become ecumenical rather
> than sectional. Our loyalties must transcend our race, our tribe, our class, and our
> nation; and this means we must develop a world perspective.

Reading that inscription took me back to April 4, 1967, when King, Andrew
Young, Civil Rights strategist Bayard Rustin, fundraiser Harry Wachtel, and I met
at Harry's office in New York City to discuss a speech that Dr. King was planning
to deliver that night at New York's Riverside Church. It was a historic speech that
would include a condemnation of the Vietnam War.

University of Maryland (Baltimore County) president Freeman Hrabowski (*center*) speaks at the 2012 national summit on black male education. President Obama appointed him chairman of a national commission on African American male achievement. As a boy, President Hrabowski was jailed for participating in Civil Rights protests.

It was a dangerous speech that would turn the powerful against King, Rustin told us. He tried to discourage Dr. King from making that address. "If you give that speech," Rustin warned, "you will make an enemy of LBJ [President Johnson] and you will never get into the White House again." The rest of us—knowing it would be dangerous—countered his advice. "Give the speech," said Wachtel. "Give it," said Andy. "Give it," I said.

When Dr. King gave his famous Riverside Church speech, I attended. There were so many people in the audience that I was forced to take a seat on the stage near the podium.

Dr. King also demonstrated bravery in the face of physical violence. His exhibitions of courage are legion, but still standing near the wall of quotations, I recalled an incident that had never been publicly disclosed.

It was the fall of 1966. I had officially finished my one-year, full-time stint with the SCLC and had returned to Michigan State. However, responding to a request from Dr. King, I traveled to Grenada, Mississippi—a hotbed of racial violence—to help the SCLC oversee the opening of an elementary school that was being integrated for the first time. Joan Baez, the folk singer, was among those who had traveled to Grenada to monitor the situation to ensure there was no violence.

On the first day of school after Labor Day, a group of us were motoring down a Grenada street. Coretta Scott King's cousin, T. Randall Osburn, was driving, and Dr. King was in the passenger-side front seat. King's aide, the Rev. Bernard Lee, Andrew Young, and I were in the back seat.

Our car stopped at a traffic light next to a Texaco gas station. A station employee, a middle-aged white man with a Texaco shirt, was pumping gas. He noticed us and began to stride quickly and deliberately toward the car. As he moved closer, I could see an angry look on his face. Suddenly, he pulled a pistol from his pocket. Before we could respond, he planted the pistol on Dr. King's temple. "Martin Luther King!" he shouted. "I will blow your brains out!"

This is the kind of racial terror that blacks had long experienced in the South. My father, Thomas J. Green, told me stories about racial terror when I was well into my adult years. My dad, who grew up in Jones County, Georgia, was fourteen years old when a close boyhood friend did not move quickly enough out of the path of a white man. A short time later, his friend was lynched. My father was sad and traumatized. However, in relating the event, he described the events in calm, measured tones.

A decade later—after my father had moved to Detroit—he returned to Jones County, Georgia, to see relatives. He was beckoned into a general store by the owner, Jim Finney, who had known my father for many years. Inside were three other men. As the store owner talked to my father, a stream of men—about thirty in all—sauntered into the store. Suddenly, one of them locked the door.

They all stared at my father as the store owner began to ask him a series of questions about his attitudes and beliefs—now that he was living in the North. My father was back in the South and knew the responses that the men expected.

"How do you refer to white people up North?" he asked.

"I call them Mr. and Mrs.—just as I was trained to do here," my father responded.

"Where do you sit when you get on a streetcar?"

"I always sit in the back."

"Do you ever speak to white women?"

"No. I do not."

The store owner then turned to the throng of men and said, "See boys—I told you Tom was OK. Now, get out of my store."

As the men left, my father noticed that two of them had ropes. It was then that

Lettie Green's parents, Inez and Willie Goree Clemens, in San Francisco, California.

he realized that he would have been lynched if he had not answered "correctly." I learned about this era of terror from my father as an adult. When I was a child, he helped my siblings and me understand the value of education. My father, who had to leave school after the fourth grade to help with the sharecropping work, talked incessantly about the importance of education.

My father helped me understand the value of education, and Dr. King—my second mentor—helped prepare me for a lifelong fight for educational opportunity for all. I recalled that they had put me on a path that helped me understand the connection between fear and the fight for Civil Rights and fear and the fight for educational equity. Many kids from low-income families have a fear of failure. They are afraid to strive upwardly because they do not believe they can excel, and they avoid disappointment by foregoing the effort.

Standing at the memorial, I felt grateful. "Thank you Dr. King, Dad, and my family," I thought, "for all you've done for me."

As we prepared to leave the memorial, my thoughts turned to the summit on black male academic achievement, the forum to be convened the following day by the CGCS and Barack Obama's Department of Education. I thought about Obama's campaign theme of "change" and noted—to myself—that there would be no President Obama if not for King. The thought resonated because Obama had, like Dr. King, talked frequently about the importance of education.

I was still thinking of Dr. King as about three hundred other scholars and school district leaders and I gathered in the U.S. Department of Education auditorium for the summit on black male education. While Dr. King had helped us close the social justice gap, we had not made much progress on his other goal—closing the education achievement gap.

Lettie, George White, and my son Kevin also attended the summit. George, Kevin, and I had documented the most recent black and white achievement disparities in our solutions brief for the summit, a report that became a chapter in an anthology published by Houghton Mifflin Harcourt. The report also made the connections between the lack of education, earning power, and incarceration. However, the bulk of the report focused on how high expectations can—and have—empowered black students to excel.

> Effective teachers not only have high expectations, but also set clear standards of attainable academic and behavioral performance and hold students to them. Students must know precisely what is expected of them and why it is expected and believe they can meet those expectations. As much as possible, they should be empowered and have played a part in setting those standards. (Council of the Great City Schools 2012, 32)

I had authored a number of books on expectations. Our solutions-focused summit report cited numerous examples of schools that had raised academic achievement by raising their standards. I explained the importance of expectations on stage as a member of a summit panel. Other scholars explored other learning issues during subsequent panels—among them, a session moderated by Arne Duncan, the U.S. secretary of education.

As the summit was coming to an end, most in the room anticipated the closing remarks by Freeman Hrabowski, president of the University of Maryland–Baltimore County. Obama had recently appointed him chair of the President's Advisory Commission on Educational Excellence for African Americans, a group that would rally support for some of the summit's recommendations. I had known Hrabowski, who is black, for several years. However, when he began to speak, I was shocked by his recounting of a seminal episode during his youth.

Hrabowski bounced on the stage, a very youthful looking man in his early sixties, a slight gloss of sweat on his face. After publicly greeting the panelists who were still on the stage from the preceding session, he launched into his address. "It was," he said, "fifty years ago that I was entering the ninth grade in Birmingham, Alabama. . . . It never occurred to me [then] that I would be in jail by the end of that year. I had no idea I would have a chance to listen to Dr. King in my church on a Wednesday night and hear him say that the country needs to understand that even children know the difference between right and wrong—that children need to be empowered to show that they want the best education possible." Referencing those comments, Hrabowski noted that he and other children had been arrested for participating in a Civil Rights protest in Birmingham, Alabama.

> The point of that story is this. I spent . . . five days in jail focused on a critical question: What do we have to do to make sure that we get a good education, so that I would never again have to get hand-me-down books . . . and no longer think that my school wasn't as good [as other] schools. . . . It never occurred to me [at that time] that I would become president of a predominantly white university with kids from more than 150 countries . . . and that we would have a wonderful man as the president of the United States who looks like me; but that a third of black children would be unable to read . . . that would not have occurred to me.

Hrabowski said the key to improving education was evaluating methods that appear to work and documenting what actually works.

> What we have found, and it has been said here today—is when you empower children . . . when you show them love and also have the high expectations, you begin to change the culture of the environment in which they find themselves.
>
> . . . Why do I still have hope? I go back to 1963. I go back to sitting in that jail. I remember Dr. King coming to that place . . . where people wanted to get out of jail. He said: "What you do this day will have an impact on generations unborn."

I was stunned and astounded. Immediately, memories of the period that Hrabowski referenced flooded back to me. I recalled one man especially—James Bevel, formerly the SCLC's director of direct action and director of nonviolent education. In 1963, after the SCLC agreed to assist one of its founders, the Reverend Fred Shuttlesworth, and other Civil Rights activists in Birmingham, Alabama, James Bevel came up with the idea of using children in the campaign.

Bevel spent weeks strategizing, organizing, and educating Birmingham's elementary and high school students in the philosophy and techniques of nonviolent protest. He then directed them to meet at and march from Birmingham's 16th Street Baptist Church to Birmingham's City Hall to talk to its mayor about segregation in the city. This action culminated in international public outrage over the police department's use of fire hoses and dogs to stop the children and the adult protesters from marching to city hall. Some adult protesters were bitten. Adults and children were arrested.

This action in Birmingham was called the Children's Campaign. The SCLC had recruited teenage students to participate in street protests. However, enthusiastic children who were younger joined in despite the efforts of SCLC organizers. Broadcast TV news images of the police response shocked much of the nation.

During the crusade, President Kennedy called Dr. King and asked him to stop involving children in the campaign. However, the SCLC decided to expand the campaign. Bevel began to ask the students to prepare to take to the highways on a march to Washington to question Kennedy about correcting the problem of racial oppression and legalized segregation in America. Bevel argued that it was better that the kids spend a short time in jail instead of spending the rest of their lives in a racial prison.

The Kennedy administration, hearing of this plan, asked the SCLC's leaders what they would want to see in a comprehensive Civil Rights bill. A draft of legislation was then composed with SCLC input, which made a children's march to Washington unnecessary. Meanwhile, Harry Belafonte, the singer-actor and activist, who was always working behind the scenes on behalf of Dr. King, was frantically raising funds to bail out the children and adult protesters arrested during the Birmingham campaign.

I know some of the leaders of the Children's Campaign—the late James Orange, the late Leon Hall, and Dorothy Tillman among them. At the time of the campaign, they were Birmingham high school students. Just one month after the Children's Campaign ended, I was actually in the midst of another student Civil Rights uprising—this one in Farmville, Virginia.

When Freeman Hrabowski ended his address, many of the scholars and education leaders surged to the stage to talk to the new Obama appointee. I greeted him and reintroduced him to my son Kevin. They had met before because I had urged Kevin to seek a teaching post under Hrabowski. I also introduced him to George. Immediately after the introduction, George asked me to explain the speech—Hrabowski's references to being jailed during King's Birmingham campaign.

I did not respond immediately. My mind's eye began to see another related image from the past. This one involved the image of a six-year-old girl in handcuffs in a photograph in Dr. King's book *Why We Can't Wait*. The girl was also a veteran of the Children's Campaign in Alabama.

It was then that I also recalled that Andrew Young once said, "A child shall lead them."

Again, my thoughts drifted to my work in Farmville, Virginia, in the summer of 1963. Farmville's Children's Campaign is not as well known, but at the time it would also have a dramatic impact on the nation. It was in Virginia half a century ago, while working with teenage activists to address an egregious educational injustice, that I witnessed a chilling training session designed to produce terror.

Two Missions for Justice

received an email in the summer of 2012 from Christopher Bonastia, a City University of New York sociology professor, requesting an interview. I recognized his name because he wrote two books on a watershed battle for educational equity, a historic five-year fight that involved me. His references to me in the two books were brief—possibly because he had not interviewed me for those books. In his email, he explained that he wanted an interview because he was now planning a third book on the subject.

I was intrigued because Bonastia's previous book on the topic, *Southern Stalemate: Five Years Without Public Education in Prince Edward County, Virginia,* was just published the year before, in 2011. That book included some references to my role as the head of an MSU research team assigned by the U.S. Department of Health, Education, and Welfare (HEW) in 1963 to assess the impact of the fourth year of a shutdown of all public schools in Prince Edward County (PEC), closures designed to thwart a school desegregation order. At that time, private schools had been established for whites, while most blacks received little or no education.

Bonastia's work and books by other authors on this seismic episode were well researched and well written; but they only told part of the story. I knew the entire *inside* story because I was part of it. As a researcher and an unofficial monitor for the Kennedy administration, I worked closely with the dynamic agents of change, the people responsible for a 1964 court order that ended the school closures: black high school students in PEC who overcame fear and intimidation and protested against injustice. The children had led us.

Ironically, it was a prior generation of young black PEC high school students who mounted 1950s-era nonviolent protests that had helped desegregate all of America's schools. Those protests against the county's substandard black schools prompted the NAACP to file a lawsuit that was later incorporated into the historic 1954 *Brown v. Board of Education* legal case.

In the 1940s, the all-black R.R. Moton High School, located in the PEC town of Farmville, did not have a gymnasium, cafeteria, or teachers' restrooms. The school was three small plywood buildings. Due to overcrowding, some students had to take classes in an immobile school bus parked outside. The school did not have desks or blackboards. The school's requests for additional funds were denied by the county's all-white school board. In 1951, students at Moton staged a walkout in protest of the conditions. The NAACP took up their case after students agreed to seek an integrated school rather than improved conditions at their black school. The NAACP filed a lawsuit.

In *Davis v. County School Board of Prince Edward County*, a state court rejected the suit, ruling that the state of Virginia was in the process of equalizing black and white schools. The verdict was appealed to the U.S. Supreme Court. Subsequently, it was one of five cases incorporated into *Brown v. Board of Education*, the landmark 1954 case that overturned school segregation in the United States as inherently unequal.

In response to the *Brown* decision, the PEC Board of Supervisors in 1959 refused to appropriate *any* funds for the county school board. They effectively closed all public schools rather than integrate them. PEC Public Schools remained closed for five years. At the beginning of the shutdown, a new entity—the Prince Edward Foundation—created a series of private schools to educate the county's white children. These schools were supported by tuition grants from the state and tax credits from the county. Effectively, these institutions were "segregation academies" that were supported with the tax dollars of blacks.

More than two thousand black students had to go to school elsewhere or forgo their education altogether. Some moved to homes of relatives in other cities to attend school. Some were educated out of state by the Quakers' Society of Friends. Some received some instruction at makeshift schools in churches. In 1963–64, some attended the Prince Edward Free Schools Association created by the NAACP. However, many black students missed part or all of their education during the five-year shutdown.

It was in 1963 that I, responding to a Kennedy administration initiative, won a research grant for a project to produce a report on the impact of missed education on black youth. The Kennedy administration planned to use that report as a cudgel in the fight to reopen the schools and end segregated education in PEC. The Kennedy administration decided to offer the research grant after the U.S. Justice Department failed in its bid to obtain a role as a coplaintiff in an NAACP lawsuit against the school closings in PEC. The schools had been closed for two years when U.S. attorney general Robert Kennedy tried get the U.S. Justice Department included as a coplaintiff in the suit in April 1961, just three months after the presidential inauguration of his brother, John F. Kennedy. It was the first attempt by the federal government to become a plaintiff in a school desegregation case, but it failed when the court rejected the bid.

John F. Kennedy was determined to find a way to help support the lawsuit and end the impasse in PEC because it was a national and international embarrassment and because he had promised to support Civil Rights during his campaign. He tossed the ball to his brother, who then tasked William vanden Heuvel, special assistant to the attorney general, to find a way to reopen the public schools. Bill vanden Heuvel then asked HEW to fund research that would gauge the negative impact of the school closings on blacks, a report that would support the lawsuit. It was Bill vanden Heuvel's job—in partnership with the education office within HEW—to act as a low-profile monitor of the work of the researcher.

David Krathwohl, associate dean of education at MSU, had connections in the federal government and learned of the grant for the PEC project. He called on me—a promising professor but untested research leader—and asked if I had an interest. I told him yes and briefly discussed my interest in social justice issues.

I knew there would be great competition for this research grant and decided on a course of action that would enable me to obtain the funding. I flew to Richmond, Virginia, and took a bus to Farmville, the county seat of PEC. There, I met and interviewed the Reverend L. Francis Griffin, head of the NAACP in PEC. I also interviewed some students and parents. I included reports on my interviews in the grant application and subsequently received the $75,000 research grant sought by many other national scholars.

Officially, my research team was to conduct studies to measure the impact of the school closings on blacks. However, I also understood the broader underlying second mission: to help get the courts to reopen the schools on behalf of the NAACP, the Justice Department, and the youths of PEC.

As I recalled that 1963 visit—my first trip to Farmville, the county seat of PEC—I began to remember my last visit to that community. It was October 28, 1999, the fortieth anniversary of the county-ordered school closings in 1959. I was attending a symposium at Hampden-Sydney College called "Prince Edward Stories: Race and Schools in America." It was an exciting event with an audience of about three hundred people. The famed actor James Earl Jones was among the speakers. He delivered an address on Vernon Johns, considered by some as the grandfather of the American Civil Rights Movement because he laid a foundation for Martin Luther King Jr. Born in PEC in 1892, the grandson of slaves, Vernon Johns graduated from Oberlin Seminary in 1918 and attended the University of Chicago. He helped lead the movement for Civil Rights in the 1920s. Also, he was Dr. King's predecessor as pastor of the Dexter Avenue Baptist Church in Montgomery, Alabama, from 1947 to 1952 and was a mentor of Ralph David Abernathy and many other leaders in the Southern Christian Leadership Conference.

It was difficult being the follow-up speaker after James Earl Jones, with his deep, sonorous voice and dramatic delivery. Despite this, I generated great interest and enthusiasm after relating my role in ending school desegregation in my official and undercover roles in PEC. However, the biggest buzz of the symposium occurred when Marjorie "Marcie" Wall, daughter of J. Barrye "Bo" Wall—the highly influential editor of the *Farmville Herald* and the leading defender of school segregation in PEC in the 1950s and 1960s—rose to speak at the conference. She began tearing up as she began to speak. When she spoke, her was voice choked with emotion. "On behalf of me—for my father," she said, now openly crying, "forgive us."

I was stunned and so were many members of the audience, which included many black adults who had been formerly shut out from school as teens. During the symposium, some of these individuals expressed the love and grace that Dr. King had advocated. "I forgive you." "I forgive your father." "Let's move on and improve education and justice for all." These were some of the comments from those who had been the victims of educational apartheid. This was grace that I fully valued, and hearing these comments, I, too, became choked with emotion. I could also understand the gravity of her request for forgiveness. After all, her father had made me a target of segregationist forces when I was appointed the federal government's researcher on the PEC impasse.

A day after the U.S. Office of Education announced the winner of the PEC research project, there was a story on the federal education department research grant and on me on the front page in a June 1963 edition of Wall's *Farmville Herald*. Despite the announcement about my official role as a researcher, the story suggested that I would be working to end the school closings. I realized immediately that the editor of the paper, Barrye Wall, suspected that there were connections between me and the Justice Department.

J. Barrye Wall was a force. He was the highly influential editor of the *Farmville Herald*, the only newspaper that focused on PEC. He was also one of the state's most high-profile opponents of desegregation and a major supporter of the school closings. He used his newspaper as a platform to disseminate his views. "Stand Fast, Prince Edward" was the headline of one of Wall's editorials.

Wall was also very active behind the scenes. For example, he used his many political connections to urge the county and the state to fight the lawsuit that sought to reopen and desegregate the schools. The stakes, he realized, were national. He explained this in a letter to the state's governor: "This suit is the last legal barrier to total racial integration and no expense should be saved in winning it. Not only is the County of Prince Edward involved but every state in the Union and particularly the South where tensions are growing daily" (Bonastia 2012, 164).

When Wall learned about the "research" project, so did the local power structure. While gathering information on the impact of the school closing in the month of June, I was stopped three times by deputies for allegedly speeding. On each occasion, each deputy said, "How are you, professor?" Clearly, they knew my identity. One deputy went further. He said, "Be careful. People in this county know who you are." Each deputy eyeballed the interior of my car, but I was never ticketed. It was a warning. "We're watching you."

During my research, I learned that the idled students were very forthcoming about their substandard schools. They talked about hand-me-down textbooks inscribed with the names of the white students who previously owned them. They talked about schools with no heating systems and how black adult residents had to make repairs on shoddy structures that the county refused to fix.

I also measured their academic capabilities and determined that their achievement levels had stagnated with limited or no educational instruction. The idled students of all ages expressed their frustration about not being allowed to continue their education. They were upset and talked about their eagerness and willingness to launch protests about their plight.

The parents were outraged and concerned but not nearly so outspoken about the need for protests. Many of them had been intimidated when they had made their views on injustices known previously. The repercussions were often financial. Adult "agitators" would suddenly have loans for tractors, seeds, fertilizer, or other bank financing cancelled. If that didn't work, there was always the threat of arrest on bogus charges. Some of the more elderly residents could also recall more brutal means of coercion.

I did not share the fears of the adults. After all, I was not a local who was subject to financial intimidation, and I also knew that those who might engage in violent acts of repression were now reluctant to do so because the national media—particularly the *New York Times* and *Washington Post*—were closely covering the situation.

In addition, I had the security of my unofficial relationship with the Justice Department. By telephone, I frequently discussed my work and the welfare of idled students and their parents with Bill vanden Heuvel, my liaison at the Justice Department. However, my status did not shield me or my family from the racist attitudes of whites who did not know us. I had brought my family—my wife, Lettie, and my two sons, six-year old Vince and four-year-old Kurt—to Farmville. On one occasion Lettie was shopping for a dress at a local store. When she found a dress she liked and headed for the dressing room to check the fit, a saleswoman issued a warning.

"If you try on that dress, you'll have to buy it," she said.

Lettie gave her a bewildered look.

"No whites will buy that dress if you don't buy it after trying it on," the saleswoman told her.

Taken aback, Lettie put the dress back on the rack. "I'm not buying anything here," she said.

Lettie was a practicing Catholic. Shortly after our family arrived in Farmville, we went to a Sunday mass at a church. However, before we could sit, a priest rushed down the aisle. "Come outside with me," he said. Outside, after we complied, the priest exhaled loudly. "You must not be from around here," he said. "You have to come back at seven o'clock tonight, when we hold service for coloreds." Lettie was shocked. At that point, she decided she would never again attend a service at a Catholic church. For Vince and Kurt, these were life lessons on being black in the South in the early 1960s. I had not tried to shield them from racism. On the contrary, I had calmly explained racism and the country's legacy of slavery to them on previous occasions.

Subsequently, I began to attend protest planning sessions at the church of Pastor L. Francis Griffin, who was also the local NAACP leader. The idled students were pushing for action, and Rev. Griffin was advising them to be cautious and to rely on nonviolent tactics. One night, on July 9, when it was clear that some of the outraged teens were ready to take action, I decided to join a sit-in they were planning to stage at the College Shoppe restaurant, one of many "whites-only" commercial institutions in Farmville.

Among the activists on the scene was Ivanhoe Donaldson, one of my former students at MSU. He was very involved in the Civil Rights movement. On one occasion, he was arrested in Mississippi for sleeping in his truck after picking up pharmaceuticals in Michigan and delivering them to black Mississippians. The supplies were delivered to Aaron Henry, a Civil Rights activist who owned a pharmacy in Clarksdale, Mississippi. The pharmacy had been firebombed by white terrorists. Ivanhoe never referenced an affiliation, but I believe he was working for the Student Nonviolent Coordinating Committee.

At 9:30 P.M., I joined a contingent of about forty teens who marched to the restaurant with the intent of staging a sit-in that would lead to arrests. When the restaurant manager asked us to leave, we refused. However, when the manager then pointed out that the restaurant was in the process of closing—noting that there were no other customers—we left. The action did not result in arrest; however, the students now knew they had the courage to make a stand.

While I was encouraging students to learn the nonviolent tactics of social change in mid-July, the leading practitioner and inheritor of the mantle of Gandhi—Martin Luther King Jr.—was meeting with President Kennedy in the White House. Kennedy warned Dr. King to be careful because FBI chief J. Edgar Hoover, who had carved a fiefdom based on secret surveillance and blackmail, was spying on him and other Civil Rights activists. However, it should be noted that it was the president's brother, Robert Kennedy, who authorized FBI spying on Dr. King, his associate Bayard Rustin, and the other Civil Rights leaders.

At times, I sensed I was being watched by strangers who were not local residents. However, those occasions were rare. Eventually, I realized that most of the FBI "eyes" were paid local informants—both white and black. I realized that I was the subject of FBI surveillance when David Krathwohl, the associate dean at Michigan State who had given me an opportunity to compete for the PEC project, called me. Krathwohl referenced my attendance at protest-planning sessions at the Farmville church and cited my involvement at the student protest at the restaurant and "other Civil Rights" work. "Be careful," he said. "You don't want to lose the grant."

I was shocked. With information from informants, the FBI must have contacted Krathwohl in an attempt to neutralize me. I responded diplomatically to the well-intentioned advice. "I'll be careful," I said. However, I would not be deterred. I had read Gunnar Myrdal's award-winning book on racism, *The American Dilemma*, and understood that scholarly neutrality was a myth. I also knew that Dr. Ralph Bunche, one of my heroes, was a graduate student who studied under Myrdal. I would continue to gather information on the impact of the school closings on academic achievement levels. However, I decided I would also continue to monitor the youths and advise them on protest strategies.

Later that month, Ivanhoe Donaldson became more active as a provider of nonviolent protest training. I monitored the training that Ivanhoe provided. A Youth Council was organized, and I allowed members to use my office copying machine to produce leaflets and flyers. One of flyers, titled "Now Is the Time," was a call to action that said the following to black residents of PEC:

> The Negro children of Prince Edward have gone without schools for a long, long time. The Negro citizens of class have had indignities heaped upon them. . . . The local merchants have gladly taken their money but have refused to treat them as decent human beings . . . [and police] are now in the process of arresting the Negro citizens of Prince Edward County for protesting against human injustice.

As activism planning expanded, Bill vanden Heuvel began to make visits to Farmville because he was becoming more concerned about the well-being of the youths and their education. He wanted to know how the idled youths were doing and if local authorities might be violating their Civil Rights. He also met with NAACP lawyers about work on the lawsuit to reopen the schools during those visits.

He and his wife, noted author and philanthropist Jean Stein vanden Heuvel, later met with the victimized youths and—moved by the injustices—provided books and encouragement to individual students. They were empathetic and caring people. As parents, they would pass those values to their daughter, Katrina, who would become editor of *The Nation* magazine and a trustee of the Nation Institute, a leader in social justice advocacy.

In my testing and assessment program for school-excluded blacks, Farmville's middle-school-aged Beauregard Lee recorded the highest on the Stanford-Benet intelligence test in the county. When Jean vanden Heuvel learned about Beauregard's score, she sent a special set of books to him.

During the last weekend of July, the idled teenagers launched the civil disobedience actions that they had been planning. About 125 protesters marched through the main commercial district, calling for boycotts of business. Then, about thirty of the more experienced activists attempted another sit-in at the College Shoppe restaurant, where police arrested them. When the arrests were made, I rushed to the county jail. I asked to see and meet with the youths, requests that were granted. (Lawyers affiliated with the NAACP would also arrive shortly after to provide bail for the students.) The youths were held two to a cell. A third of the arrested teens were female. They were sequestered separately.

As I met with the Farmville teens, their faces lit up with smiles. I asked if they were OK. They all nodded affirmatively, and some offered comments. It was when I asked if they were afraid that they responded most verbally. "No, we're not afraid," many of them said, before responding articulately on why they were willing to be arrested. (That civil disobedience would pay off later when the U.S. Supreme Court—in a 1964 ruling—reopened and desegregated the county's schools.) At the time of their arrest, I was buoyed by their responses. I realized that the youths had and would continue to be agents for social change. They would continue to help America become a more just society.

When I visited the cell of Melvin Moore Jr., my mood changed. Melvin would later earn a PhD in psychology from Harvard, but at that time he was an MSU student who was serving as a member of my research team. Melvin was upset about his arrest. With anger in his voice, he told me that a deputy had kicked and assaulted him. I fought back a surge of fury. "Swear out a complaint for a warrant," I said to Melvin.

While sitting on the bunk in his jail cell, a containment unit with a barred window, I heard and saw something remarkably disturbing. The loud barking of dogs prompted me to look through the window at the scene outside. A tall, strapping white deputy was vigorously restraining two huge Doberman pinschers on a leash as a black man with gloves and leather sleeves that extended to his elbow punched the snarling dogs in their snouts and taunted them.

I had a PhD in educational psychology and quickly assessed the situation. It was basic psychological conditioning. The dogs were being trained to hate and attack blacks. They were being trained to terrorize people of color. This was my first experience in the crucible of the struggle for Civil Rights in the South, and I now understood how far the enforcers of unjust laws would go to engender fear in those who called for change.

I had not seen dogs used against blacks in Virginia. However, on television news reports, I had seen them unleashed on Civil Rights activists in Alabama and Mississippi. At that time, I did not know that Mississippi would be my next southern destination.

CHAPTER THREE

The March against Fear

was always glad to speak with Dr. Reginald T. W. Nichols, a long-time president of Piney Woods, a private black high school in Mississippi that has been a national leader in student achievement for more than one hundred years. I called Dr. Nichols in August 2012 for a progress report. Nothing had changed. Graduation rates and college placement rates were still near 100 percent. I was pleased, but not surprised.

My relationship with Piney Woods began when I became a member of the board of trustees in 1985, after I left the presidency of the University of District of Columbia in Washington, DC. At that time, I served on the board that oversaw the administration of school president Charles H. Beady, a MSU grad and one of my former students. Charles, who obtained his BA, MA, and PhD from Michigan State, headed Piney Woods for about two decades. Piney Woods was important because schools for blacks were scarce in that part of Mississippi.

One of my most memorable experiences occurred in 2004 during my trip to Piney Woods after being voted in as the first black board chairman of the institution. Piney Woods had always sent a driver to pick me up at the airport in Jackson, Mississippi. However, when this driver arrived, the revelations began. The driver pulled up in a civilian car, but he was a Mississippi State patrolman. "Morning, Dr. Green," he said.

Even though I had come to Mississippi as a Piney Woods board member for seven years, I continued to have uneasy feelings and concern about the state patrol. Based on my early history in this state, I had every reason to not want to see a Mississippi State trooper ever. It was a history with that state police force I would never forget. But this was a new and unexpected face—a face of a black state trooper.

I wasn't the only Piney Woods board member who had horrific experiences with law enforcement in that state. One of Piney Woods' most important financial donors, Hank Thomas, a successful black businessman who also served on the Piney Woods board, told me about his experiences. As a nineteen-year-old student at Howard University, Hank joined the Freedom Riders, activists who challenged the status quo by riding various forms of public transportation in the South to challenge local laws or customs that enforced segregation—the law that required blacks to sit at the back of a bus among them. On May 24, 1961, Hank moved to a seat near the front of a bus as it traveled from Montgomery, Alabama, to Jackson, Mississippi. When he arrived in Jackson, police beat him brutally, arrested him, and put him jail.

The black Mississippi State trooper assigned to drive me knew a bit about me and wanted me to know about this *new Mississippi*. As we traveled Highway 51, we passed a number of marked patrol vehicles. My driver waved when they appeared on the road. Like him, a number of these state troopers were black.

At that point, I realized Mississippi's affirmative action federal consent decree was working. Under a federal court order, Mississippi had been required to hire one African American for every white that was hired. Ironically, as a consultant for the Michigan State police and the Memphis and Detroit police departments, I had been providing staff development training to help troopers in that state improve their relationships with minorities. It was clear that Mississippi—a segregationist citadel for decades—now had more black state troopers than Michigan. This was an example of the impact of Civil Rights laws. Laws are important. I recall Dr. King telling me, "You can't always change attitudes, but you can change behavior."

As we drew close to the Piney Woods campus, I began to reflect on the school's amazing history. The institution, the nation's largest African American boarding school, was founded in 1909 by Laurence C. Jones. Jones also founded the Mississippi School of the Blind for Negroes in the early 1920s. In 1929, with the arrival of Martha Louise Morrow Foxx as principal, the Mississippi Blind School for Negroes relocated to Piney Woods.

Robert L. Green, Floyd McKissick, Martin Luther King Jr., and Stokely Carmichael lock arms during the March against Fear and sing "We Shall Overcome"—June 7, 1966.

Piney Woods was where the International Sweethearts of Rhythm were formed in 1937 to raise money for the school. The famous Five Blind Boys of Mississippi, who later changed their name to the Blind Boys, are also associated with the school. In the 1930s, Piney Woods sponsored baseball teams as part of the fund-raising efforts. Inventor George Washington Carver is among the many famous African Americans who have delivered addresses at the school.

Piney Woods has been an anomaly, a rare oasis of peace for blacks in a state where African Americans had been the victims of lynchings, illegal property appropriations, and terror and intimidation from the end of Reconstruction through the 1960s. For more than a century, black institutions—churches and schools among them—have been burned or razed by white supremacists and usurpers. Black ministers were also the victims of racial harassment, discrimination, and deadly attacks.

Piney Woods had survived and thrived because the founder had recruited a rich, white local banker to serve as the first chairman of its board. Through the decades, that chairman and other prominent whites who have served on the board protected the school. The students were required to wear T-shirts bearing the Piney Woods name when they ventured into nearby towns. To my knowledge, no student or faculty member at Piney Woods has ever been subject to murder and terror.

In addition, the founder generated national support and recognition in 1954 when he appeared on the *This Is Your Life* television show. During the show the host asked viewers to each send in $1 to support the school, eventually raising $700,000. With those funds, Jones created the school's endowment fund, reported to be at $7,000,000 when Jones died in 1975.

In more recent years, Morley Safer reported on the school in 1992 and again in 2005 for the CBS television show *60 Minutes*. The family legacy of success has been extended by Cathy Hughes, founder of black broadcasting networks Radio One and TV One. She is a granddaughter of Laurence Jones.

As I arrived on the grounds of this treasured institution in 2004 as its first black chairman of the board, I considered the irony. Robert Lee Green, who had spent most of his adult life fighting for equity for blacks in public schools, was now providing leadership to a renowned private school. In my mind, there was no contradiction. After all, I have always believed that alternative schools should be supported if they have a proven record of high expectations and excellence.

My memories of my first day as Piney Woods's chairman were interrupted when I noticed an email note from Reggie Nichols, the school's president. It was a pleasant follow-up to our conversation. Among other things, he asked if I might be returning to Mississippi any time soon. In my mind, I began to return to the past—to a very different Mississippi.

When Dr. King called on me in 1966 to provide leadership for an important march to and through Mississippi, I was well aware of the state's heinous history. At that time, the more notable recent state history included the notorious murder of Emmett Till, a fourteen-year-old black boy who was tortured and then killed in a racially motivated incident in 1955. The same year, the Reverends George W. Lee of Belzoni and Lamar Smith of Brookhaven were murdered. Later that same year, three more black ministers were killed for Civil Rights activities.

Also, there was the tumult that followed a federal court ruling that paved the way for James Meredith, a black student, to enroll at the then segregated University of Mississippi (Ole Miss) in 1962. People died in violence related to that event. That was followed in 1963 by shocking murder of Medgar Evers, a local NAACP leader who had the temerity to investigate the Emmett Till killing. Evers was killed just

Robert L. Green, Floyd McKissick, Martin Luther King Jr., and Stokely Carmichael wave to a supportive crowd while marching through Mississippi in the March against Fear in June 1966.

hours after President John F. Kennedy's nationally televised speech in support of Civil Rights.

Those two events—the Evers murder and the anti-integration violence at Ole Miss—along with the infamous 1964 police-supervised lynching of a trio of young Civil Rights workers, gave the state a well-earned reputation for terrorism. The three murdered activists were James Chaney, a twenty-one-year-old black man from Meridian, Mississippi; Andrew Goodman, a twenty-year-old Jewish anthropology student from New York; and Michael Schwerner, a twenty-four-year-old Jewish organizer for the Congress of Racial Equality (CORE), also from New York.

It was clear to me that most of the major modern Civil Rights battles were connected to education issues, beginning with the 1954 *Brown v. Board of Education* Supreme Court decision that officially struck down the "separate but equal" sham of Jim Crow schooling. After all, Chaney, Goodman, and Schwerner were lynched shortly before midnight on June 21, 1964, after they had investigated the burning of a church that had agreed to provide facilities for a freedom school. Freedom schools were designed to provide elementary and high school students instruction on social change advocacy as well as traditional studies.

Education has been and continues to be a key to ending subjugation because you cannot enslave or abuse a large population of educated and literate people. Education was also the cause in subsequent Civil Rights battles in the state. Medgar Evers had become an activist after the segregated University of Mississippi Law School rejected his application in 1954. He submitted his application to help the NAACP file a suit that eventually enabled James Meredith to be admitted to the university in 1962.

Meredith, galvanized by his own experience in the education rights crucible, decided to fight back against Mississippi's culture of terror. With the fame he garnered for fighting for the right to a university education—including a face-off with the state's lieutenant governor on the Ole Miss campus—he had declared on June 1, 1966, that he would undertake a March against Fear from Memphis, Tennessee, to Jackson, Mississippi. Ironically, the lieutenant governor who had tried to turn him away at the University of Mississippi four years earlier was now governor of that state.

Meredith had made his decision at the crossroads of fear and freedom when he applied to become the first black student at Ole Miss. His decision to march against fear in Mississippi was another crossroads decision that transfixed the nation.

I had joined SCLC for a one-year post as education director in 1965, buoyed by my success in 1963 and 1964 in my roles as a U.S. Office of Education researcher who oversaw student activism that helped the NAACP reopen and desegregate schools in Prince Edward County, Virginia.

In conversations with me and other associates, such as Andrew Young, and in comments during his sermons at the Ebenezer Baptist Church in Atlanta, Dr. King often said, "Unless we overcome the love of wealth and the fear of death, we will have difficulty obtaining our freedom." By that, he meant those with financial resources or property should not allow a love of wealth to make them complacent about social justice and that people should be willing to die for freedom.

The senior staff at the SCLC gather regularly gathered for meetings. Sometimes staffers shared stories about violence or injustice. For example, I related a story involving Moon Song Lee, a Civil Rights activist from Hawaii. She was tasked with confirming that blacks working for a Mississippi farmer were being paid in scrip that could only be redeemed at the farmer's company store. This was peonage.

Moon chartered a small plane, and she joined senior SCLC staff member Randolph Blackwell and me on a flight to the site, where we talked to the black farm workers. They confirmed the peonage arrangement. We spent the night at

COURTESY CORBIS IMAGES.

Robert L. Green, Floyd McKissick, Martin Luther King Jr., and Stokely Carmichael confronting Mississippi highway patrolmen at the beginning of the Meredith March against Fear in June 1966.

the home of one of farm workers. We returned to the plane the following morning. However, before we took off, the white farmer appeared in a truck and stopped the vehicle in front of the plane. He had a shotgun. Angry, he demanded to know why we were on his property.

We kept mum while our pilot, who was also white, told the farmer that we had landed there by mistake. That was good enough for the farmer; he allowed us to leave. Later, I submitted a report on the situation to the U.S. Justice Department.

Also, I recalled a story told by Harry Boyte, a white Civil Rights activist who worked with Dr. King. Dr. King and many members of the SCLC staff were in a conference room. We were exchanging stories when Harry said, "Let me tell you about attack dogs." Harry was marching with Dr. King and other Civil Rights activists in Birmingham, Alabama, when police arrived with attack dogs. They unleashed the dogs on the activists, and the canines began to bite some people around Harry. One dog, in the frenzy, bit through Harry's pants, exposing his white skin. However, when the dog saw his skin color, he refused to bite Harry.

When Harry completed the story, many of those in room told him that they didn't believe his story. However, the story rang very true to me because I saw a black man taunting a dog on a policeman's leash in Farmville, Virginia, part of a session to train dogs to be vicious toward blacks. I related that story to the group. "In psychology," I told them, "we call this classical conditioning." Dr. King smiled when I completed my explanation. He was very happy to have me on board.

I had been working at the SCLC for nearly a year when—during a June 6, 1966, staff meeting with Dr. King—his secretary, Dora McDonald, burst into the room. "Meredith!" she said. It was late afternoon and she told us what the TV network evening news broadcasters would be telling the rest of the nation shortly: a few minutes after four o'clock, James Meredith was shot in the back and legs as he walked south on Highway 51 two miles south of Hernando, Mississippi, during his March against Fear.

Meredith was taken to a hospital in Memphis and treated for three shotgun wounds. Immediately after the shooting, police arrested a middle-aged white man who identified himself as Tim Norrell of Memphis. The shooting occurred as Meredith was completing the first thirty-mile leg of a 220-mile Civil Rights walk from Memphis to Jackson, Mississippi, to encourage black voter registration and combat the fear of white authority in the state.

The next day, Dr. King, Floyd McKissick of CORE, Hosea Williams, and I met with Meredith in his hospital room as he prepared to be discharged the morning after his surgery. I was at the hospital with Dr. King when he announced that a coalition of Civil Rights groups would resume Meredith's March against Fear. Dr. King had commitments throughout the nation. He was raising support and money in the North, managing SCLC campaigns in the South, and lobbying the president and Congress for a comprehensive Civil Rights bill in Washington.

He knew this march against fear was important—but he needed help. He collared me and Hosea Williams, a veteran SCLC manager of campaigns in Mississippi

Some March against Fear leaders met in June 1966 to discuss strategy at the Canton, Mississippi, home of George Washington after police attacked marchers with tear gas: Ralph Abernathy, Bernard Lee, Andrew Young, Robert L. Green, Martin Luther King Jr., and Stokely Carmichael.

and Alabama, and told us of this united front plan to continue Meredith's march. "I will be involved," he said. "When I'm not, I want the two of you to be SCLC's representatives in the march."

Planning for the march took place at the Lorraine Hotel in Memphis, which is where Dr. King would be assassinated two years later. All of the mainstream Civil Rights leaders attended—Dr. King, Roy Wilkins of the NAACP, Floyd McKissick of CORE, Whitney Young of the Urban League, and James Orange of the SCLC. However, there was a new wildcard in the mix—the Student Nonviolent Coordinating Committee (SNCC). The SNCC was now led by Stokely Carmichael, a firebrand who was ready to eschew the tactic that was part of his organization's name. He made it clear that this would not be a traditional Civil Rights march when he said, "We're going to test nonviolence." Referring to the forces of terror in Mississippi, he said, "They're not nonviolent and neither am I."

Roy Wilkins, executive director of the national office of the NAACP, decided not to formally involve the NAACP in the march because he was concerned and worried about the radical remarks made by Stokely Carmichael. However, Wilkins did provide financial donations for march-related expenses.

King picked up the gauntlet and organized a 220-mile walk from Memphis to Jackson, Mississippi. Charles Evers, brother of murdered Civil Rights activist Medgar Evers, decided not to join the march but said he and Civil Rights supporters would meet the marchers when they arrived in Jackson. This was at a meeting that Roy Wilkins and King had organized at the Centenary Methodist Church in Memphis, which drew a crowd of six hundred. Again, all of the major Civil Rights leaders attended. Dr. King told the gathering that the Civil Rights movement had a "great indebtedness to Meredith because of his dedication to what we believe." Wilkins said the shooting was "disgusting, incredible and cowardly."

Later, Hosea Williams and I met the first wave of arriving marchers at transportation centers in Memphis. We began to organize by phone by contacting Mississippi and Memphis homeowners who might provide sleeping quarters for the marchers because no white hotel would give lodging to blacks. This housing experience reminded me of my childhood. When I was ten years of age I attended, with my father, an annual meeting of the Church of God in Christ in Memphis. Blacks had to stay with local black residents because hotels and motels would not provide lodging.

Sensing the urge to respond to violence and provocations, Hosea spoke to the organizers. "This is a nonviolent march. If you decide you want to be violent, you go ahead. But you're on your own. You are not part of this march."

One member of CORE, Herb Callender, told the group he was in agreement with Williams, "but," Callender said, "I'm not going to let anyone push me around. I want to live, and I'm going to do that the best way I can."

A flyer produced for the march announced the stakes and the goals.

The Reign of Terror still exists in the South!

Dr. Martin Luther King Jr. calls YOU to join him in the James Meredith Mississippi March now in progress from Memphis to Jackson, Miss.

Now is the time to make your witness for a lifting of the veils of intimidation, violence, deprivation and fear.

We Demand:

· Federal registrars in every Mississippi County
· A chance to work for a decent wage

- Housing for every family
- Aid to Farmers

Hernando, Mississippi, June 7

The march began at the bloodstained spot on the highway where Meredith had been shot, three miles south of Hernando, Mississippi. Many potential marchers watched on the side of the road as about thirty of us began the march. Dr. King, Stokely Carmichael, Floyd McKissick, and I locked arms and began to lead the march. We had moved only about two hundred yards when we were confronted by a dozen Mississippi highway patrolmen—three in the vanguard and nine behind them. Suddenly, the three lead officers ran toward us and ordered us off the pavement. One of them said, "You can walk as far as you want to, all the way to China if you like, as long as you are unarmed and walk single file on the shoulder!" Dr. King responded calmly. "We don't want to go to China, just to Jackson." We then locked our arms together at elbows to create a nonviolent resistance circle.

At that point, the officer put his hand on Dr. King's chest and pushed him. Dr. King shrugged off the push, and the four of us kept our arms locked. Stokely then responded by lunging at the trooper. I grabbed Stokely and wrestled him to the ground. When Stokely and I looked up, we noticed that the trooper's gun was a foot away—aimed at Stokely's head. Stokely would later tell me that I saved his life. As a result of the incident, we began to forge a strong bond.

Responding to the provocation, Dr. King referred to the famous Montgomery to Selma, Alabama, march of the previous year. "When we walked from Montgomery, we walked in the middle of the road," he told the trooper.

Another trooper unbuckled his pistol and said, "Do you have a permit for this march?" Dr. King started to reply, but before he could, one trooper said, "Let's get 'em off the road." Another added, "Yeah." The three officers moved in a line and began shoving the four of us. McKissick fell down and nearly pulled Dr. King down with him. After that, the four of us huddled and conferred. Dr. King told us that we had to minimize conflict and that we should—for now—march on the side of road.

The four of us moved to the shoulder, locked arms again, and resumed the march, even when it meant walking through mud created by a brief thunder shower the previous day. However, by the second day of the trek, the ranks of the marchers were in the hundreds as supporters streamed in—some by foot and others dropped off by drivers. By that second day, the group was too large to stay on the shoulder of the road. Some moved onto the highway despite the presence of a small motorized contingent of troopers.

In the state capitol, Governor Paul Johnson, who as lieutenant governor made a trip to the University of Mississippi in 1962 to personally try to block James Meredith's attempt to enroll, issued a chilling statement, promising to provide "sufficient policemen and any *other* state forces" to deal with the marchers.

Batesville, Mississippi, June 11

After a few days of marching, we reached Batesville, our major first stop. We celebrated by organizing a hand-clapping, singing demonstration in front of the white-columned Panola County Courthouse in Batesville. We were a contingent of about 450 at that time; whites accounted for about a tenth of the marchers.

All the white-owned restaurants in Batesville were closed during our visit. They did not want us to challenge the "whites-only" laws. We focused on one of our main objectives—to register blacks to vote. It started slow. However, when we registered El Fondren, a 106-year-old retired farmer who had never voted, we had momentum. After he registered, I and others put him on our shoulders and carried him down the street. The crowd of marchers and local residents cheered him as a hero.

While the Selma to Montgomery march of 1965 was protected by the U.S. Army, the March against Fear was followed and threatened by antagonists—the highway patrol and local police in each city. However, there was a contingent of about fifteen to twenty journalists—newspaper and TV network reporters who diligently reported on every step, every stop, and every threat. I realized, early on, that they were our only protection.

On the evening of June 12, 1966, the second and last day of our stay in Batesville, a message from the Ku Klux Klan was circulated. It declared, "We have been invaded by the biggest band of renegades in this country today."

However, even the Klan—or some group impersonating the Klan—may have realized that the media was closely covering the march. The message concluded with this caution: "The best way to deal with this bunch of scum and alley rats is strictly a hands-off policy." On the other hand, was this a message designed to absolve the Klan of attacks that they were actually planning?

Robert L. Green addresses a June 1966 rally during the March against Fear in Yazoo, Mississippi.

Charleston, Mississippi, June 13

We marched through rain and mud on the road to Charleston. As we reached Oakland, Mississippi, a community near Charleston, we passed a misspelled painted sign on the side of the road. It was an old racial taunt that said:

KKK
Red [read] Nigger, and run
If you can't red [read], run anyway.

Grenada, Mississippi, June 14

By the time we reached Grenada, the county seat of Grenada County, we were a force of about five thousand—most of them black Mississippians who had arrived to support us. There were also about five hundred white marchers, most of them from the North. Dr. King was away to deliver an address in Chicago. As we entered

Grenada the media contingent had doubled, matching the twenty or so who covered the start of the march. News organizations had reduced their staff coverage but were now resending staff. I was emboldened. We needed a demonstration that would inspire the marchers and the local black population.

As we moved toward Grenada's town square with this huge contingent, I could sense that the crowd was emboldened. Fear was diminishing. I borrowed a small American flag from a local black child who was watching our procession. I spotted the Confederate monument at the courthouse, moved toward it, and motioned marchers to follow.

Most major towns and cities in the South had such a monument, which was typically enshrined with a statue, a bust, or emblematic image of Jefferson Davis, the Confederate president. In this case, it was an oblong eight-foot sculpture with an engraved facial image of Davis at the top. Like comparable shrines, this monument was considered sacred by southern whites. To me, it was a symbol of slavery, segregation, and southern terrorism. I then saw it as a prop for an opportunity to help blacks overcome their fear of Confederate symbols.

With the flag in hand, I scaled the monument, found a crevice at the top, and inserted the American flag. Nicholas von Hoffman, a *Washington Post* reporter who had taken an interest in my role, wrote the following about the incident:

> After arriving in Grenada, a town of about 12,000, Robert Green stuck an American flag on top of Jeff Davis' head. "We're tired of rebel flags. This is the flag we want to see!" The marchers and local blacks responded with cheers. Some local whites looked on quietly. (von Hoffman 1966a)

I then told the crowd that the public segregation accommodations laws would be tested in Grenada. It was a milestone in social history in the town. I knew that the toilets in restaurants and government buildings were marked "1" for whites and "2" for blacks. Speaking to the marchers and local black residents, I said, "I want every Negro who hasn't gone to the toilet to go down to the courthouse."

Many of the marchers surged to the courthouse to use the toilets. Inside the courthouse—now surrounded by TV cameras and reporters—was Sheriff Suggs Ingram, a heavy drinker who had mercilessly beat blacks with a club in the past. Ingram falsely claimed that there were no segregated toilets. "We didn't take the numbers down from the doors."

There was a rally outside of a black church that night. About five hundred

Robert L. Green plants an American flag on the Jefferson Davis Monument in Grenada, Mississippi, during the June 1966 March against Fear, telling the crowd, "The South must and will change!"

people attended, about a fifth of them white marchers. There were a series of spontaneous speeches, comments from Floyd McKissick among them. A young SNCC activist from Chattanooga and Atlanta, Willie Ricks, stepped forward and said blacks should not depend on whites for their freedom. "We need the power to make change," he said. "We need black power!"

This was the first time this phrase was so publicly used. I was concerned that the phrase and the sentiment was the voice of anger, that it would alienate whites—including white volunteers in the march. I walked to the front of the gathering and spoke. I felt it was important to ensure white students and adults, most from urban northern communities, that we cared for them and did not associate them with racist whites. "We need people power," I told the marchers. "We need power from everyone. Power from everyone can end institutional racism."

After the rally, some of the leaders met to discuss the route ahead. There was a debate on whether to proceed to Jackson or veer off into the delta counties, where blacks were frequently terrorized, to register more voters. The Mississippi Freedom Democratic Party, a Civil Rights offshoot, and SNCC—led by Stokely Carmichael—wanted to take the detour. I didn't take a position, but I understood and supported Stokely's passionate desire to register voters because blacks were a majority in many Mississippi counties, and if they registered and voted—without the fear of police intimidation—they could gain power.

However, after the meeting, I was still concerned about how the "black power" message might be perceived. I talked to Willie Ricks privately. "We need to make it clear that we are not afraid," Ricks told me. On that we agreed. However, I told Ricks that a great deal of our power was derived from the media—primarily white journalists who exposed racial injustice, terrorist tactics, and our nonviolent resistance to racism.

Dr. King returned the next day from a speech in Chicago, and I informed him of Ricks's speech. I noted that we were being covered by national media and there could be reports on the growing militancy of the SNCC contingent and their willingness to confront and fight local white authorities. Dr. King expressed concern because he wanted the march to be nonviolent. Dr. King also valued the role of the media because it had given sympathetic coverage to the struggle for Civil Rights. He wanted that positive coverage to continue during the march.

That evening, Dr. King gave a press conference and discussed the results of his negotiations with county officials. There was the smell of magnolia trees and the smell of an early victory. The county, he said, had agreed to appoint four black

Robert L. Green challenging Sheriff Suggs Ingram about police brutality against blacks in Grenada, Mississippi, in June 1966.

registrars and to send them to register blacks to vote. King continued. "This is a significant victory for no other reason than that so many people turned out to register today and that the county officials made concessions that they had never made before."

Meanwhile, on that same day, more than twenty African Americans registered without incident for the summer term at the University of Mississippi. Black enrollment at Ole Miss was becoming a norm—and that was a victory too.

However, on June 15, we learned that three Ku Klux Klansmen were arrested and charged in Natchez, Mississippi, that day for the slaying of an elderly black man whose body was riddled by seventeen rifle slugs and a shotgun blast. It was another example of terrorism and white intimidation. I was convinced that such tactics would no longer work.

I firmly believed in nonviolence as a political tactic for change. However, I also had to guard against my learned instincts to respond to any personal attack. I was also concerned about SNCC. I knew that the organization was becoming more militant. After all, two months before the march, Stokely had withdrawn SNCC from any participation in the White House Conference on Civil Rights. I constantly reminded myself that Dr. King expected me to help ensure that the march would remain nonviolent.

Greenwood, Mississippi, June 15

Stokely and two SNCC aides were arrested on the evening of June 15 while trying to set up a campsite for marchers on the grounds of a black school in Greenwood. They were arrested for disobeying police who told them not to pitch tents. When I learned of Stokely's arrest, I was alarmed because I knew about the history of Civil Rights activists in Mississippi jails. My friend Andrew Young had told me about one of those harrowing episodes.

On the day Medgar Evers was murdered in a terrorist attack, Dr. King and Andy became concerned about the safety of Civil Rights activists imprisoned in jail cells in Winona, Mississippi. In the wake of the Evers murder, they concluded that these devotees to nonviolent change could be killed by sheriff's deputies who would falsely claim in police records that violent people had tried to escape. It had happened to many innocent blacks in Mississippi over the decades.

Dr. King sent Andy Young and SCLC associates James Bevel and Dorothy Cotton to Winona to arrange the release of Annelle Ponder, an SCLC field worker in Mississippi. Ponder, an Atlanta native who had an MA from Atlanta University, was a voter registration worker. Ponder and eleven other men and women had been arrested for using "whites only" restrooms at a bus station despite the fact that the Interstate Commerce Commission (ICC) had banned segregation at interstate travel facilities in 1961. (The ICC ban was prompted by the Freedom Riders, black and white college students who had defied segregation on buses and bus facilities.)

Andy Young was Dr. King's top negotiator. However, the jailers refused to release the group. Andy then called Wiley Branton, a black SCLC attorney in Arkansas who helped desegregate the University of Arkansas School of Law more than a decade earlier. Branton told Andy to hand the phone to the deputy. When the deputy put the phone to his ear, he heard the dialect and intonations of an authoritative white man. "Get those Niggers out of there," a posing Branton said. "They're my Niggers

Robert L. Green stops a train before it hits Civil Rights marchers during the June 1966 March against Fear in Jackson, Mississippi.

and I want them back. They can only get into more trouble there. I want them back in Atlanta right away."

Thinking that the order was coming from white law enforcement in Atlanta, the deputy told Branton he would release the activists. At Branton's request, the deputy then handed the phone back to Andy. "When he releases our people," said Branton, "say 'Thank you,' and get everyone out of town as fast as you can."

Among the three liberated women was Fannie Lou Hamer, a Mississippian who worked for SNCC. Weeks later, I would conduct voter registration work with her in the state. She would become nationally known a year later when she led members of the Mississippi Freedom Democratic Party in a challenge of the all-white Democratic Party contingent at the party's 1964 national convention in Atlantic City, New Jersey.

Andy, Dorothy, and James were shocked when they saw Annelle Ponder. They did not recognize her because her face had been disfigured, the result of a severe beating for refusing to address a deputy as "sir."

That episode rolled through my mind when I learned that Stokely, a firebrand, had been arrested. If they beat mild-mannered Annelle Ponder, what would they do to Stokely? I had to get him out of jail as soon as possible. In the station where Stokely was jailed, there was a commemoration for a local folk hero of the racist power structure—a fierce German shepherd dog named Tiger. The dog is commemorated with a plaque for its role in quelling Civil Rights demonstrations in the city in 1963.

I went to the jail to seek Stokely's release. I told the sheriff that Stokely was well known and that if anything happened to him, "you will have a major problem on your hands." They released Stokely to me. After his release Stokely reappeared to speak to about seven hundred marchers. Standing on the back of a pickup, his face lit by television camera lights, he gave one of his more fiery addresses.

> Today is the twenty-seventh time I've been arrested. I ain't gonna be arrested no more. . . . I ain't gonna be arrested no more. . . . I'm gonna tell you baby, that the only way we're going to get justice is when we have a black sheriff. . . . Every courthouse in Mississippi should be burnt down tomorrow so we can get rid of the dirt! (Carmichael and Thelwell 2003, 166)

I was standing next to Stokely when he leaned forward toward the crowd, raised a fist, and shouted, "We want black power! We want black power!" I whispered to Stokely, "Easy, Stokely. Easy, easy on 'black power.'" Some of the younger members among the marchers shouted back the refrain "black power!" However, most of the older marchers stood mute, looking about uneasily. Some white residents were not far away. Some of them were sitting on their porches. Some had dogs trained to attack blacks. This was, after all, Greenwood "the Gateway to the Delta." (It was cotton country and the home of Byron De La Beckwith, the man who would, in 1994, be arrested and convicted for the murder of Medgar Evers.)

The next day, Governor Paul Johnson held a press conference and announced that he was reducing the number of state troopers protecting the marchers because "we are not going to be in the position of wet-nursing a group of showmen."

Greenwood, Mississippi, June 17

Bristling like a Confederate infantry, a huge contingent of about sixty sheriff's deputies in gray uniforms—many of them recently deputized—formed a line in

At an SCLC convention in Jackson, Mississippi, during the summer of 1967: Walter Fauntroy, Coretta Scott King, Martin Luther King Jr., Ted Kennedy, Charles Evers, and Robert L. Green (*behind Evers*).

front of the wide county courthouse lawn in Greenwood, the seat of Leflore County. They were there to keep us away from the Confederate monument behind them. There were also six black prisoners, county jail "trustees" pressed into service as an auxiliary backup for the deputies. Greenwood's authorities had heard about my flag replacement in Grenada a few days previous and were determined to "protect" the Stars and Bars. It was hot and humid and about to become even hotter and stickier.

Hosea Williams was next to me as we observed the long gray line of officers. He smiled broadly and said kiddingly, "OK, Mr. Professor. You're so brave. Break through those lines and plant another American flag."

Again, the media—with their TV cameras, still photo cameras, and reporters with notepads—were on the scene. The commanding officer spoke, but—with all the media attention—his tone was polite. He asked us to stay off the grass and warned that trespassers would be arrested. Stokely, who had been arrested the night before, was undaunted and defiant. He marched up to the largest deputy in the contingent—a man of about six feet four—and said, "I've been in your jail more than you, and I don't even work there."

Willie Ricks, another leading member of the SNCC contingent, walked up to another officer and said in an indignant tone, "Why don't you get out of the way?"

Another young marcher, who had been beaten in a previous protest in Greenwood, walked up to the commanding officer and said, "I got my jaw broken on those courthouse steps!"

"No one is going to put a foot on this lawn!" the officer shouted. Meanwhile, three little white boys in red sweaters were playing on the grass.

It seemed that the standoff would end in violence until Dr. King intervened and waved everyone toward the courthouse steps. We all followed, creating a surge that put the deputies on a hair trigger. They all pulled out their clubs. One of them slid his hand up and down his club and muttered, "I'm ready to start this now."

Andy Young began to defuse the situation. "Walk easy," he said loudly but in a calming tone. "Walk easy. Don't push." The marchers responded by slowing down and stopped in front of Dr. King who stood before the steps of the courthouse. The deputies relaxed, and most holstered their clubs. It started almost as a whisper and grew in volume until much of the crowd joined in the chant: "Black Power!" Many clenched black fists rose and fell in time with the chant.

This was the biggest demonstration of the SNCC-inspired chant. When the demonstration ended, Dr. King faced a throng of reporters and cameras and tried to put it in context. "You can always tell where the Negro community begins because that is where the pavement ends," he told them. "We're going to change that when we get the ballot. That's what we mean when we say we want power. Power is the ability to make the power structure say 'Yes' when it wants to say 'No.'"

Meanwhile, Stokely was holding court with his own contingent of reporters.

> Black nationalism only means one thing in this country, that you're antiwhite. That's the trick bag the press is trying to get me into. But I'm not antiwhite.
>
> Every group in this country owns its own neighborhoods—but us. . . . The Jews, the Italians, the Germans. The Irish took over Boston and nobody asked them what they were going to do statewide where they weren't in a majority. Well, we're going to elect sheriffs where we can, where we're in a majority.

Meanwhile, Hosea Williams was leading the marchers in singing "We Shall Overcome." However, later that day, a truck with a loud audio system was driven slowly

Robert L. Green, with Andrew Young and Martin Luther King Jr., talks to a highway patrolman during the March against Fear.

past the marchers, blaring a Klan song. Also, I will never forget the small white kids—youngsters trained to hate blacks—waving Confederate flags.

Itta Bena, Mississippi, June 18

Early the next morning, as we were packing and preparing to leave Greenwood for the trip to Itta Bena, I heard yelling from one of the media trucks. I ran over to investigate the commotion. As I reached the truck, I could see about half a dozen large snakes inside an open metal TV camera case, bobbing their venomous heads to and fro. Nearby, a reporter was shouting, "Snakes! Snakes!"

Immediately, I knew some local white racists had planted the snakes. Our opponents hated the news media, and this was an attempt to terrorize them. Someone dispatched the snakes. A group of journalists—all of them from the North, all of them white, and all of them shocked—gathered around me. "This is the South," I said. "They've been doing this to blacks for years. It's an attempt to intimidate you."

I was concerned that some of the reporters would be fearful. Instead, they were angry and more determined to cover the march. It also gave them a sense of kinship with the marchers. Previously, they thought they would not be attacked because they were white and male. They now had a new perspective—that they could be victims too.

We moved out of Greenwood. Just south of the city we encountered a flaming cross, the symbol of the Klan. Some of the marchers stopped at the spot and knelt in prayer.

As the march continued into Itta Bena, the hometown of SCLC activist James Bevel, we expected to spend the night on the grounds of Mississippi Valley State College, a black school near the swamps. However, when we arrived we learned the school president would not allow us to camp there. I met with the president of the school, and he told me his school would lose state funding if he allowed the marchers to camp. I relayed that information to the marchers and asked everyone to prepare to leave because we didn't want the school to lose funding. At that point, Dr. King was back from a trip to Detroit. He arranged for the marchers to rest at the banks of a river, just south of Itta Bena. The next day, he decided the march would proceed to Belzoni, twenty-seven miles away.

Belzoni, Mississippi, June 19

Trucks were brought in to transport most of marchers to Belzoni because a Baptist church in the town of 4,100 had offered a site to camp and sleep. Black youths among the marchers held an impromptu rally in the church parking lot, many of them shouting "black power." They decided to march to the courthouse. Nearby, local white youth gathered at a filling station and began to shout racial epithets. The two groups appeared to be on the verge of a clash until the SCLC's Hosea Williams intervened, telling them turn the march around because their adversaries had "chains and clubs."

As the marchers receded, one young local activist told me that a local police officer had been harassing him. The following day, that young marcher ran up to me and pointed to a white man standing a few yards from a green Pontiac. "That's the policeman who's been harassing you?" I asked. The young man nodded affirmative. "Okay," I said. "Let's go over and talk to him."

As we approached, the man, dressed in plain clothes with a badge, began to run for his car. "Hey, hey," I said, calling out. "We want to talk to you." He reached the car door as we reached him. The man immediately removed his engraved identification badge so that I would not be able to read it. Quickly, four other Belzoni police officers rushed over to the scene. Now inside the car, the man sped off in the Pontiac. As he did, one of the police officers unbuttoned his holster. "Don't go for your gun!" I shouted. "Your gun doesn't frighten us." The officer dropped his hand away from the weapon.

The city's police chief and Willie Ricks had now come to the scene of the flare-up. I told Leon Hall, a student activist, to go to the courthouse to get John Doar, a U.S. Justice Department liaison to the march, to help settle the situation. An agitated Ricks said, "We'll protect our own people. If somebody touches one of us, we'll tear this place up." Ricks then looked at the chief. "You'll protect us if you don't want the courthouse burnt, baby, 'cause we'll burn it down for you."

"You can't," the chief said, "because it's fireproof."

"Then we'll bomb it!" Ricks responded.

I stepped in between the two and extended my arms in a calming, separating motion. I said, "The argument is over. It's over. . . . They know one thing for sure: we're not going to take any more of that crap."

Observing the scene was *Washington Post* reporter Nicholas von Hoffman. Noting the tension between the more militant SNCC members and the SCLC, he wrote the following: "It's the ubiquitous fear of mayhem that keeps this march of many philosophies united" (von Hoffman 1966b).

The same day, during a quick visit to Atlanta, Dr. King appealed for an end to talk of "black power." "It is," he said, "absolutely necessary for the Negro to gain power, but the term 'black power' is unfortunate because it tends to give the impression of black nationalism" (King 1967, 29–30). He spoke of "grave consequences" if his nonviolent approach to social change should be abandoned.

Philadelphia, Mississippi, June 21

When the marchers moved into Philadelphia, they visited the courthouse to honor the three young Civil Rights workers—James Chaney, Michael Schwerner, and Andrew Goodman—who were detained in the courthouse jail briefly before they were murdered and left at the earthen dam where they had been killed. When the marchers arrived—on the second anniversary of their murders—they were assaulted by jeering white men who hurled firecrackers at us.

About a half dozen of the marchers broke away and engaged in a brawl with ten assailants. Meanwhile, some of the whites attacked the media contingent, roughing up journalists and shattering their equipment. King was outraged. He blamed the federal government and the state of Mississippi for not preventing the violence and compared it to the vicious attacks he and other activists suffered in St. Augustine, Florida, in 1964.

Meanwhile, the march began to receive a lot of high-profile support. Vocalist and dancer Sammy Davis Jr. announced that he and actors Marlon Brando and Burt Lancaster would join us later that week just outside of Jackson. Davis said he and his troupe would perform in Tougaloo at a black college near Jackson on the night before the final leg into Jackson.

The violence continued the evening of June 21. That night, whites in cars drove by the Freedom Democratic Party headquarters in a black neighborhood. Someone in the first car shot at Jim Letherer, a white one-legged veteran of previous Civil Rights marches, as he walked in front of the party headquarters. They missed. Later, other cars drove by and the passengers fired into the windows of the party headquarters. Inside were a few marchers and many local blacks. The local blacks, who had weapons, returned fire. A white man who had been in one of the cars was wounded.

Dr. King was in Yazoo City during the incident. Speaking to reporters, he said, "I think this is by far the worst situation I've ever been in. This is a complete climate of terror and breakdown in law and order."

The next day, Dr. King was back in Philadelphia, and he made plans to give an address in front of the city courthouse. When the marchers arrived, agitated local whites were in lines on each side of the courthouse, and they also surrounded the square. Standing in front of the courthouse was a contingent of about a dozen deputies. In the center of this group was Deputy Sheriff Cecil Price, known then as one of seventeen men suspected of orchestrating the murder of Chaney, Schwerner, and Goodman two years before this confrontation. (Price was later among the men convicted for the murders.)

Undaunted, Dr. King approached the courthouse steps, paused, and began by saying something he would say later in life: "I'm not afraid of any man!" The white resisters on the sidelines began to heckle him, but he continued. "Before I will be a slave, I will be in my grave!" he said. "We'll help you!" several local white residents shouted. Another yelled, "Hey Luther! Thought you wasn't scared of anybody. Come up here alone and prove it!"

Robert L. Green (*center*) steps in to reduce tension between highway patrolmen and young marchers.

Dr. King ignored the taunts. The marchers moved forward toward the court-house steps behind Dr. King. It seemed a confrontation was imminent. This time, it was the Reverend Ralph Abernathy, an SCLC veteran who had joined the march, who brought peace. Speaking to Deputy Sheriff Price, he said, "We have come peacefully. We have people here who want to register." Price said the registrar's office was closed until 1:00 P.M.

"Then we will have a peaceful, orderly prayer meeting," Rev. Abernathy said.

Responding, Dr. King addressed the marchers in the form of a prayer. The marchers were vastly outnumbered by an angry crowd of whites. "The witness," Dr. King said, "you are making here today will go down in the history books. We have seen the violence of misguided men. Today, we have seen men with hatred on their faces who want to turn this country backwards."

Many of the whites surrounding the marchers jeered, laughed, and threw sticks at us. When Dr. King completed his comments, the marchers were directed to head to a church. As they moved peacefully, some local white residents followed and threw more sticks. Meanwhile, the main contingent of marchers, who were not at the town square in Philadelphia, began to move out, stepping off sixteen miles from the nearby town of Louise to Yazoo City, where they were quietly received at a campsite at a "Negro" baseball park owned by the city.

Canton, Mississippi, June 23

There was a rally in front of the courthouse in Canton. It was dusk when about three hundred marchers moved to a school grounds eight blocks away to camp and spend the night. I conferred with Dr. King and other leaders about the upcoming march to Jackson. I also spent time with my wife, Lettie, and my three boys—Vince, Kurt, and Kevin—who had traveled from Atlanta to join the march. Meanwhile, many of the marchers were setting up tents to spend the night at a local school for blacks.

A contingent of highway state police had—at a distance—followed us to the school grounds. As we settled on the grounds, a cohort of about forty troopers moved toward us, and one of the officers, using a bullhorn, said, "You are not authorized to be here. Clear the grounds!" The troopers, who were moving forward, were about twenty-five yards away when I noticed they had tear gas canisters in their utility belts. I told Lettie that a tear gas attack was likely and that we had to take the children to the nearby home of George Washington, a well-known local black resident. I walked with them to the home and returned to the school grounds.

When I returned the marchers were still huddled. No one had left. Suddenly, I heard a pop-pop-pop! It was tear gas canisters exploding. I could smell the pungent scent and the burning sensation. I had learned from my training in the army how to respond to tear gas. I dropped to the ground on my hands and knees to keep below the clouds of gas. I saw Stokely running, staggering, and coughing—his face wet from the tear-inducing gas. I immediately began to look for Dr. King. When I saw him, I crawled to him and said, "Dr. King. Come with me. I'll lead you out of this." At my urging, he dropped to the ground, and together we crawled off the school grounds to the side of a road.

The troopers, who were wearing gas masks, ran amok. They kicked some marchers, slugged others with rifle butts, and cursed the marchers as they pulled up and flattened their tents. The press covered much of the melee. According to a United Press International report, one black marcher was kicked simultaneously by four officers. "God pity you because I can't," a white marcher yelled, the report said. One officer struck a white Roman Catholic priest in the stomach with the butt of his rifle, bowling him over. According to an Associated Press report, another marcher approached the officer and complained about an assault on a "man of God." According to the report, the officer said, "I put him with his God."

Standing on the edge of the grounds with Dr. King, I yelled, "Get off the grounds. Keep your head down and get off the grounds!"

In about twenty minutes, they had cleared the school grounds. About two hours later, many of us reassembled in a nearby church. As a result of the gas attack, some of my hair had an orange tint, and all of us had watery eyes. It was clear that the attack was intended to hurt us and instill fear. Dr. King wanted to show that we were not intimidated. "We've got to do something tonight," he said. We decided to conduct a night march in the neighborhood. About one thousand people joined us.

Reflecting on the day, Dr. King called the assault, "one of the best expressions of a police state I have ever seen." However, he also found a silver lining. "It was a marvelous display of nonviolence in the midst of the most brutal inhumanity" (Stanton 2011, 197).

The following day, we had an important morning planning meeting in the home of George Washington, the local resident. The braintrust included Andy Young, Ralph Abernathy, Stokely Carmichael, and me. We discussed how we would move on to the city of Jackson, how we could keep the march nonviolent, and how we would maintain our voter registration momentum. That same day, a recovering James Meredith arrived in Canton to join the march he had inspired.

"I don't know what's happening," he said after he arrived by car. Meredith was welcomed by Ralph Abernathy, who led him to a meeting with Dr. King and other leaders. Dr. King thanked Meredith for his leadership and his sacrifice. However, Meredith seemed to be resentful and declined to speak at a rally organized to give him a platform. With a small cohort, he later left, driving a car toward Tougaloo, the next stop on our march.

Media accounts and images of the tear gas attack unsettled the nation. President Lyndon Johnson conferred with U.S. attorney general Nicholas Katzenbach on June 24 in the wake of the Canton tear gas assault. The press reported that Katzenbach told Johnson that Mississippi authorities were doing an adequate job. I read that report. Frustrated, I talked to Andy Young about that and told him that "the troopers were doing a good job of intimidating the marchers."

While we were in Canton preparing our march plans for Jackson, Gov. Paul Johnson on June 24 agreed to permit a massive Civil Rights rally on the capitol grounds but not in the capitol building. Workers erected a fence about midway between the capitol building and the sidewalk surrounding the grounds.

A group of church leaders on June 25 sought unsuccessfully to meet with President Johnson. They wanted to warn him that a failure to protect the marchers might touch off racial explosions elsewhere in the country. President Johnson was known to be watching situation closely but said little.

Tougaloo, our next stop, was to be a celebrity-organized celebration featuring major entertainers. However, as we prepared to leave Canton, I was more focused on the fact that we had survived another stop without the loss of a marcher. The tear gas incident had given us the fuel to move ahead. We were more determined than ever. We felt we were winning the war against fear.

Tougaloo, Mississippi, June 25

We passed Piney Woods, the famous black boarding school, on our way to Tougaloo. Vocalists Sammy Davis, James Brown, Eartha Kitt, and Nina Simone and actors Marlon Brando and Burt Lancaster were among the celebrities waiting for us at Tougaloo's Southern Christian College, a black institution. The organizers of this celebration and local farmers had erected a makeshift wooden stage in a cotton field. Lettie and I and our three young sons were on stage with the stars. When James Brown came on with his big band, the stage began to sway. Fearing for their safety, I helped usher Lettie and the kids off the stage.

There were about five thousand people—locals included—at the concert. James Brown, dressed in blue jeans, a blue denim shirt, cowboy boots, and cowboy hat, performed "Please, Please, Please" and other hits to raucous cheering from the crowd. Brown was a supporter of the Civil Rights movement. His concert, nearly three hours long, lifted our spirits. In a field near the stage, I met Sammy Davis Jr. "I'm glad you had the courage to come," I said. "We're glad you're here." Marlon Brando and Burt Lancaster were huddled with Dr. King. To these famous Hollywood actors, Dr. King was the star.

Meanwhile, I was aware of the involvement of another famous entertainer— Harry Belafonte. He was not at the march but was behind the scenes raising money for funds for our medical support, food, lodging, and transportation throughout the march. He was especially busy as we prepared to enter Jackson.

Most significantly, it was in Tougaloo that Dr. King reconciled with James

Robert L. Green talks to marchers—activist Fannie Lou Hamer (*far right*) among them—during the Meredith march.

Meredith, who had arrived and abruptly left Canton in a snit. King reassured Meredith that this was "his march" and that he would be needed in the final stop in Jackson.

It was a night of harmony and fun. However, I was still apprehensive about our final stop.

Jackson, Mississippi, June 26

I was driving a small bus that had been adjusted to serve as a makeshift ambulance when I entered Jackson at the head of a march that now numbered about fifteen thousand and stretched for miles. Waiting along the road and in the heart of the city was at least another fifteen thousand—many supporters and many opponents. About twenty marchers, victims of heat prostration, heart palpations, and fatigue, were in the bus.

Suddenly, a young Jackson police officer was at the driver's side of the bus cab.

Yelling at me, he said, "Goddamn you, Nigger! Move that truck or I'll blow your goddamn head off!"

Some local whites on the side of the road responded. "Shoot! Shoot!" they said.

Considering the importance of the event and the media coverage, I remained calm. I ignored the officer and drove on. However, a day or so later, I saw the same officer with another officer. I and others approached him, and I said, "You threatened to blow my head off the other day." Although he was armed and we were unarmed, he felt threatened by our presence. He picked up his pace and kept moving.

As we moved further into Jackson, I had another trusted march manager relieve me as the ambulance driver to join Dr. King and the other leaders on foot—now at the front of the procession. As we approached railroad tracks on the city's periphery, I noticed a train moving slowly toward the first wave of marchers crossing the tracks. My immediate reaction was shock. My next reaction was to move. I ran toward the head of the train, mounted it, and confronted the engineer, a red-faced man in his fifties. "Mister!" I shouted. "We have thousands of people about to cross those tracks. If you hit one person, we're going to have a major problem—and it will center around you!"

Suddenly, I heard the high-pitched voice of Willie Ricks, making the same demands with profane expletives. The engineer stopped the train. Determined to stop any potential conflict, I leaned my head outside the train and told a contingent of angry SNCC members, activists who had also chased the train, to fall back into line with the other marchers. While doing so, I noticed *Washington Post* reporter Nick von Hoffman was running alongside. He had witnessed the entire train incident.

There were thousands of state troopers and a large contingent of the National Guard when we reached the capitol grounds. But there was no sense of confrontation. Instead, it was a celebration of solidarity. United Automobile Workers president Walter Reuther brought a huge contingent of union members, many of them carrying placards that announced "UAW Safety and Security." Celebrities—Burt Lancaster and Marlon Brando among them—marched in step with veterans of the long campaign. We were greeted by other entertainers—singers Lena Horne and Josh White, who performed on stages.

When the cheering subsided, the leaders of the march assembled to speak. Stokely Carmichael had his largest audience. He told the throng, "Stop being ashamed of being black," which prompted chants of "black power."

Floyd McKissick tried to bridge the gap between the more militant and the devotees of nonviolence. He told the crowd that there was nothing wrong with black power but also said, trying to unify black contingents, "we're going out there and we're going to be together."

King spoke to blacks and whites. He talked of shattered dreams of equality spoiled by northern riots and southern bushwackings, but added, "I still have a dream this afternoon of when whites and Negroes will live side by side in decent, sanitary housing." Speaking of the "evils of this state," he called on "all Americans to see the needs of the black people of Mississippi who are poverty stricken."

Meredith drew great cheers by denouncing white supremacy and warned the crowd to "not forget that the issue here is the power structure."

I sat quietly on the speakers' stage—relieved. I told myself that we had done something special. We had helped end an era of fear in Mississippi. I knew this was a campaign that would also change the mood in Alabama, another state with an extreme reign of terror.

Aftermath and Insight

Two days after the march ended I traveled to Grenada, Mississippi, to attend a Civil Rights rally in support of school desegregation, an issue that a local court was considering. Suddenly, a mob of white residents began to hurl bottles and rocks and—using slingshots—shot fishhooks at us. I saw one fishhook strike the forehead of a pretty young teenage girl.

I realized we were near a major store in the city. Recognizing the power of the heads of commerce, I told the activists to march to the store—not be afraid—and stand in front of the building. Our assailants realized that they would damage the store if they continued their attack. They stopped. Suddenly, my old nemesis—Sheriff Suggs Ingram—appeared and demanded that we move away from the store. We stood our ground until, minutes later, federal officials—led by John Doar, the U.S. Justice Department liaison to the Civil Rights movement—arrived and dispersed the mob of assailants.

By the end of August, I had completed my one-year stint at the SCLC and returned to Michigan State, where students and faculty members clamored for stories about my experiences.

Dr. King asked me to return to Mississippi later that year to help the SCLC oversee the September opening of an elementary school in the city of Grenada that was being integrated for the first time in the wake of a 1966 desegregation ruling by a court. My good friend Andrew Young and folk singer Joan Baez were among those in the state helping the SCLC ensure there would be no harassment of black children.

On September 7, 1966, two days after the Labor Day holiday, a group of us were traveling by car along a Grenada street. Coretta Scott King's cousin, T. Randall Osburn, was driving, and Dr. King was in the passenger's side front seat. King's aide, the Reverend Bernard Lee, Andrew Young, and I were in the back seat.

Our car stopped at a traffic light next to a Texaco gas station. James Belk, a white middle-aged station employee, was pumping gas. He noticed us and began to stride quickly and deliberately toward the car. As he moved closer, I could see an angry look on his face. Suddenly, he pulled a pistol from his pocket. Before we could respond, he planted the pistol on Dr. King's temple. "Martin Luther King!" he shouted. "I will blow your brains out!"

Dr. King did not flinch. Instead, he turned to the potential assailant, the gun still on his temple, and said in his always resonant voice, "Brother, I love you." The man displayed a look of stunned disbelief. Slowly, he lowered the weapon and walked away. Before the would-be assailant could change his mind and return, Randall Osburn drove the car slowly forward even as our hearts raced rapidly.

After we had travelled about a half mile, Andy, who was agitated, broke the silence. "Martin," he said, exhaling before he continued. "We've asked you, for safety reasons, to sit in the back seat, in the middle." Dr. King turned around to address Andy and said, "John Fitzgerald Kennedy had the Army, Navy, the Air Force, Coast Guard and the Secret Service, and they killed him. When they are ready, they will get me."

There was no fear in the man. I heard him say on several occasions: "There's a bullet out there with my name on it." He had been threatened hundreds of times. However, it was the first time anyone had come so close to killing him. King's reaction to Andy made it imminently clear that he knew he could be killed at any time. It would not be the last time he would indicate that he might be assassinated. For King, there was no crossroads of fear and freedom. He always ignored the fear-induced detour of accommodation and marched steadily and resolutely down the path toward freedom.

Dr. King was not alarmed, but I felt an urge to take some kind of action. I sent a letter about the incident to Texaco headquarters. In a letter dated November 14, 1966, Texaco vice president Annon M. Card responded, calling the gun incident "distressing," and promised action. "I am having an immediate investigation made of the circumstances cited in your letter," Card wrote.

Those two postmarch events—the aborted assassination of Dr. King and Sheriff Ingram's coordinated mob attack on Civil Rights activists—were attempts to thwart the early phases of school integration in Mississippi. It was then that I realized that the most important battle lines were at the schools where children could mix, end the cycle of hate, and obtain a comparable education. Our march and our subsequent support for integrated schools had helped black parents in the South overcome their fear. They were now willing to send their children to schools that could offer the equal educational opportunities required to remake America.

It was now time to take on the more sophisticated system of housing discrimination and educational injustice in the North. Education and housing were connected. After all, blacks sought homes in better neighborhoods partly because those communities had better schools.

CHAPTER FOUR

Crises and Change at Home

W hen Lettie and I completed the packing for a trip from our home in Las Vegas to East Lansing, I went to my computer to double-check our flight's departure time for the following day, August 22, 2014. We would be headed back to MSU for one in a series of very important events called Project 60/50.

That series, monthly public events from January 2014 through January 2015, was referenced by Lou Anna Simon, president of MSU, in a message on the university's website.

> We are approaching a pivotal time in our nation's history and one that gives each of us reason to pause to share our opinions and to learn from each other by joining important conversations. As we approach 2014, Michigan State University is gearing up to acknowledge the 60th Anniversary of the Supreme Court Decision in *Brown v. the Topeka Board of Education* and the 50th Anniversary of the Civil Rights Act of 1964 (CRA of 1964).

I then reflected on my experience at a previous Project 60/50 event, my contributions as a speaker at a May 2014 *Brown v. Board* retrospective at MSU.

Memories of that visit, which included a separate meeting with President Simon, flashed through my mind until I began to read her comments on the Civil Rights Act (CRA).

> Michigan State University is in a unique position to acknowledge the role that former MSU President John A. Hannah played with the passage of the CRA of 1964 when he was appointed as the first chairman of the United States Commission on Civil Rights by President Dwight D. Eisenhower in 1957. In demonstrating leadership and focusing on these important events in our nation's and institution's history, Michigan State University will facilitate many conversations around civil and human rights.

The message was cosigned by President Simon and Paulette Granberry Russell, senior advisor to the president for diversity. Paulette was one of many black students I knew during my first thirty-plus years at MSU as a professor, urban studies center director, and college dean. Also, I have known President Simon since she was a young graduate student in MSU's College of Education in the early 1970s.

President Simon didn't give lip service to diversity. Through her appointments and with the help of a responsive university community—faculty, staff, and board of trustees—she has helped MSU demonstrate a strong commitment to equal opportunity in hiring, professional development, and advancement. For example, she presided over a process that culminated in the appointments of two distinguished black women: the selection of Denise Maybank for the high-ranking post of vice president of student affairs and the appointment of Cynthia Jackson-Elmoore to the prestigious position of dean of MSU's Honors College.

Indeed, I knew that African Americans held quite a few top-level positions at MSU—among them Terry Curry, associate provost and associate vice president for academic human resources; Dr. Glynda Moorer, director of Olin Student Health Center; and Vennie Gore, a vice president who presides over State's vast residence hall systems and the university's hospitality services.

President Simon was simply adding to MSU's legacy of promoting high expectations and equal opportunity in its deeds and its leadership. MSU has a legacy of valuing diversity. After all, the iconic Clifton R. Wharton Jr., MSU president from 1970 to 1978, was the first African American to lead a major, predominantly white university in the United States.

President Wharton was distinguished for his achievements at MSU and admired for his subsequent work as chancellor of the State University of New York, as chairman of the Rockefeller Foundation, and as head of a national educators' pension fund that ranks among the largest institutional investors in the nation. In addition, in his last major leadership post—as a senior advisor within President Clinton's State Department—he was held in great esteem by his colleagues.

Like President Wharton and all great MSU presidents, President Simon established a record as a designer and promoter of programs that extend a unique Spartan scholarship legacy—engagement with and assistance to the developing world. For example, her Spartans Will. 360 initiative is a communications campaign that, beginning in 2013, produced stories on Spartan faculty, students, and alumni making a difference in the world—particularly in countries in Africa, Asia, and Latin America.

This global consciousness and diversity-valuing ethos originated under the legendary John Hannah, who had breathtaking skills as a university capacity builder. In 1941, Hannah was elected president of Michigan State College (MSC). Founded in 1855, it was the nation's first federal land-grant college. Throughout much of its early history, MSC distinguished itself in agriculture research and agricultural-outreach assistance to farmers in the United States, prompting some to dub the school "Moo-U." Some used it as an expression of derision, but many Spartans later embraced it as a term of endearment.

To the horror of MSC's university competitors and the snobby, and to the hurrahs of the supporters of this upstart publicly chartered institution, John Hannah, in the transformational post–World War II period, managed to help grow a rapidly expanding Moo U into the global leader in agriculture research and farming applications abroad.

During Hannah's tenure, which ended in 1969, MSU leveraged its position as a global leader in agriculture development into a world-class university with one of the nation's top international studies programs. Hannah also launched MSU on a path that would make it an institution that had and continues to have one of the largest and most diverse student bodies in the nation.

I learned a lot about John Hannah by working with him in the 1960s. I first met him in 1962 when I was doctoral candidate. I was walking to the library when a car pulled up. Out stepped a big man in a suit with a smile on his face. He walked toward me and beckoned me. We shook hands. "Who are you?" he said. "I'm Robert Green, I'm a graduate student," I replied. He said, "I'm John Hannah, president of the university. If you ever need anything, come to see me."

I've learned more recently from articles and books about how Hannah addressed problems and avoided taking credit by doing things behind the scenes. I was very aware of one of his attempts to intervene behind the scenes. When he offered to privately help me resolve a situation involving housing discrimination in 1964, I had to make a decision. For me, the first crossroads of fear and freedom was housing discrimination in East Lansing. The Fair Housing Act was not enacted until 1968. That was more than ten years after Hannah was appointed chairman of President Eisenhower's Commission on Civil Rights, and it was four years after the Civil Rights Act was enacted.

With President Hannah, his contemporaries, and subsequent campus leaders—students among them—I would come to a crossroads of fear and freedom many times. We would make decisions that would impact the nation. However, the matter of housing discrimination was on my mind because Lettie and I were returning to MSU to take part in a Project 60/50 retrospective on that subject. That's where my fight for justice began—but that's not where it ended.

After we arrived in Michigan, Lettie and I had dinner with our eldest son, Vince, a prominent Lansing-area attorney, and his wife, Valerie. As we dined at an upscale East Lansing restaurant, I began to think about 1963, my first year as an MSU faculty member. Things were so different then. Today, a black woman, Robyne Thompson, serves as superintendent of the East Lansing School District. In 1963, Vince was the only black child in his elementary school and may have been the only African American student in the school district. This was largely due to written and unwritten covenants by real estate agencies that prohibited selling East Lansing homes to blacks.

Vince interrupted my thoughts with a question. "Dad," he said, "what's it like to be back?" "It's great," I said. Looking at Lettie, I added, "Maybe we should move back?" Lettie shook her head from side to side, indicating "no" to a proposition made in jest. I then considered the fact that we would have no trouble buying a home in East Lansing today. However, fifty years ago, black adults at Michigan State and campus-employed African Americans at most majority-white universities could not buy a home in their college towns.

Even simply living off campus in East Lansing and other major college towns could be a challenge for African Americans. Our young family discovered this in 1963 when we arranged to move from MSU's Spartan Village apartment complex to rent a house in East Lansing. Now that we were back in this bucolic community, the memories of challenges and change in the 1960s were revived.

Thomas J. Green (1918) and Alberta Green (1915), parents of Robert L. Green, in Detroit, Michigan.

Located in mid-Michigan near the state's capitol, the institution now known as Michigan State University began to admit black students well before most other predominantly white institutions of higher learning partly because of its federal land-grant mandate. It was known as State Agriculture College in 1899 when it admitted William O. Thompson, an African American student. After graduation, Thompson taught at the Tuskegee Institute in Alabama, which is now known as Tuskegee University, also a land grant institution.

The first president of the Tuskegee Institute, the famed black educator Booker T. Washington, served as commencement speaker at Michigan's "State" school of the class of 1900. The following year, Washington and President Theodore Roosevelt were heavily criticized for dining together at the White House.

Roosevelt was the target of savage attacks by politicians and newspapers in the South. For example, Senator James Vardaman of Mississippi complained that the White House was now "so saturated with the odor of nigger that the rats had taken refuge in the stable" (Wickham 2002). Meanwhile, some black activists criticized the socially conservative Washington. For example, William Monroe Trotter, a Boston-based newspaper publisher, called him "a hypocrite who supports social segregation between blacks and whites while he himself dines at the White House" (Lusane 2013, 255).

A few years later, Myrtle Craig became the first black woman to enroll at the college. Myrtle and the other members of the class of 1907 received their degrees from President Roosevelt, the commencement speaker that year. The City of East Lansing was incorporated the same year. Two years later, the school changed its name to Michigan Agricultural College.

In the early 1900s, housing was a challenge for many blacks at the college and in the broader Lansing area. Housing discrimination and "redlining" were actually institutionalized by the federal government when it created in 1934 a Federal Housing Administration and, a year later, a Federal Home Loan Bank Board. The federal home loan bank used maps that included red lines around certain communities. These neighborhoods, primarily black, would be ineligible to receive mortgage financing.

Without access to bank loans, renters in Lansing's small black neighborhood could not become homeowners, and those who owned homes could not get home-improvement financing. African Americans could not buy homes in tony East Lansing or white neighborhoods in Lansing. Also, managers of apartments in East Lansing refused to rent to blacks.

In the late 1950s, the Lansing chapter of the NAACP helped a group of MSU students open their own chapter in East Lansing. That chapter organized marches against housing discrimination.

At the time, I didn't know all of this history, and I'm sure Orion Ulrey, an MSU professor of agricultural economics, didn't know it all either. However, Orion knew that there would be complaints when he agreed in the spring of 1963 to rent a house he owned to me and my family. I had just completed my PhD and had accepted a teaching position at MSU.

"This is the right thing to do because you're on the faculty," he said.

After my family moved into the house, some neighbors were friendly, some were indifferent, and some were rude and nasty, exhibiting the kind of racism that roiled Malcolm X, the Lansing-born black nationalist.

There was a great deal of campus interest in Martin Luther King Jr. and Malcolm X. Universities have always provided platforms for the discussion of public affairs. Malcolm X was born in Lansing, and I knew he monitored developments in his home state. I was sure he was aware of my successful fight against housing discrimination in East Lansing. I decided to invite Malcolm to speak at MSU, and he accepted the offer.

On June 22, 1963, he arrived at the auditorium in Erickson Hall. The room was packed, but the crowd was quiet and tense in anticipation of hearing from the black firebrand. Malcolm, who always had a sharp sense of humor, inadvertently disarmed the audience as I put a microphone with a string around his neck on stage. Not knowing that the microphone was turned on, he said, "Brother, I would only let a black man put a rope around my neck." The nervous audience broke out in laughter and applause. Malcolm also began to relax and made a frank presentation on how he and Dr. King agreed and disagreed on liberation tactics—his primary point being "blacks should not turn the other cheek."

After his presentation, he thanked me privately for arranging the forum and congratulated me for my academic achievements. I respected Malcolm, but I was more supportive of Dr. King's position and philosophy on race and social change. Moreover, I believed that individual blacks had a right to defend themselves if attacked by violent whites. I also believed that we had basic human rights, including the right to buy a home in the neighborhood of our choosing. I had grown up in a house because my parents were homeowners. My wife and my three young sons also deserved a home.

Despite my status as a rising star among young scholars at MSU, my initial efforts to buy a home were thwarted by real estate agents who would inform me that the homes of interest were no longer available. On one occasion, I learned from a colleague—a progressive white professor—that a high-level MSU administrator lived in one neighborhood that included a house I had sought. In March 1964 I learned that this administrator and some of his neighbors had pressured a real estate company not to sell the house to me.

I was enraged when I learned this. I decided to confront this man, who worked at the university's administration building. Upon arrival, I learned that the administrator and other top-level managers were meeting with President Hannah. I knew that Hannah did not tolerate interruptions of his meetings. However, I whisked past his protesting receptionist, entered Hannah's conference room, and called out my antagonist.

Hannah stood up, asked me to calm down, and then asked me to join him outside the conference room. When I explained the situation to him outside the conference room, he asked me to wait in his office so that we could chat after his meeting. He ended that meeting quickly and joined me in his office.

I knew Hannah would be sympathetic. After all, President Eisenhower had selected him to serve as the first chairman of the U.S. Commission on Civil Rights, and President Kennedy kept Hannah in that position.

That was the public John Hannah. The private John Hannah frequently helped African Americans behind the scenes. For example, Ernie Green was a member of the Little Rock Nine in 1957, the first blacks to attend the previously segregated Little Rock High School in Arkansas. Eisenhower had to send in the National Guard to protect them and maintain peace. When Green graduated, he received an offer of a full scholarship to attend Michigan State. He would learn years later that President Hannah had paid for that scholarship.

I knew Ernie. He was one of my students when I was a young professor. Ernie was also one of my assistants in Prince Edward County, Virginia, during that harrowing 1963 Justice Department research project on the impact of the county's public school shutdown.

Ernie earned a BA and MA in sociology from MSU and would go on to have great careers in government and business. From 1977 to 1981, he served as assistant secretary in Jimmy Carter's Labor Department. He retired in 2009 from his position as managing director of the municipal finance section of Barclays Capital (formerly Lehman Brothers). John Hannah would have been proud.

Hannah also personally intervened if he could address a problem. For example, there was the black athlete at MSU who was turned away when he tried to get a haircut at the MSU Union Building. When Hannah learned about the incident, he went to the athlete and they went to the barbershop together. Both received haircuts, and the barbershop ended its exclusionary practices.

After I briefed President Hannah fully on my situation, he leaned forward, his hands on the edge of his desk. "We can fix this," he said. He then offered to personally buy an East Lansing home, which he would then sell to me. I thought about it only a moment before demurring. "That would fix my problem," I said, "but it doesn't help the next black family seeking a home. Discrimination must be challenged."

Hannah crossed his arms, sighed, and then nodded. "As you pursue this," he said, "let me know if I can help."

Not long after that meeting, East Lansing mayor Gordon Thomas invited Lettie and me to dinner at his home. I did not know at the time that John Hannah had secretly asked Thomas to make the invitation. Subsequently, I began to call black faculty members at other schools in the Big Ten coalition—professors at Indiana University, Northwestern University, and the universities of Wisconsin, Illinois, and Michigan. All of them informed me that blacks could not buy homes in their college towns.

I wanted to make this a high-profile fight so that it might have an impact on other communities. I decided to send a letter about my situation to George Romney, then the governor of Michigan. Romney was a progressive Republican, but I had no idea if he would respond. To my surprise, Romney wrote back. In a letter dated March 20, 1964, Romney advised me that I could "file a complaint with the Michigan Civil Rights Commission which has general authority to investigate alleged racial discrimination."

Following the governor's advice, I filed a complaint with the Civil Rights Commission. I realized that my fight would become a public issue if the commission decided to launch an investigation. I had just filed the complaint with the commission and was awaiting a response when I received a phone call from an aide to Governor Romney. He told me privately that the governor hoped that I would be able to own a home in the community of my employment.

Subsequently, I was contacted by some local members of the Mormon community—among them Darryl Hart who, like me, had recently earned his PhD at MSU. He knew about my housing discrimination fight and arranged for me to discuss the issue at a meeting in East Lansing of a Mormon "stake," an administrative unit composed of congregations of the Church of Latter Day Saints. After my presentation to the stake about my housing discrimination experience, many Mormons approached me and expressed an interest in helping me.

Hart and Romney were Mormons, a religion that prohibited the ordination of blacks into their priesthood because of a belief that people of African descent inherited a so-called Curse of Ham. At the time, I did not know about the church's official position on the ordination of blacks. When I read about it, I realized that I could not consider becoming a Mormon, but I maintained cordial relations with my Mormon friends. It was then that I realized that social justice as it relates to religion is best defined by more enlightened believers, not doctrine. That Mormon doctrine on race was later struck down by the church leadership.

I very much valued Romney's advice when the Civil Rights Commission responded to my complaint by assigning a staff attorney to investigate my case. The investigator was Carl Levin, who later became a U.S. senator in 1979, a post he would hold for more than three decades. Levin was highly intelligent. We were both from Detroit. He was indignant that a young black with a PhD could not buy a home in East Lansing. He conducted research and filed a request for a cease and desist order from the commission, naming Walter Neller, the realtor who had blocked my home-buying efforts.

The local news media reported the legal action, and coverage expanded nationwide. The action was public, and I became a public figure—a target for bigoted whites. I received anonymous hate mail and hateful calls at my office. I could deal with that.

However, the conflict literally came home when Walter Neller and his wife appeared on the doorstep of my rented home a week after Levin filed the legal action. I let them in. Neller was a big imposing man. His wife had a troubled, uncomfortable look on her face. I offered them a seat. She sat, but he remained standing. Neller got right to the point. "I just wanted to see who you are because you're causing problems in this community," he said, his face reddening and his voice filled with anger. "You pup. I ought to hit you!" I was not afraid. I had placed third in the heavyweight division of the 1954 Association of American Universities national wresting championship. His wife stood and tugged at his arm. "You're wrong," she said. "Let's go."

My stress levels rose dramatically when I learned that threatening phone calls were made to my home. Like most very young children, my son Vince was eager to answer the phone. When he did, on several occasions, the caller threatened to kill me. On one occasion, the caller called Vince "nigger" and said, "We're going to kill you."

However, many fair-minded whites joined blacks in public demonstrations in support of me and open housing. For example, during this period several hundred students—blacks and whites—demonstrated against housing discrimination in front of East Lansing City Hall.

Also, when the city held hearings on housing discrimination, many MSU faculty and staff attended and demanded change. No one was more vociferous then than Betty Duley and her husband John, a university chaplain and local minister.

March 20, 1964

Mr. Robert Lee Green
221 Durand Street
East Lansing, Michigan

Dear Mr. Green:

In response to your letter of March 18, I wish to
advise you to file a complaint with the Michigan
Civil Rights Commission which has general authority
to investigate alleged racial discrimination.

The Lansing office of the Commission is located
on the first floor of the Mason Building.

Sincerely,

George Romney

In a letter, Michigan governor Romney offers Robert L. Green advice regarding his
housing discrimination complaint.

The Civil Rights Commission ruled in my favor and ordered Neller to sell to me. However, I declined to buy because I did not want to help the hostile Neller make money. A short time later, I arranged to buy the home of an MSU professor who was moving to take a department chair position at the University of Idaho. I was able to make the down payment of $2,500 because Jerry Wish, a PhD candidate who was from a wealthy family in Ohio loaned me $1,000. Jerry believed that racism was antithetical to Christianity.

Jerry later became a Civil Rights activist and antiwar activist. I encountered many whites like that—conscientious people who believed in social justice. To conservative elements in the country at that time, these people were radicals. When you're at the crossroads—and you take the more difficult path toward freedom—these are the kind of people you want at your side.

My battles for equal rights drew the attention of the FBI. At the time, though, I did not know that I had an FBI agent in one of my classes, a special agent who was gathering information to determine if I was a "subversive." The agent found no such evidence.

To be sure, the fight had stirred the public locally and nationally. For example, the City of East Lansing created a human relations commission, a group that advised Mayor Gordon Thomas after investigating conflict. I was very pleased that Robert Morgan, a doctoral student, was appointed to the commission. Robert was a former student who joined me in Farmville, Virginia, during the public school shutdown in 1963. He helped me write the report on the situation for the Office of Education, now known as Department of Education. He was also one of the most active protestors against housing discrimination in East Lansing. Mayor Thomas knew this.

I turned from integrating a community to integrating schoolbooks. As a boy, I had never understood why there were no black characters in my school readers. This fight began in the fall of 1963, when I spoke out against schoolbook publishing policies that limited the expectations of young black children. That year, at a conference of publishers of elementary schoolbooks at MSU, I asked executives how black children could have a positive vision of themselves and their future when they are not even represented in the "Dick and Jane" stories that introduced them to reading.

Book publishers frequently meet on campuses because university professors often help the companies produce books for K–12 students. I made my remarks during a question-and-answer period. "I'm a professor in the College of Education," I told the publishing executives. "I train future teachers. I have four hundred future teachers, and I want them to leave my class believing that integrated books would be a good thing. It would be good for the self-esteem of many children and—in the long run—it will be good for sales."

There was no serious discussion of my comments. However, when the meeting ended, I was approached by Jane Creeden, an executive with the Chicago-based Follett Corporation, a major academic book publisher. "Good job," she said. "My company agrees with you. I'd like you to talk to Dwight Follett, head of the company."

I learned that Follett had actually published the first series of school readers with black characters in 1959. The sales had been anemic, and six years later, no other publishing company had integrated the world of schoolbooks.

About a month later, I went to Chicago to meet Dwight Follett and his son, Bob, an executive at the company. I noticed many blacks at work stations. We met in Dwight's office, which was tastefully appointed with mahogany furniture. Dwight was a medium-sized man of athletic build. He had heard about my housing discrimination fight. Bob had also heard about the case. Bob told me that he and his wife, Nancy, had spoken out and worked against housing segregation in Oak Park, Illinois.

We then talked about the integration of school readers, reinforcing our respective views about how such books could prepare white children for a more diverse, more democratic society and help lift the self-esteem of black students. However, Follett was having difficulty convincing school districts to purchase his integrated series. He did not expect school districts in the South to buy his books, but he was disappointed by the responses in districts in the North and West. He thought I could help.

Follett wanted me to help motivate his sales team. After our meeting, I addressed a Follett sales group of about one hundred people. I talked about attitudes, values, and shaping young minds in a democratic direction. This was the beginning of a relationship with the Follett family that would last for decades.

I realized that Follett and other potential trailblazers might produce more books with black characters if professors at universities expressed interest in producing such readers. With funding from the National Defense Education Act, I served as a guest lecturer at many universities, and I always included comments about the value of integrating books during those lectures to encourage potential producers of schoolbook content.

However, when it came to oratory about the need to remove racial barriers of all kinds, no one was more eloquent than Martin Luther King Jr. I decided to invite Dr. King to speak at MSU. I had been occasionally sending notes to Dr. King, often with a small check donation to the SCLC, since I had met him in San Francisco as a student in 1956. I was thrilled, but not surprised, that he accepted because he was very interested in connecting with college students and university communities.

MSU chaplain John Duley, with the help of his wife, Betty, helped me raise the money to cover King's expenses. John, an ardent social justice activist, would in the early 1970s successfully advocate for the creation of the first subsidized housing in East Lansing.

Whites in northern university communities—especially students—overwhelmingly embraced the call for change when it was delivered by Martin Luther King Jr. When John Duley and I brought Dr. King to speak at MSU on February 11, 1965, more than 4,500 people—students, faculty, and community residents—attended the lecture. They filled the campus auditorium, and the overflow crowd went to the campus theater for the arts, where audio from his speech was transmitted.

The event was a fundraiser for MSU's Student Educational Project (STEP). STEP was the first student-administered educational outreach program of its kind in the country. The King address raised the funds that would finance volunteer programs that enabled MSU students to spend the following summer (1966) as instructors and tutors at Rust College, a black school in Holly Springs, Mississippi. MSU students would also tutor students at resource-poor black elementary and secondary schools in that Deep South community.

It was in the immediate aftermath of his speech that Dr. King asked me to take a one-year leave of absence and move my family to SCLC headquarters in Atlanta to work with him nationwide on education projects designed to help blacks register to vote in the South. John Hannah granted the leave, which would begin a few months later in September 1965. Before I started work at SCLC, I made a STEP-related trip to Holly Springs, Mississippi. During the visit, I tried to desegregate the local library by attempting to check out books for my two young sons; but they turned us away.

SCLC did not have the money to pay my $14,000 salary. The Marshall Field Foundation stepped up and provided the funds. In addition, the Follett family contributed another $200 a month, which covered the cost of rent as I continued to make my monthly mortgage payment on my new home.

In the 1960s, I would occasionally help Dr. King raise money for his Civil Rights work. For example, William vanden Heuvel, whom I came to know during my Farmville, Virginia, study when he was a special assistant to Attorney General Robert Kennedy, became involved in fundraising for Dr. King at my behest.

In the fall of 1967, Bill vanden Heuvel, who was then a senior partner at a prestigious law firm, organized a fundraising dinner in New York at a swank Fifth Avenue apartment owned by Allen Funt, the creator and host of the popular *Candid Camera* TV program. Dr. King, Andy Young, and I attended.

There were about twenty-five people at the gathering, many of them movers and shakers in the communications industries. The food and drink were top-notch. There was caviar, shrimp, lobster, champagne, and the best liquor. After about a half hour of mingling, Bill quieted the gathering and, glancing at Dr. King, said, "We're not here to hear a speech. We're here to write checks." Dr. King did give a brief speech, and the guests began to write checks. Among those in attendance was Neil Sullivan, an educator. I had met Neil shortly after I had completed the study on the impact of the public school closings by segregationists in Prince Edward County, Virginia, in 1963. Neil had used data from my study to design plans for instruction for a school he was managing in Farmville, Virginia. The school, financed by foundations and individuals, provided education to those affected by the public school shutdown. Bill vanden Heuvel had recruited Neil for the job. Most of the students who attended were black. He would later write a book about those experiences (Sullivan 1965).

Neil knew I had a PhD in educational psychology and gave me the name and phone number of one of his friends, Allen Calvin, founder and president of Pacific Graduate School of Psychology, later renamed Palo Alto University. Calvin and I would later collaborate on education projects.

Also in attendance was Harry Oppenheimer, a South African who chaired the Anglo American Corporation, an international mining company. He also served as chairman of De Beers Consolidated Mines, which dominated the diamond industry. He was one of the world's richest men. He was also, like many Jews in South Africa, opposed to apartheid. I leaned forward when Oppenheimer stepped forward with a $5,000 check in his hand.

The day after the fundraiser, a number of Dr. King's closest associates gathered in another New York apartment. Bernard Lee of the SCLC was among those there. So was Jack O'Dell, an SCLC staff member. In addition, singer and actor Harry Belafonte and heavyweight champion Muhammad Ali came to the apartment together, the last to arrive. The charismatic Ali was joking and laughing when he entered the room, but his demeanor changed and he became serious when the discussion began.

Immediately, talk turned to whether the SCLC should keep Oppenheimer's check. Some said the check should be returned, calling it "dirty money" made off the backs of blacks in South African diamond mines. I was among those who argued that the SCLC should keep the money, noting that it could be used to help the voter registration campaign in the South.

King was very democratic. He would usually let his associates debate issues, encourage everyone to speak, and then make a decision. However, in this case, he was noncommittal. He talked about the possibility of using part of the money to fight apartheid and part of it for voter registration. (It was a tough decision—one that Dr. King would never make. When he was assassinated about a year later, on April 4, 1968, Oppenheimer's check was still in his wallet.)

As the gathering ended, I approached Ali, who had condemned the Vietnam War. I told him that I also opposed the war.

The Vietnam War was a subject of contention when I first met with Allen Calvin at his Los Altos home in the summer of 1967. He had a company that produced and sold educational materials designed to help students improve in reading and math. I knew many school district superintendents, and Calvin wanted me to help engage them as a consultant for his operation. However, our conversation became heated when Calvin told me that Dr. King should not have given the April 4, 1967, speech against the Vietnam War at the Riverside Church in New York. To be sure, most of the establishment—white liberals included—felt the same way. "He should stick to Civil Rights," Calvin said.

As I got to know Calvin, who had previously taught at Michigan State, I learned that he was very progressive and that he had many blacks on his staff. He later changed his mind on that King speech, and I introduced him to Robert Morgan, who had a PhD in psychology from Michigan State and experience as a fair housing activist in East Lansing. Calvin hired Robert. (After Dr. King's assassination a year later, Calvin and I became even closer as friends. I introduced him to Coretta Scott King, and they also became friends.)

The year 1967 was also one of mounting militancy among black students at Michigan State and many other universities. I talked frequently with militant students. It reminded me of my disagreements with Stokely Carmichael during the March against Fear, conflicts that were resolved as he and I developed mutual respect.

I recall a spring 1967 forum involving some black activists and Robert Little, brother of Malcolm X, who had been assassinated February 21, 1965. Little had given a fiery address. As he moved to his closing comments, he looked directly at me and criticized me for "opposing" the black nationalism espoused by his brother. There was silence as everyone in the room turned to look at me. I stood up to respond.

Bob and Lettie Green discuss issues with Senator Robert F. Kennedy in Lansing, Michigan, in April 1968, shortly after King's assassination.

Malcolm X is unquestionably one of the greatest leaders of the modern Civil Rights movement. But I say now—as I said when he was here in East Lansing—that I believe in an integrated society. I believe in an America that includes equal opportunity for both blacks and whites in housing, employment, education—in all realms of American life. I believed then and I believe now that an integrated society offers the best hope for freedom and equality for black people in this country.

I then looked around the room at some of the students—Richard Thomas, Jason LaVette, Barry Amos, and LaMarr Thomas. I pointed to each of them as I continued.

> And to you, Richard, and to you, Jason, to you, Barry, and to you, LaMarr," I said, "to any of you who say you believe in black nationalism, I accuse you of being hypocrites for being here on this white campus, rather than out on the streets putting your lives on the line, like Malcolm X did; like Martin Luther King Jr. and Andrew Young and Stokely Carmichael are doing at this very moment!

After chastising the students, I complimented them for being socially conscious and active and reminded them that young people and their organizations—the SNCC among them—were making a difference. This was sincere because these thoughtful students gave me hope for the nation's future. However, over the next twelve months, I felt powerless during tragic events that would sadden me deeply.

Trouble was brewing in my hometown of Detroit where the lack of opportunity along with tension between a police force that was 93 percent white and a population that was 30 percent black.

The 1967 Detroit riot was prompted by a police action. It began on a Saturday night in the early morning hours of July 23. The precipitating event was a police raid of an unlicensed, after-hours bar then known as a blind pig. To help end the disturbance, Governor Romney called in the Michigan National Guard, and President Lyndon Johnson sent in U.S. Army troops. The results of the disturbance included 43 dead, 1,189 injured, more than 7,200 arrests and more than 2,000 buildings destroyed. At that time, the scale of the riot was surpassed only by the Civil War draft riots in New York City.

I was surprised and disturbed by the 1967 Detroit riot. During the riot, I discussed the situation by phone with Dr. King and members of his staff. He was also very distressed about it. He was very opposed to rioting because inevitably innocent people were hurt and because it also hurt the Civil Rights movement.

However, the greatest threat to Dr. King and the Civil Rights Movement was the FBI. FBI director J. Edgar Hoover had expressed his enmity toward King during a press conference on November 18, 1964, calling him "the most notorious liar in the country" (Bruns 2006, 67). Dr. King had responded by issuing a press release that suggested that Hoover was senile. That angered Hoover even more, and his pursuit of King became a vendetta.

There were FBI spies on the outside and FBI-paid informers on the inside. For example, the world would learn in 1981 that a top SCLC associate, James Harrison, was an FBI informer. Harrison handled payroll for the SCLC and personally handed me my salary checks. I did not know he was an informer, but I was suspicious during my one-year full-time stint with the SCLC because he frequently left his office to use a nearby pay phone. To track Dr. King, FBI agents would contact associates such as Harrison or call airlines to get his departure and arrival times and would determine where he would be staying. We did not think the agents were a lethal threat, but we knew that they were frequently using third parties in attempts to "set up" SCLC leaders—bids to entrap us in illegal or compromising situations. Information from FBI files shows that FBI Director J. Edgar Hoover and his agency were actively working to incite hatred toward Dr. King. Some believe that Hoover helped create a climate that led to the assassination of Dr. King.

By August 1967, the FBI's monitoring activities were intense. It would become evident when Lettie and I traveled to Chicago to rendezvous with Dr. King and Andy Young. Dr. King was to give a speech to the Council of Federated Organizations, a coalition opposed to the Vietnam War.

Dr. King did not travel with an entourage. When he was on the road, he traveled only with Andy Young and/or Bernard Lee, another SCLC associate. He had no bodyguards. For that reason, I had a clear view of the people observing us as we moved about. Some eyes stayed on us beyond the customary stares Dr. King's presence generated. "Hey," I thought at one point during the Chicago visit, "didn't I see that face before?"

When we convened for his speech to the Council of Federated Organizations, I could sense unease and some hostility in the crowd. That was confirmed when there was only moderate applause when Dr. King was introduced.

We were not caught totally off guard because we knew the coalition was very progressive and adamantly against the war. Before the speech, I looked around the hall and noticed some of the black and white faces in the audience. Some of them were some of the most militant members of the March against Fear that I had helped lead from Memphis to Mississippi. Despite the fact that Dr. King had taken the courageous step of denouncing the Vietnam War in his famous Riverside Church speech, some members of the council believed that his stance was not adequately antiwar.

A few minutes into the speech, the interruptions began—catcalls such as, "What about the war?" and "What about the people dying?"

Dr. King was a graceful, polite, and patient man who could not be flustered.

King responded by saying, "OK, I hear you. Now give me a chance to tell you where I stand."

The heckling disturbed me because Dr. King was in a vice. At one end were those urging Dr. King to devote much more of his time to the antiwar effort. Squeezing him from the other end of the vice were more conservative Civil Rights leaders, the mainstream media, and most politicians, people who believed he should not further involve himself in foreign affairs issues.

Dr. King had maintained his calm demeanor during the speech. The four of us—Martin, Andy, Lettie, and I—boarded a plane the next morning, September 1, 1967. It was then that Dr. King told us, "These days, the only place I feel comfortable as a public speaker is in black churches in the South."

The four of us were bound for Washington, DC, where Dr. King was scheduled to speak to the American Psychological Association. When we arrived at the DC airport, Andy said, "Our friends are tailing us."

Dr. King gave his address, "The Role of the Behavioral Scientist in the Civil Rights Movement," at a hall in the Washington Hilton hotel. He began by distinguishing the work of social scientists from other scientific work.

> For social scientists, the opportunity to serve in a life-giving purpose is a humanist challenge of rare distinction. Negroes too are eager for a rendezvous with truth and discovery. We are aware that social scientists, unlike some of their colleagues in the physical sciences, have been spared the grim feelings of guilt that attended the invention of nuclear weapons of destruction. Social scientists, in the main, are fortunate to be able to extirpate evil, not to invent it. (American Psychological Association 1999)

I was surprised and proud when he then made reference to me, an expert in educational psychology.

> From its inception, the Southern Christian Leadership Conference, which I have the privilege of serving as president, has recognized the value of social scientists—and welcomed the vast support. It must be added, however, that in ten years only one social scientist left a university to engage in full-time activity with us. Dr. Robert Green of Michigan State University spent more than a year with us and is presently a part-time member of our staff.

Later in the speech, Dr. King spoke bluntly.

If the Negro needs social sciences for direction and for self-understanding, the white society is in even more urgent need. White America needs to understand that it is poisoned to its soul by racism, and the understanding needs to be carefully documented and consequently more difficult to reject. The present crisis arises because although it is historically imperative that our society take the next step to equality, we find ourselves psychologically and socially imprisoned. All too many white Americans are horrified not with conditions of Negro life but with the product of these conditions—the Negro himself.

White America is seeking to keep the walls of segregation substantially intact while the evolution of society and the Negro's desperation is causing them to crumble. The white majority, unprepared and unwilling to accept radical structural change, is resisting and producing chaos while complaining that if there were no chaos orderly change would come.

Negroes want the social scientist to address the white community and "tell it like it is." White America has an appalling lack of knowledge concerning the reality of Negro life. One reason some advances were made in the South during the past decade was the discovery by northern whites of the brutal facts of southern segregated life. It was the Negro who educated the nation by dramatizing the evils through nonviolent protest. The social scientist played little or no role in disclosing truth. The Negro action movement, with raw courage, did it virtually alone. When the majority of the country could not live with the extremes of brutality they witnessed, political remedies were enacted and customs were altered.

These partial advances were, however, limited principally to the South, and progress did not automatically spread throughout the nation.

He then explained why he opposed the Vietnam War.

I am convinced that the war in Vietnam has played havoc with our domestic destinies. The bombs that fall in Vietnam explode at home. It does not take much to see what great damage this war has done to the image of our nation. It has left our country politically and morally isolated in the world, where our only friends happen to be puppet nations like Taiwan, Thailand, and South Korea. The major allies in the world that have been with us in war and peace are not with us in this war. As a result we find ourselves socially and politically isolated. (American Psychological Association 1999)

Dr. King ended his speech by noting that his recent travails had not robbed him of optimism.

> I have not lost hope. I must confess that these have been very difficult days for me personally. And these have been difficult days for every civil rights leader, for every lover of justice and peace.

The speech was very well received. When it ended, we attended a reception. It was hosted by Kenneth Clark, the psychologist who had conducted groundbreaking studies on race and child development, and Milton Rokeach, a noted MSU professor psychology.

When the reception ended, Dr. King and Andy, leery of FBI monitors, exited through a hotel backdoor and took a taxi to the airport for a trip to New York.

My next visit with Dr. King was on March 14, 1968, when he arrived in the Detroit suburb of Grosse Pointe to give a speech. We discussed the impact of the riots that had occurred in Detroit in the summer of 1967. It would be last time I would see him.

I can't describe the shock and grief I felt when, less than a month later, my friend and mentor, Martin Luther King Jr., was assassinated on April 4, 1968, at the Lorraine Hotel in Memphis during a campaign to help striking sanitation workers. I had actually met with Dr. King in that hotel during our planning for the March against Fear.

My wife and I and our children had always been close to Coretta Scott King and her children. We all became even closer after the assassination. King's death inspired me to expand my efforts as a social change activist.

The evening of King's assassination, about thirty black student activists came to my home to express anger and grief. They wanted to do something, but they didn't know what. Violence was already breaking out in many cities, and I wanted to ensure that the students had an outlet so that they would not engage in violence.

I had that in mind when I proposed to these activists that we should hold a campus memorial meeting the following day involving faculty and students. Some of the students said they wanted an all-black meeting, and I insisted that it would be an integrated gathering, in the spirit of Dr. King.

I told them, "I don't care what you think. I care what King would think!"

Robert L. Green, father Thomas Green Sr., brother Dr. Thomas Green Jr., and son Kevin attend the dedication of the MSU Community Outreach Building in Lansing, Michigan, in 1969.

At this crucial period, word of my insistence on inclusion spread to many faculty members about my effort to unite the Spartan community—black and white—in a postassassination gathering at the ballroom of the Student Union Building. Most of the black students who came to my home appeared to acquiesce to my call for a peaceful united front, but I was concerned about a few hard-core black nationalists.

Lettie and I arrived at the Student Union Building early the next day to ensure that angrier blacks did not keep whites out. The gathering was about 40 percent white. I chaired a discussion involving faculty and students regarding the meaning of King's death and its impact on the nation. After the gathering, about six hundred students marched with me from the Union Building to the Administrative Building. I took a few of the students to meet with John Hannah. President Hannah expressed grief and concern at the meeting. When the students left his office, he told me that he wanted to arrange to pay the expenses of some MSU students who would attend the King funeral in Atlanta. I later selected fifteen students, including a few white students, who would be reimbursed. Knowing President Hannah's pattern, he probably did not use university funds and may have financed it himself.

Lettie and I encountered George Romney and his wife, Lenore, immediately after the memorial service at Morehouse College, which had followed the funeral services held at Ebenezer Baptist Church. He recognized me because we had met previously and because my name and photo had been in the news regarding my housing discrimination ordeal. The four of us talked on the way to the parking lot. He asked me to discuss my experiences as a black homeowner in East Lansing. He also expressed his great concern about the assassination of Dr. King and praised him as a great leader for nonviolent change.

Shortly after Dr. King's death new racial tensions on campus began to emerge. First, many of the black student-athletes on MSU's football team were unhappy for a number of reasons. Some of them—LaMarr Thomas, a very bright star running back from Chicago, among them—had discussed the situation with me. They alleged that the coaches were "stacking" some of the team's best black players, forcing them to compete against each other for similar positions to ensure that whites would have a clear path to be starters at other positions.

Black football players often confided in me because I had helped recruit some of them and served as mentor to many of them. Lettie and I often hosted student-athletes at our home for food and talk. They sometimes visited without an invitation.

The allegations would have shocked many at the institution, which changed its name from Michigan State University of Agriculture and Applied Science to Michigan State University in 1964. It would have been surprising because State had a well-earned reputation as a magnet for some of nation's top African American athletes. Football coach Duffy Daugherty recruited talented black players from around the country—including the South, where black players were not recruited by local universities.

There were many black standouts on the 1965 team, which won a share of the national title. Running back Clinton Jones, wide receiver Gene Washington, and two All-Americans—defensive lineman Charles Aaron "Bubba" Smith and linebacker George Webster—were among the stars.

The following season, Jimmy Raye became one the few blacks to ever play quarterback for a major university. One of the back-up quarterbacks, Eric Marshall, was also black. He was from Oxford, Mississippi, the home of the University of Mississippi. The coach of "Ole Miss" was not allowed to recruit blacks. Instead, he called MSU coach Daugherty who gave Eric a scholarship. (Lettie, my sons, and I visited Eric's family after we completed the March against Fear in Jackson, Mississippi.)

Jimmy Raye led the Spartans to an undefeated season. That season included the "Game of the Century," a 10–10 against rival Notre Dame. The 1966 team also won a share of the national championship.

Duffy was not only a great recruiter and coach, he was a legendary wit known for the following quips: "A tie is like kissing your sister." "When you're playing for the national championship, it's not a matter of life or death. It's more important than that." "Football is not a contact sport. Football is a collision sport. Dancing is a contact sport."

I was an unpaid recruiter and counselor to many black student-athletes. Working with Duffy, who had a green light from President Hannah, we created an Underground Railroad for southern black athletes.

In all, the 1965 and 1966 teams had twenty black players, far more than most integrated college teams. In contrast, major southern universities such as Alabama, Mississippi, and Mississippi State had none.

However, I knew there were problems. One of them related to Jack Pitts, a Georgia high school quarterback I had just helped recruit during my off-hours from the SCLC in 1965. Jack was one of the top collegiate prospects in the country. Not long after I helped recruit Jack, the football coach of North Carolina's Wake Forest made a visit. He told me that he was trying to recruit Jack but that Jack mentioned my name when he explained he had already committed to Michigan State. The coach then asked me if I could confirm what Jack told him. I kept it short. "Jack has decided to go to Michigan State," I said. The coach left my office, but he made one other stop before leaving the building. A few minutes later, Ralph David Abernathy, a top King associate, approached me, smiling. "I understand that you were paid to recruit Jack. Where's my cut?" he quipped. Of course, I had received no payment.

Unfortunately, when Jack arrived on campus, there were several players already competing for the quarterback position. Jack was reassigned to play defensive back, a position a number of black players were attempting to win. As a defensive back, Jack would later suffer an injury that essentially ended the possibility of a promising athletic career. (Jack would work for me as finance director of the College of Urban Development and subsequently had a good career as a medical insurance executive.)

Considering that blacks were playing key positions at MSU, quarterback among them, I wasn't sure that there was a lack of opportunities because of "stacking." However, I sensed the underlying concern of black players. To me, the core problem was apparent. Michigan State, like most major universities, had no black assistant coaches. Something had to be done, and I knew a black qualified to join the Spartan staff—Don Edwin Coleman.

Don Coleman in 1951 was an All-American football player at what was then called Michigan State College, when he played tackle for legendary coach Clarence Lester "Biggie" Munn. He was also the first MSU football player to have his number retired and would later be inducted into the College Football Hall of Fame. Don graduated in 1952, then served in the military and came back to Michigan as a high school coach in the city of Flint.

At that time, Biggie Munn was athletic director. He had been head football coach at Syracuse University before taking the reins at Michigan State in 1947. His early success and the academic growth on campus enabled Michigan State to join the prestigious Big Ten Conference in 1949. Under Munn, the Spartans beat the famous Frank Leahy's Fighting Irish three years in a row (1950–52), the only team to have done so. In 1952, Michigan State won the national championship.

Munn retired from coaching in 1953 to assume duties as Michigan State's athletic director, and his assistant coach, Duffy Daugherty, took over as the leader of the football team. Munn was inducted into the College Football Hall of Fame in 1959.

I made plans to meet Munn in 1968 to ask him to consider hiring Don Coleman, a famous Spartan, as an assistant coach. As I headed to Munn's office, I wondered how he would react. I was hopeful. After all, under Munn, Willie Thrower became the first African American to play quarterback in the Big Ten. Coming in as a replacement for an injured teammate, Thrower led the Spartans to victories in the final two conference games of that 1952 championship season. (Thrower later became the first black to play quarterback in the National Football League.)

I entered Munn's office and we shook hands. Munn was literally and figuratively a big man on campus and a big man in college athletics. He was tall and had huge shoulders. I made my pitch for Don Coleman, noting that he had been successful coaching on the high school level. Munn was quiet until I made additional comments about the need for black coaches at a major university. "I'm sorry, professor," Munn said, looking dour. He told me, "I know football." He then said, without a pause, that blacks "do not have the ability to coach." I knew this attitude persisted, but I was shocked and disappointed by Munn's comments. I was also undaunted. I decided to make the same request of head football coach Duffy Daugherty.

I was not the only one to meet with Biggie Munn about equal opportunity. Black activists on the football team, led by running back LaMarr Thomas, wanted some specific actions. For example, they wanted the athletic department to hire some blacks for positions at the university's sports arenas and they wanted the all-white cheerleading team to add some blacks to their squad.

The gridiron players added to their ranks by recruiting some black athletes from the basketball and track-and-field teams to support their demands—about forty athletes in all. The football players then threw down the gauntlet by abruptly quitting a spring practice session to meet with Munn about their concerns. The players said they would sit out the football season if their demands were not met. The threat made national news.

This turned up the heat. When I met with Duffy, he told me he had actually hoped to hire a black assistant coach and that Don Coleman was an excellent candidate. He told me he would try to bypass Munn by going directly to John Hannah. He did so, and I also met with Hannah separately on the same subject. In the spring of 1968, Don Coleman was hired as an assistant coach.

I participated in several meetings with the athletes, discussions that also involved John Hannah and his senior advisor, Jack Breslin. During the initial meeting, I noted that Don Coleman had been hired. During both meetings, I served as a kind of interpreter, explaining the players' concerns to the administration and explaining how the university wanted to resolve any possible problems.

When it was over, the players agreed to resume practices. I felt somewhat gratified. When it came to fear or freedom at the crossroads of equal opportunity and racial bias in sports, Michigan State was continuing as a pioneer—always taking the right path.

(Team activist LaMarr Thomas, who was recovering from knee surgery at the time, later decided not to return to the football team in order to concentrate on his studies. Duffy allowed him to keep his scholarship. He would later become a noted researcher and historian.)

The following year, 1969, I spent a lot of time building MSU's Center for Urban Affairs (CUA), an institute that I had founded the year before. CUA was beginning to conduct research to address problems in major Michigan cities. I was expanding the staff. Maxie Jackson, then an administrator at MSU's volunteer bureau, joined me that year.

Maxie replaced Nolan Ellison, a doctoral candidate and one of my former students. He left CUA to work as an administrative aide for President Wharton. Nolan would later become president of Cuyahoga Community College in Cleveland, a post he held from 1974 to 1991. His successor at CUA, Maxie, was a hard-working administrator. He would work with me until I left MSU many years later.

About one year after I hired Maxie, I brought in Eric Winston, an MSU Library employee. Eric was director of student affairs for CUA. He was very good with students. Like Maxie, he was also with me until I left the university.

I would eventually build a CUA faculty that included sociologists, psychologists, political scientists, economists, a physician, and an urban planner. Within CUA, there was the Department of Urban and Metropolitan Studies, which conducted research on health and education issues.

University financial support for a CUA transition to a new College of Urban Development (CUD) increased partly as a result of student activism. The great John Hannah resigned in 1969 to become head of the U.S. Agency for International Development. Walter Adams, a prominent economist at the university, became interim president. Adams, a progressive who wore bow ties and smoked cigars, was attentive to the concerns of black students.

Shortly after assuming office, Adams met with black student leaders. They had a number of requests. They wanted Adams to speak at an April 4 memorial on the first anniversary of Dr. King's assassination. Adams agreed. They also wanted the university to admit more black students, employ more African American faculty and staff, and offer more courses on African American history.

The students also told Adams that a blue-ribbon faculty committee had been tasked to address the requests that had been made the previous year and lamented that no action had been taken. Adams moved quickly, taking steps to show support for human rights without hijacking the mission of the faculty committee. The university excused students from afternoon classes on April 4 for meditation, religious devotion, or attendance at the King memorial.

Adams spoke eloquently at the memorial. In addition, two weeks later, on April 18, the university dramatically increased its financial support for CUA, which

Tom Gunnings, Joseph McMillian, and Robert L. Green formed the Civil Rights troika during the Civil Rights movement on the campus of MSU during the 1960s and 1970s.

would lead to the creation of a CUD. The action was well received by the student activists—and by me.

However, ten days later, black students had occupied the cafeteria at the Wilson Hall dorm. Many of them were students affiliated with the Black Student Alliance, an organization that students founded during a meeting in my house earlier that year. Walter Adams went to Wilson and discussed the situation with the black students. The activists were barring white students from the cafeteria because two white supervisors had mistreated and verbally insulted some black sanitation and cafeteria employees. They wanted the supervisors fired. (Some of the activists had told me the day before the protest that they were planning to take direct action, but they did not provide any details.)

Adams told one of the students that the supervisors were entitled to a fair hearing and could not be summarily dismissed. He asked the protestors to consider the supervisors' rights and to contact him after giving the situation more thought.

Adams then met with about two hundred white Wilson Hall students, many of them angry because they did not know why the cafeteria was being occupied. One student asked Adams if he would contact the police to have the protestors forcibly removed. However, Adams decided not to call the police because it could escalate the problem—and certainly not solve it.

I liked Walter Adams and knew him well. I was very glad that he was showing restraint. For my part, I felt the protesters needed support. On the third day of the occupation, Adams accepted a proposal to resolve the situation. Under it, a biracial investigating committee consisting of an equal number of administration and Black Student Alliance representatives was constituted to conduct a hearing and make recommendations to the interim president.

The hearing was held at Wilson Hall, and I attended as a representative of the black faculty. I was concerned about the abuse of black employees. The protesting students had no reason to make erroneous claims about mistreatment. I spoke up at the hearing. "In the future—and this is a warning—when racism exists in any component of this university, we will close that component down," I said. When the hearing ended, the committee came forward with unanimous recommendations.

- That a black person be appointed in the central MSU personnel office with the general assignment of recruiting more blacks
- That steps be taken to upgrade blacks in residence hall employment with on-the-job training, if necessary
- That an arbitration system be established to adjudicate the sort of conflict involved in Wilson Hall
- That a black college graduate be recruited and trained for one of the managerial posts at Wilson Hall
- That the two white supervisors be transferred out of Wilson and placed in nonsupervisory positions

The two supervisors threatened legal action against the university, charging libel and defamation. The university offered them a new hearing to be conducted by professional, outside arbitrators. One rejected the offer. The other accepted and subsequently filed a lawsuit that was dropped six months later.

Adams was the target of media criticism during the crisis and after the resolution. Many critics said Adams should not have bargained with students. Adams answered them in *The Test*, his 1971 memoir.

The students alone—among all the "constituencies"—came closest to understanding what was involved. Wilson Hall was no panty raid, no casual fling, no night on the town, no search for kicks. Nor was it an act of violence, either by intent or execution. It was an angry cry, born of long suffering—a reaction to what more mature minds had labeled white racism, not alone in white universities but in this white society. It was black people shouting so loud because for so long no had listened. With the passage of time, the initial indignation of white students gave way to questioning—to attempts at understanding. (Adams 1971, 77)

Adams was also an advocate of affirmative action in college admissions. Like John Hannah, he understood the need to address the nation's legacy of institutional racism. When Michigan State selected its next leader, it made a statement that would be heard around the world.

With an impressive personal academic background—enrolled at Harvard at age sixteen, an MA from Johns Hopkins University, and an MA and a PhD in economics from the University of Chicago—Clifton R. Wharton Jr. also had career experience perfectly suited to be president of MSU, a global leader in research and applied sciences in international development.

He had gained great experience and expertise on Third World development as an analyst during his five years (1948–53) at the American International Association for Economic and Social Development, working his way up through that organization over five years. At that time, most of his work centered on Latin America.

After earning his advanced economics degrees, Wharton went to work for American business mogul and philanthropist John D. Rockefeller III's Agricultural Development Council (ADC). He joined as an ADC associate in 1957 and later served as ADC's director of its Southeast Asia operations (1958–64). While representing the ADC in Malaysia and other Southeast Asian countries, Wharton became an acknowledged expert on agrarian reform. He taught economics at the most prestigious university in Malaysia. In an interview with the *New York Times Magazine*, the Boston-born Wharton reminisced fondly about his six years in Asia, saying, "Three of my friends and I formed an organization called CBCBCRAEA. It stands for City-Born, City-Bred, City-Raised Agricultural Economics Association."

Subsequently, Wharton became ADC's director of American university research (1964–67), a post that made him even more qualified to lead a university with global reach. He was serving as vice president of ADC (1967–69) when he became a candidate for the MSU presidency.

Pedigreed? Yes. Qualified? Yes. However, when the MSU Board of Trustees decided in a 1969 vote to elect Clifton R. Wharton Jr. the president of MSU, news of that action circulated the globe because in 1970 he would also be the first black man to lead a major, majority-white university in the United States.

In the United States, his selection was cited as an unexpected and hopeful harbinger of actual national progress toward a more color-blind society. There was a front-page report in the *New York Times* and a cover page article in *Jet* magazine—just two of many examples of the importance American media ascribed to this event.

Some of the mainstream and more conservative media narrative suggested that Wharton was someone relatively new in American public life: a black member of the *establishment*—not a member of the *black establishment*. However, few were aware that Wharton had been a member of the Tuskegee Airmen, the first African American military aviators in the U.S. armed forces. During World War II, black Americans in many U.S. states were still subject to Jim Crow laws and the American military was racially segregated, as was much of the federal government.

Also, before his election as president of MSU, few were aware of the quality of our association. I did not know Wharton before he was nominated for the presidency. I had heard of him, but I knew more about his father, Clifton R. Wharton Sr. The elder Wharton was the first African American diplomat to become an ambassador by rising through the ranks of the U.S. Foreign Service, rather than by political appointment.

I learned that Wharton was a finalist for the presidency from Edgar Schuler, an MSU sociologist who worked with me on my report on the public school shutdown in Prince Edward County, Virginia. When Edgar mentioned Wharton, I initially thought he was referring to the diplomat. I was encouraged when I learned it was Wharton Jr. because he could lead MSU long enough to make a major difference.

The presidency of MSU was a plum position that was highly contested. The other major finalist was the iconic G. Mennen Williams. Williams, nicknamed "Soapy" because he was an heir of the family that founded the Mennen personal care products company, was elected governor of Michigan in 1948 and served six two-year terms in office. Williams was a political reformer who helped forge the long-standing Democratic Michigan alliance that included blacks and the state's strong labor unions. He gained prominence for his refusal in 1950 to extradite to Alabama prison escapee Haywood Patterson, one of the nine Scottsboro Boys who, in a miscarriage of justice, had been convicted of rape. As governor, he appeared on the cover of *Time* magazine's September 15, 1952, issue, sporting his signature bow tie. During the 1952, 1956, and 1960 national Democratic conventions, he fought for insertion of a strong Civil Rights plank in the party platform.

After Williams left office in 1961, President Kennedy appointed him to the post of assistant secretary of state for African affairs. At a post-appointment press conference statement, Williams said, "what we want for the Africans is what they want for themselves," sparking controversy because it was reported in the press as "Africa for the Africans" (Muehlenbeck 2012, 45).

Whites in South Africa and Rhodesia, another country controlled by a white-minority government, along with white leaders in British and Portuguese colonies in Africa, contended that Williams wanted them expelled from the continent. Williams and President Kennedy defended the remark, saying that the reference included white Africans as well as black Africans. Williams wrote *Africa for the Africans*, a book published in 1969, the same year the MSU Board of Trustees would elect a new president.

Williams and Wharton were both great candidates. However, I was intrigued by Wharton because he was an international development expert with ties to the Rockefellers who happened to be black. That impressed me because of MSU's claim to fame as a "global university." I was leaning toward supporting Wharton, but I wanted to know more about him.

I contacted Hope Spencer, daughter of John D. Rockefeller III and younger sister of Jay Rockefeller, who would later become a West Virginia senator. We had met when we were both graduate students living on campus at Spartan Village and had developed a friendship. When Hope told me she didn't personally know Wharton, I asked her to check with her Rockefeller associates and to let me know if I should have any reason to be concerned about a Wharton presidency. She agreed but did not contact me on that question—a sign that there were no problems. (Hope would later spend her career as a journalist in New York, Beijing, and Washington, DC, before joining and later buying the *Santa Fe Reporter* and becoming its publisher.)

I decided I wanted to meet Wharton. I called him, told him that Lettie and I would be visiting New York soon and that we would like to meet him and his wife, Dolores. He welcomed the opportunity. We had a number of meetings over a two-day period. Once, the four of us had lunch in the Rockefeller box of an upscale New York restaurant. I was impressed by his poise and his intellect.

He also demonstrated great knowledge of Michigan State's history and recent developments at the university. In addition, he was familiar with my work at the CUA and my role as unofficial counselor to black student leaders on campus. He even named some of those students.

During our last meeting, he asked for my support, and I pledged it. He then surprised me by suggesting that I might be an excellent candidate for the position of vice president for student affairs. I immediately declined politely, telling him that I wanted to write books on urban problems and discrimination and that I could not do that as a vice president.

Winning out over Williams would be a challenge. "Governor Williams can get the university more funding from the state legislature" was a very persuasive argument. Also, as former head of the party, Williams could count on a lot of Democratic support. With his connection to the Rockefellers, Wharton could count on Republican support, but he would need the votes of Democrats, a majority on the board of trustees, to get elected.

I did my part by supporting his candidacy in talks with Dr. Blanche Martin, a black member of the MSU Board of Trustees. I also obtained positive responses from Basil Brown and Coleman Young, influential members of the Michigan State Senate. (In those days, Coleman would occasionally visit our home because he loved Lettie's collard greens and the Pinch scotch we would provide.) Also, when some black student activists expressed support for Williams after they became aware of the former governor's vast African arts collection, I talked to them, explaining my support for Wharton.

Wharton and I talked frequently on the days leading to the vote. With a vote from Don Stevens, a white Democrat on the board, Wharton was elected by one vote. I was elated!

When Wharton arrived as president, many white faculty and staff members were apprehensive and unsure what to expect. They soon learned that he was a good leader. Although he was very confident, he was also self-effacing. In addition, he was also a great listener and excellent consensus-builder.

Except for complaints about property damage during a major MSU campus demonstration against the Vietnam War in 1970—the same year many other campuses erupted with protests against an unjust war—that first year was a "honeymoon" for Wharton in terms of the support and admiration he engendered. He had challenges, many priorities, and plans for new initiatives. However, we managed to talk frequently—usually by phone—during his first year in office. I also saw him at monthly administrative meetings. He gave me the impression that the CUA appeared to be on track to becoming a college.

However, I had some opponents on campus. Some faculty members and students questioned the need for the CUA and opposed its creation because they believed that universities should be insulated learning centers, not compromised by involvement in or engagement with outside communities. Some assumed it would

Sociologist Kenneth Clark, Robert L. Green, famed network news anchor Walter Cronkite, Lettie Green, and MSU trustee Pat Carrigan chat at the 1973 MSU commencement.

not have high standards because they knew only about Robert L. Green the activist and not Green the scholar. They did not know that I had produced two books and numerous articles in prestigious, refereed academic journals. I didn't hear these comments directly from my critics. Progressive white friends on the faculty relayed this information to me.

However, one of my severest critics was very public. Barney White, a columnist with the *State News* student newspaper, frequently attacked me. White never interviewed me. As a columnist, he was not required to do so. However, to me, he demonstrated ignorance about the historic role of universities in community affairs.

The *State News* had been fair in its coverage of my fight against housing discrimination, and the paper had chronicled my work for Dr. King and the campus forums I had organized on Civil Rights. Editorially, the *State News* also supported Walter Adams's handling of the Wilson Hall crisis during a period when he was being savaged by the nonstudent media. However, the *State News*—like most newspapers at major universities—had never had a black staff member.

I had expressed my concern about the absence of blacks on the staff in a meeting with John Hannah in 1968. However, Hannah was concerned about taking any action that might be seen as interference with the editorial independence of the *State News*, widely recognized as one of the best student newspapers in the country.

When Barney White attacked me again in a *State News* edition in the fall of 1971, I concluded that it was time to confront the paper's leaders about the absence of staff diversity. This was a pivotal decision that would have a great impact on George White, a black freshman from Detroit, and other black journalism students at Michigan State.

MSU was a great match for George. He intended to get BA in both journalism and African history as a double major. MSU was his best option because it was and continues to be a leader in communications and African studies. MSU also appealed to George because it had the Honors College, a prestigious unit that allowed undergraduates to waive customary freshman and sophomore prerequisites to tailor studies to earn double majors.

George was a late academic bloomer, and his grades were not good enough for initial admission to the Honors College. He was accepted under the MSU Development Program designed to help increase the enrollment of black students and other underrepresented groups. This program and other initiatives had generated some positive outcomes. There were about 690 black students at MSU during the fall of 1967. There were about two thousand black students in a forty thousand–student MSU population when George, a (Detroit) Mumford High School graduate, enrolled in the fall of 1971.

A few other black Mumford alums at MSU welcomed George when he arrived. One of them, Gerald Evelyn, was a student activist who was eager to get George involved because young Mr. White had helped organize a successful student protest at Mumford High School in Detroit. The high school protestors obtained the classes that their protests had prompted the administration to provide: a black literature course and a black history course.

When the new black history teacher had George and his classmates study the ancient African civilizations of Ghana, Mali, and Songhai during the first few weeks of a course that focused primarily on African Americans, George developed a great yearning to learn more African history. He knew MSU could provide a valuable education in journalism and international affairs.

His fellow Mumford alum Gerald Evelyn and another black student activist, Walter Thomas, arranged for George—a first-term freshman—to become director of the Office of Black Affairs (OBA), a part-time job. OBA was a student services group that organized campus programs and represented the interests of African American students and black organizations—activist groups such as the Black United Front and the Black Student Alliance among them.

The OBA, like the Associated Students of MSU, received university funding. The OBA, also like the *State News*, was located on the third floor of the Student Services Building. George was at his desk in the OBA office when a colleague raced in from the hallway.

Looking at George, he yelled, "Dr. Green is in the *State News* office raising hell!" George knew of me and my work, but we had not met. Curious, George rushed to the *State News* office as I was confronting the student editor of the paper. George's activist friends, Gerald Evelyn and Walter Thomas, were already on the scene standing near me. Standing in front of the editor of the paper, I said, "You don't have one black person working here." The editor, clearly shaken, said, "No blacks have applied." Walter Thomas noticed that George had entered the newsroom. He pointed to him and said, "Here's George. He's a journalism major. He's applied."

George had a surprised look on his face and appeared to be ready to speak when I spoke instead. "Hire him," I said. "Hire him right now." The editor looked at George and said, "George, if you're still interested, come to the office tomorrow and we'll do the paperwork to get you started." George nodded, and we all left the newsroom. George thanked me and headed back to the OBA office with Walter and Gerald. I overheard an exchange between George and Walter.

George said, "But I hadn't applied. Students have to be in their junior year to be eligible for the staff." Walter said, "That's OK. You'll be applying tomorrow." The following day, George became the first black student and the first modern-era freshman to join the *State News* staff. During his first year, he distinguished himself as a reporter and columnist. For example, he produced a column on the Environmental Protection Agency and the urban health threat of lead paint poisoning.

Considering his interest, it was no surprise that his first article was on developments in Africa, an interview with an East Indian refugee from Uganda who had fled the tyrannical rule of Idi Amin. The following year, 1972, Amin expelled eighty thousand Asians and expropriated their businesses, doling them out to supporters.

By early 1972, George was frustrated because no other blacks had been added to the staff. Other black journalism students were not getting the experience they needed to get internships. For that reason, George—while continuing his work at the *State News*—also began to help improve a fledgling black newspaper called the *Grapevine Journal*.

He would later relinquish his position at the *State News* to become editor of the *Grapevine Journal*. The *Grapevine* would thrive. One fall orientation issue had sixty-four pages. *Grapevine Journal* staff members would go on to work as professionals at a number of outlets—the Associated Press, the *Washington Post*, the *Detroit Free Press*, the *Detroit News*, and *Ebony* magazine among them.

In addition, George would later lead a multiracial coalition that successfully pushed for a student fee to support all student media, a registration assessment that had previously been reserved for only the *State News*. (Over a period of time, many other universities followed suit and provided student fee money to alternative campus media to ensure diversity and fairness in communications.)

George was prompted, in part, to work with the *Grapevine Journal* because he believed there should have been more in-depth coverage of a report I produced on racism in Big Ten athletics. Working with two other MSU scholars—psychiatry professor Tom Gunnings and Joseph McMillan, assistant vice president for human relations—I began working on the Big Ten report in 1971. Racism in sports had always disturbed me because playing fields and courts had been touted as meritocracies.

Both McMillan and Gunnings had experience in college sports. Gunnings had played football at a college in South Carolina, and McMillan had been a member of a college track team. The three of us had been meeting at the end of each day to talk about campus developments. Those meetings became more focused when we decided in 1971 to do a study on college sports and race. I had the funds, and we began to gather information from contacts throughout the Big Ten Conference, although we suspected there was evidence of bias nationwide.

The study would examine Big Ten universities' hiring records as it related to coaches and assistant coaches. It would also explore the treatment of black athletes in the conference—from their education to practices such as "black-athlete stacking" to their financial situations. Most of them were poor and, like all athletes, received no compensation. The no-compensation rule would be challenged in court decades later.

The questionnaire for the study was designed by John Schweitzer, one of my promising graduate students. All of the Big Ten schools cooperated. (I would continue to work with John Schweitzer, an analytics expert, decades later in my consulting work for public school districts.) I didn't go into the Big Ten study willy-nilly. I realized that billions were being generated by college football and basketball and that there might be stiff resistance to our findings and possible criticism of Michigan State for being the source of the study.

We knew there would be a lot of media coverage, and we didn't want President Wharton to have to defend the study; we would do that. Wharton had always quietly supported my work. But Wharton had to be the president of the entire student body, and we didn't want to unnecessarily involve him in race-related issues. When we completed the study, we determined when Wharton would be out of town and scheduled a press conference on that day.

The 1972 report documented how coaches pushed athletes to achieve in sports but did little to enable them to cope academically. The report also documented the lack of opportunity for blacks as coaches and game referees. There was a near absence of black referees. Of the seventy-six football and basketball game officials, only two were black. There was also underrepresentation in athletic department offices. There were many secretaries in the offices of Big Ten athletic directors, but none of them were black.

The report also made some recommendations to address the concerns of black athletes. It called on schools to provide black counselors for African American athletes. It also recommended that a fifth-year plan of financial aid be instituted to enable many athletes to obtain their degrees after four years of toiling on behalf of their schools.

The report was titled "The Status of Blacks in the Big Ten Athletic Conference: Issues and Concerns." It generated huge coverage. It also generated a lot of hate mail, delivered in huge bundles to my office. Some accused me of trying to get unqualified blacks to officiate games. Others accused me of race-baiting. Some of the media commentary was also negative. Some of the newspapers that had published positive reports about my leadership during the March against Fear in Mississippi were now critical of me.

However, the famed author James Michener was very impressed with this report. He wrote about it in a 1976 book titled *Michener on Sport*.

[This] confrontation was more to my liking, because it was intellectual, orderly and responsible. In early 1972 blacks at Michigan State University, athletes and faculty alike, decided to compile a document that would inform Wayne Duke, Big Ten Athletic Commissioner, of the actual state of affairs in his conference. Drafting a preliminary paper listing grievances, they circulated it among the other Big Ten schools, soliciting their counsel. Finally, three black faculty members from Michigan State, Robert Green, Joseph McMillan and Thomas Gunnings, drafted the final report using scholarly procedures and non-inflammatory language:

Of the black-student athletes in the study, 100 percent reported that their coaches expected them to remain eligible, but only 7 percent reported that their coaches expected them to receive their degrees. Seventy percent reported that their white coaches and professors and white students expected them to be weak academically.

... Black athletes from several Big Ten schools commented that severe punishment was meted out for missing practice, yet no real concern was exhibited when classes were missed. (Michener 2014, 159–60)

We also heard, through sources, that there was some positive reaction in the office of the Big Ten commissioner Wayne Duke. We had made some strong recommendations to address hiring bias.

Our report recommended that blacks be hired at every officiating level, particularly in basketball and football. It recommended that a Big Ten Equal Opportunity Committee be established, each university having two representatives on the committee, one from each school being black. The committee would work to insure that each athletic department was desegregated at all levels of employment. In a final, bold gesture, we recommended that the Big Ten hire a black associate commissioner with a major responsibility for implementing the recommendations.

Emboldened by some positive reaction to the recommendations, I took a gamble to ensure that they would be adopted. I expanded the stakes by contacting a few black athletes throughout the conference to get their support for a conference-wide football sit-out if the Big Ten failed to respond. I did not know whether I had enough support to actually initiate such an action, but I believed the threat would move the Big Ten.

The Big Ten had reviewed coverage of our report. On March 7, the three of us traveled to Big Ten headquarters in Chicago to meet with Commissioner Duke about the report. It would be a meeting with consequences. Although the media was not invited to the meeting, a resourceful photographer from *Jet* magazine managed to get in to take a few shots.

Duke and his staff didn't say much during our presentation. At the end, Gunnings told Duke that a football sit-out might be called if the conference didn't act. Again, I wasn't sure that we could pull off such a boycott, but I had already

MSU president Clifton R. Wharton Jr., Andrew Young, Maudine Dobbins (a graduate and former Green student), and Robert L. Green at MSU graduation ceremony on June 11, 1977.

seen young college students and high school pupils take action for social justice. I believed that the athletes—like the young people who had engaged in actions that had propelled the Civil Rights movement—would also take a stand.

The Big Ten took immediate and more thoughtful longer term action. The next day it created an advisory commission to address the issues we raised. The commission, which was not informed about our findings, was then tasked to conduct a similar study, and it came to the same conclusions. There was a problem.

When it came to remedies, the Big Ten followed our roadmap. As we advised, the Big Ten extended financial aid to all athletes for a fifth year and set up monitoring programs to track their academic progress. The conference also established other remedies that we proposed.

- Counseling programs for all student-athletes
- Professional training programs for coaches to help them better understand the needs of minority athletes
- The compilation, by the Big Ten, of a list of blacks who could be employed as coaches, athletic administrators, game officials, trainers, and other athletic department personnel

Finally, the Big Ten checked off our last major recommendation by appointing a black assistant commissioner to oversee the initiatives.

This was a landmark response that prompted collegiate conferences throughout the nation to follow suit. This, I thought at the time, is what activists—with the support of young people—could achieve when they overcome the fear of confrontation with injustice. While our report received heavy coverage, the media produced very few reports on the Big Ten reforms. I was always conscious of media coverage of issues because it framed how the public understood problems.

At this time in the spring of 1972, George was very happy because he was excelling academically and would be admitted to the Honors College the following fall. He was also appreciative of the opportunity that Wharton had given him: membership on a small group that served the president's student advisory committee. The committee members, who were invited to attend some of the president's staff meetings, kept Wharton in touch with student interests and concerns. Wharton also believed that if talented students obtained more access to the workings of university administration, some future university leaders would emerge.

Although Wharton did not discuss all major issues with his student advisors, committee members were aware of the major priorities: maintaining the quality of academic programs despite fiscal problems resulting from budget cuts, the integration of the School of Osteopathic Medicine with MSU's medical school, and more progress on efforts to provide more opportunities for the economically disadvantaged. (He had created the Presidential Commission on Admissions and Study Body Composition.)

Also, student unrest over the Vietnam War was a major issue at Michigan State and many other major campuses at that time. However, the response of MSU leaders was very different than the heads of most universities. Interim president Walter Adams actually marched with campus protesters in October 1969. (I participated in that march.) As for Wharton, he took a bold stance by offering to personally take student petitions against the war to Michigan's congressional delegation in the wake of protests following the April 30, 1970, invasion of Cambodia.

After President Nixon ordered the mining of all North Vietnamese ports on May 8, 1972, MSU and some other major campuses erupted with protests again. The protest started slow and then spread throughout much of the campus and spilled out into East Lansing as many protesters blocked traffic along Grand River Avenue, a major artery.

The Michigan State police were called in to clear Grand River, and troopers then moved onto the campus. When the state police arrived, the flow of protesting students increased. It was during this crisis that Wharton met with key staff and student advisors—George among them.

When asked for their thoughts on the situation, the students and some key staff told President Wharton that the state police were inflaming the situation. They suggested that he ask the state police to withdraw from campus. Subsequently, Wharton did so. The police left, and the demonstration dwindled and died.

May 1972 was also the month that the university funded the launch of the new CUD. President Wharton had advised me keep a low profile—to rely on other faculty members to help make the case for the creation of the college. An ad hoc group of distinguished faculty members led by sociologist John Useem made the case for the college in the Faculty Senate. Also, Walter Adams was a vocal advocate for the college. When it was created, I was initially selected as acting dean and appointed dean a short time later by Adams's successor, Clifton Wharton.

Elated, I began to assemble a faculty for the college. For example, I convinced esteemed sociologist Wilbur Brookover, who had retired several years before, to return to MSU. I had also hired Jack Bain, an extremely articulate former MSU dean, to manage communications and other CUD issues on an ad-hoc basis. After the vote, the faculty and staff who had worked at the CUA became employees of the CUD. We did not offer classes immediately. Instead, we prepared curricula as we planned to offer classes in September 1973.

The CUD would have two major units. The Department of Urban and Metropolitan Studies would provide instruction on addressing health and education issues in cities. Students in CUD's racial and ethnic studies department would study bias and conflict resolution. All CUD majors would be required to do field work in cities.

As the acting dean, and later appointed dean, of the new college, I was able to marshal resources to launch economic development and education-improvement initiatives in major cities—my native Detroit among them.

At this point, it was clear to me that an activist-scholar could create great change at a university and also prompt a university to become a force for social justice in the world. However, some in the academic community considered me more of a rabble-rouser than a scholar. That burned inside me because, at the time, I was frequently published in refereed scholarly journals.

Still, I was very upbeat about MSU as a leader in excellence and diversity. This was also confirmed in 1972 when I attended a meeting on black enrollment in graduate programs at Michigan State. The presentation was made by future MSU president Lou Anna Simon, then a graduate student in the College of Education. She made the presentation on behalf of Lee Winder, the university provost.

It was clear to me that she was a good researcher and a calm presenter with an understanding of the value of diversity. When she completed her presentation, I was among the faculty members who commended her for her work. "Here," I thought, "is a person who could be a university leader."

Some wondered why I spent so much time helping the university with outreach to black students. It was because I knew these students could make a difference in our world.

Those who didn't understand my passion about the power of education did not know my family background. They didn't know that I was actually compelled to help others obtain educational opportunities. Considering my upbringing, I simply had to be involved in educational outreach.

CHAPTER FIVE

The Power of Education

had just completed an email message on plans for launching "Each One, Read One," a new program that promotes literacy by encouraging adults to read to Las Vegas children, when I thought of my late brother Havious Vinson Green. The reading program is designed for all children, but it's especially important for at-risk children and those with behavioral problems. I thought of Havious, who died at age ninety-two on July 17, 2014, because he began his career as a special education teacher helping "problem" kids. I also thought of him because, as the oldest of nine siblings, he set an example: study hard and work hard. It was good to have an older sibling you could admire—and I had one in Havious.

Havious worked full time while attending Wayne State University in Detroit part time, obtaining an MA in education at the age of twenty-four. He was determined to get that advanced degree because my father, Thomas, made it very clear that all his sons and daughters must be high academic achievers.

I saw my three surviving siblings—Naomi, Bertha, and Richard—and dozens of nieces and nephews at Havious's funeral. That memory prompted me to pick up a copy of a 1982 article on the Green clan in *The Crisis* magazine, published by the NAACP. The article summarized the Green family belief in the power of education and our dedication to learning and social justice.

The Green family of Michigan State University puts a premium on learning and social involvement.

Robert L. Green remembers his father's hardheaded philosophy: go to school and worship the Lord. Through the years it has stuck with him and eight brothers and sisters and their offspring, more than 35 in all, who have gone on to attain, or are in the process of attaining undergraduate and advanced college degrees. (Higgins 1982)

I paused at that point and smiled because the article had been published twenty-two years ago and the number of my nieces and nephews with degrees is much higher now. In all, my sons, nieces, and nephews have earned 120 degrees—eight PhDs, eight medical degrees, and three MBAs among them. I am Uncle Bob to men and women who have obtained advanced degrees at major universities—Michigan State, Yale Law School, Harvard, Stanford, Notre Dame, University of Colorado, University of South Florida, University of Michigan, and Columbia Law School among them. My eldest brother, Havious, had eight daughters, and they all obtained PhDs or MDs.

My nieces and nephews have become high achievers because their parents—my brothers and sisters—set high standards for their sons and daughters and were well-educated role models. The article makes a reference to the accomplishments of my brothers and sisters.

For example, all of his brothers and sisters have degrees. One of them is a doctor, one is a university administrator, three are teachers [and] two are registered nurses. . . . A remarkable accomplishment, when it is considered that Green's father, Thomas, was born to an ex-slave in dirt-poor, Jones County, Georgia, was self-educated himself, but became a Pentecostal minister. With his wife, Alberta, he came north to Detroit, lured by the "astronomical" offer of $5 a day to work in an auto plant. There he established a church, worked days in the Fisher body plant, sold coal from a wagon to better feed and clothe his large and growing family. (Higgins 1982)

I paused and thought about my dad. My father had only completed the fourth grade, and my mother had completed the sixth grade. However, they valued education and made it clear to us that educated blacks would have opportunities. They made sure we completed our homework, ensured that we had supplies and

Lettie and Robert L. Green with their dog, Otto, in 1966 in Atlanta, Georgia.

books—and not just the textbooks required by schools. In addition, they made it clear that they had high expectations and that we should also adopt high standards. My parents had an unshakable faith in education. They often told us, their children, that if you're educated, you can get a job.

They were also very religious, and my father was pastor of a Church of God in Christ (COGIC) in Detroit. We attended church all day on Sunday and on Tuesday, Thursday, and Friday evenings. If we were sick, we came to church to get healed. If we were tired, church was the place to rest. If we had homework, we were advised to bring it along and do it under the watchful eye of the Lord.

Our church tried to meet physical needs as well as spiritual. On many Sundays, for example, a dinner was served following the church service. (At that time, blacks were generally unwelcome in restaurants.) The cost of those Sunday meals was nominal, and those who could not pay ate free. I loved those great dinners and looked forward to them.

Churches also provided a forum and a religious pedagogy that met some of the social-psychological needs of African Americans. For example, testimonies were and continue to be a part of church services. As a boy, I saw folks testify. The testifying "witnesses" would first give thanks to the Lord, then reflect on their experiences—their trials, troubles, and triumphs. In my youth, I also occasionally testified with the fervor that characterized witnessing.

The black church was a venue that met desire for arts and entertainment. At that time, blacks were barred from movie theaters or required to sit in the balcony. My father's church sponsored programs that encouraged young people to participate in performing arts programs sponsored by the church. Another COGIC church we sometimes attended also had music programs, and some of those parishioners later excelled and became professionals. For example, the family of Milt Jackson, later to gain fame as a member of the Modern Jazz Quartet, was active in our church. Both churches provided a platform for educationally valuable programs such as public speaking. Among the young speakers in the church we sometimes attended was Berry Gordy, who would later launch and lead Motown Records. There were also a number entertainment icons who were raised in COGIC churches, including rocker Sly Stone of Sly and the Family Stone and gospel singer Andre Crouch.

Many prominent black leaders had similar experiences in the church. Dr. Benjamin Mays, who later became president of Morehouse College and mentor of Dr. Martin Luther King Jr., recalled an event that occurred when he was about eight years old. He took part in a public speaking context in his church and diligently prepared for the event. When he finished his speech, the congregation exploded with applause. That inspired Mays to become an educator and a great orator.

This was the only venue for such youth development. The racially segregated Rotary, Kiwanis, Optimist, and Lions Clubs—all notable for their support for fledgling orators—did not sponsor speaking contests for blacks. However, it was clear to me that religion was a force for evil as well as good. After all, passages from the Bible had been interpreted in a way to justify slavery. Also, some of the most religious whites in the South were also among the most bigoted with attitudes encouraged by churches.

In addition, it was clear to me that my parents did not believe that religious conviction alone would lead to opportunities. I recall comments my father made

Robert L. Green (*front left*) touches the casket of Martin Luther King Jr. during the funeral procession on April 9, 1968, in Atlanta, Georgia.

to my brothers and sisters when I was only ten years old. He made the comments after a regional service involving a number of COGIC churches. The speaker at that service was expounding on the power of faith with a litany that included "You don't need education. All you need is Jesus!" When the service was over, my dad drove us about two blocks from the church, pulled to a curb, and turned to face us, his sons and daughters. "Just remember," he said. "You need education as much as you need Jesus."

My wife's family also understood the power and importance of education. Lettie Clement grew up in San Francisco, where I met her during my military service. Her parents were Willie and Inez. Lettie had three sisters—Ruby (deceased), Catherine, and Willie Mae. She also had one brother, James Henry. Her mother divorced Willie and married Fred Cornelius.

Lettie and I were married August 10, 1956, after I finished my military service in San Francisco. Our first son, Vince, was born in 1957, and Kurt, our second son, was born in 1959. Fred and Inez Cornelius supported us by babysitting, and Fred loaned me money for books and tuition. Also, Lettie's brother-in-law, Luther Elarms, had a janitorial maintenance business and provided employment to me while I finished my bachelor's and master's studies. Of course, Lettie's family encouraged both of us to pursue our goals.

Lettie did so by getting an RN degree. She then served as nurse for Dr. Carlton Goodlett, a black physician whom I admired because of his activism. Dr. Goodlett had obtained a PhD in psychology from the University of California, Berkeley, and subsequently earned an MD from Meharry Medical College in Nashville, Tennessee. He then moved and set up a practice in San Francisco, becoming one of only three black physicians in the city.

At that time those three physicians could only see patients in their offices because blacks could not practice in any hospitals in San Francisco. Dr. Goodlett took the lead in ending that ban. Realizing that the black press could be an effective force for change, Dr. Goodlett saved enough money from three years of practice to buy a small weekly, the *Reporter*. Subsequently, he bought the rival paper, the *Sun*, from its white owner. He merged the papers into a new entity called the *Sun Reporter*. He would use his position as publisher to agitate for equal access to jobs.

My admiration for Dr. Goodlett swelled after one legendary incident. He had been showered with gifts at a birthday party in his honor. When the party ended, he headed home, his car loaded with the gifts. However, he was stopped on the road by a San Francisco cop. Peering through Goodlett's car window, the officer

Robert L. Green provides skiing tips to Bernice King and Martin Luther King III in 1973 in northern Michigan.

said, "Where did you get those gifts, boy!" Dr. Goodlett responded with an expletive. The cop arrested him and took him to jail. When the commanding officer at the jail learned of Dr. Goodlett's identity, he offered him a release with no charges. However, Goodlett rejected the offer and was jailed. He used his right to one phone call to contact the head of the local NAACP chapter. The NAACP contacted the mayor, George Christopher. Christopher, a Republican, gave the police chief an earful regarding racial harassment. On the hearing date for the arrest, the arresting officer did not appear, and the court threw out the charges. Dr. Goodlett had made his point a public one. He was a model for me because he continued to push for social justice in many ways throughout his career.

In 1951, Dr. Goodlett joined the National Newspaper Publishers Association, also known as the Black Press of America, and served three terms as president. He also served as chair of the California Black Leadership Council. In addition, as president of the San Francisco NAACP, he led a protest against the Municipal Railway for job discrimination.

In 1963, Dr. Goodlett built a two-story office building that housed his medical practice and his newspaper operations. The building, located in the Fillmore district, was the center of black activism in San Francisco. It would host an array of high-profile figures—Malcolm X, Muhammad Ali, and Dick Gregory among them.

Dr. Goodlett would later become a prominent political figure. He ran for governor in 1966 and finished third in a field of six, the first black American since Reconstruction to mount a serious candidacy for the governor's office. Later many of the state's most prominent politicians would seek Goodlett's counsel and advice—among them, Governor Jerry Brown, U.S. representatives Ron Dellums and Mervyn Dymally, and my old friend Willie Brown, who would become speaker of the California House of Representatives and mayor of San Francisco. I did not know Dr. Goodlett would become a political force when Lettie, our two sons, and I prepared to leave San Francisco in 1963, but I did know that he would become even more of a change-agent.

Dr. Goodlett was a generous man. When Lettie and I began to prepare to move to Michigan for my PhD studies, he gave us $300 for travel expenses, money we sorely needed.

The night before our departure, Lettie's family hosted a big dinner for us and saw us off the following morning. They were proud and had high expectations for me.

Lettie's parents also had high expectations for their nieces, nephews, and grandchildren. They encouraged our sons—Vince, Kurt, and Kevin—to achieve. They also convinced some of their nieces and nephews to attend Michigan State during my years at the university, and they helped arrange for others to attend the Piney Woods School in Mississippi where I was chairman of the board.

Looking back on the encouragement and support I received from my own parents to achieve academically, I now realized it was very much needed considering the low expectations of many students. I attended Northern High School, which was in my neighborhood. Like many neighborhoods in Detroit, my community had transformed quickly from a predominantly white neighborhood to a predominantly black community.

I recall that our French class teacher asked us, the students in French I, who planned to take French II. Some students raised their hands, including me. She told us not to take French II because it was for students who were college bound and that we weren't going to college. At the time, I had a brother in medical school,

At a 1974 birthday party for Bernice King at Berry Gordy's Detroit home: Martin Luther King III (*kneeling*), Kurt Green; Kevin Green; Lettie Green; Bernice; Coretta Scott King; Esther Edwards, sister of Berry Gordy; and Robert, Esther's son.

another brother in undergraduate studies at Wayne State University, and two sisters in nursing school. I ignored the teacher's comments because I assumed that some teachers had also tried to lower the expectations of my older siblings.

I also learned about racism—and the fear it engenders—from my father, who witnessed police brutality in Detroit and intimidation in the state of Georgia. As a boy, I learned first-hand during a couple of drives—a trip to Memphis to attend a COGIC convocation and one to Georgia to visit our relatives. I was in the car when state troopers in both states stopped us for allegedly speeding. After collecting money from my father, they let us go. My father urged me to "avoid conflict with whites" almost as often as he told me to "get good grades." I would ignore the former and embrace the latter.

My dad, a freelance trucker who delivered coal to homeowners for home heating, warned us about "conflicts" because he didn't want us to hate whites and because he wanted us to survive and thrive.

I was an adult when I learned about the early experiences that were the source of my father's fear. When my father was fourteen years old, one his close friends was lynched in Jones County, Georgia, because his friend did not step out of the path of a white man fast enough or apologize quickly enough. They hanged him from a tree. My father and most blacks in the county quickly learned about this.

After the lynching, my dad and two friends cut down the body, and the lynching leaders told them to take it to the icehouse where blacks obtained their ice and frequently congregated. The body remained there for two days before whites allowed it to be buried. This was a warning to other blacks that they could suffer the same fate if they stepped out of line.

Four years later, my father was drafted into World War I, where he served in France for fourteen months, experienced combat, and was honorably discharged. Like many black World War I vets, he was upset that white America did not consider him a full citizen with equal rights—he was not allowed to vote—even after he had fought for his country.

Part of the problem was the federalism that allowed states to set their own laws and standards on issues of race. The federal government's role in the lives of blacks was often inconsistent and ill-defined. This is why lynchings were legal in some states, but not others. This is also why blacks were forced to ride in the back of the bus in some states, but not others.

The "states' rights" clauses in the original U.S. Constitution enabled the South to institutionalize slavery and, later, sanction legalized discrimination after abolition. These clauses were also an impediment to some of those trying to get on their feet after moving from southern states to the North. This was a burden for the millions of blacks who migrated to northern cities.

For example, when my father moved his young family from Georgia to Detroit, he was poor and had little formal education. However, he had served in France in World War I and assumed he would be treated as an American instead of a Georgian. He expected help when he went to a Michigan social services agency for temporary aid while he searched for work. However, a social worker told him he would have to get assistance in Georgia, "not here."

My father consciously straightened his posture, looked the social worker in the eye, and said, "I didn't go to France to fight for Georgia. I went over there to fight for my country." My father then politely told the social worker that returning to Georgia was out of the question. The social worker put down her pencil and regarded my father more thoughtfully. He said nothing more. He just stood before her with great

At a March 1971 event at MSU's Kellogg Center: Kurt Green, Lettie Green, Morehouse College president emeritus Benjamin Mays, Coretta Scott King, R. Vincent Green, and Robert L. Green.

dignity and waited. She then walked across the room to another desk, where she sat down and wrote a check. "You can come back next week if you need more," she said. "I hope you'll never see me here again," my father said.

By taking odd jobs, he was able to support his family and never returned for more assistance. Indeed, he would help support all of us as an odd-jobs entrepreneur. My mother also generated income as a business owner, identifying house-cleaning positions for job-seeking black women.

Shortly after arriving in Detroit, my father founded and served as pastor of a church affiliated with the COGIC, the largest Holiness Pentecostal denomination in the United States. As pastor, he tried to address the spiritual and physical needs of his congregation. I remember my father taking a young mother with three small children to the welfare office to help get them the help they needed.

He had helped others get assistance and had learned which social workers to avoid and which to turn to for help. On this day, he carefully checked each line to find a social worker who would be responsive to the needs of the young mother. He would help plead her case. After all, he had once come to this office to get assistance.

After getting destitute people welfare assistance, he would drive them to a grocery market and then take them home. The black church, under pastors such as my father, was a safe haven and advocate for people during a period when discrimination stacked the deck against them. Of course, it was the leader of a black church, Martin Luther King Jr., who nonviolently led the fight to end American apartheid.

My father's denomination, COGIC, was founded by Charles Harrison Mason (September 8, 1864–November 17, 1961), the son of former slaves who resided in Shelby County, Tennessee. As a child, Mason was greatly influenced by the religion of his parents. In 1879, when he was twelve, Mason joined the African-American Missionary Baptist Church; he was later baptized by his half-brother, Rev. I. S. Nelson. He began his ministerial career in 1891 by accepting a ministerial license from the Mount Gale Missionary Baptist Church in Preston, Arkansas. On November 1, 1893, Mason entered the Arkansas Baptist College but withdrew after three months because of his dissatisfaction with the curriculum and the interpretation of the Bible.

He was influenced by African-American Methodist evangelist Amanda Berry Smith after reading her autobiography and became a convert to the "Holiness" movement that she supported. Those who had accepted the Holiness message testified being "sanctified" and cleansed from sin. Mason embraced sanctification and began preaching the doctrine of Holiness and Sanctification in the local Baptist churches.

In 1895, Mason met Charles Price Jones, an influential Mississippi preacher who shared his enthusiasm for Holiness teachings. He would also meet Elder J. E. Jeter from Little Rock, Arkansas, and Elder W. S. Pleasant from Hazelhurst, Mississippi. The three men would be Mason's close companions in a new ministry. These men spread the doctrine of Holiness and Sanctification in African-American Baptist churches in Mississippi, Arkansas, and Tennessee. In June 1896, they conducted a revival, preaching the message of Sanctification and Holiness, which prompted the local Baptist association to excommunicate them.

In 1897, Mason and Jones formed a new fellowship of churches named simply Church of God, later amended to Church of God in Christ. In March 1907, Mason

Coretta Scott King and her daughters and sons and Robert L. and Lettie Green and their sons gather at the MSU Union Building in 1974. Robert L. Green's niece, Anne Dudley, is in the background on the left.

was sent by the church to Los Angeles to investigate the revival being led by Elder William J. Seymour and experienced the baptism of the Holy Ghost and evidence of speaking in tongues.

After his experience in Los Angeles, he returned to Mississippi preaching the new Pentecostal teachings on the baptism of the Holy Ghost, but his associate, Elder Jones, the general overseer of the group, was opposed to it. After significant debate at the general convocation in June 1907, Mason was expelled from the church.

Later in November, he established a new Pentecostal group in Memphis. He was elected the general overseer of his group. After years of conflict, he won the legal rights to the COGIC name and charter in 1915. In the years that followed, Mason directed a group of traveling evangelists who spread COGIC's message. That included evangelism in northern cities where many blacks were settling in search of work.

After moving to Memphis and establishing it as the headquarters of COGIC, Mason founded and served as pastor of Temple COGIC. He established the annual "International Holy Convocation." As the church continued to grow, he established departments and auxiliaries—among them a wing now known as the International Youth Department.

Mason's interest in global affairs was not confined to youth and development. He was an avowed pacifist, and the federal government secretly monitored him because of that conviction.

At the time of Bishop Mason's death in 1961, COGIC had spread to every state in the Union, and to many foreign countries, and had a membership of more than four hundred thousand and more than four thousand churches.

The global consciousness of COGIC appealed to my mother, Alberta.

[Alberta Green] was also a hard worker. She was a missionary in the real sense of the word. She collected clothes to ship to Africa and their church established an overseas program in Africa (Liberia) in the 1930s and '40s when most U.S. blacks, influenced by a bigoted system and Tarzan movies, looked with shame and scorn on the land of their ancestors. (Higgins 1982)

To be sure, my mother served people in the United States as well as Africa. She incorporated an employment agency called the Charitable Workers Institute and charged a small fee of twenty-five cents a week to place employment seekers in jobs. When she learned about poverty in Haiti and Liberia from COGIC missionaries, she began collecting new unsold clothing—gifts from the J. L. Hudson department store chain—and shipped them to Haiti and Liberia with funds generated from sales of homemade pies. My sisters, Naomi and Bertha, and I sold many of those pies. My mother also collected books from a middle-class school district near Detroit and shipped them to the two countries.

My brother Havious embraced my mother's global consciousness and her philanthropic work. Like her, he made a difference stateside as well. After obtaining his MA in 1959, he left his well-paying job as an automotive tool and die maker to become a special education teacher of boys who were socially and emotionally impaired. Havious, like the church founder, Mason, was a pacifist. Havious sought and obtained conscientious objector status during World War II.

After receiving religious training at a Bible college in Detroit, he founded the Antioch COGIC in 1965. At home, Havious and his wife, Julia Mae, demanded

Henry Ford II (president of Ford Motor Company) made a major donation to help fund the Martin Luther King, Jr. Center for Nonviolent Social Change during a 1974 meeting. At the gathering are Martin L. King Sr., Ford, Coretta Scott King, Detroit mayor Coleman Young, and Robert L. Green.

academic excellence. There was no TV in their home, and all his daughters were required to learn to play two musical instruments.

During some summers, Havious had to return to the factory in order to provide for his family of eight children, but he remained committed to the art and science of teaching his "boys." One of his daughters, June C. Green-Rivers, said in a eulogy, "My dad mastered the skill of teaching children to read, and so I grew up feeling that he could teach anyone to read."

In addition to tutoring children, Havious also paid a professional musician to teach youths to play musical instruments and in 1972 founded the Martin Luther King, Jr. Education Center. This academy was ranked by the Michigan Department of Education as one of the top twenty-five charter schools in the state during the start of 2012–13 school year.

It was also in 2012 that *Desert Rose: The Life and Legacy of Coretta Scott King*, a biography written by Edythe Scott Bagley about Dr. King's widow, Coretta Scott King, was published. After its publication, Coretta's daughter Bernice wrote a personal note to Lettie and me on a copy of the book.

> You are and have always been very special to me and my family. I will forever cherish the moments that me and my brothers spent with you and your boys. Thanks for providing incredible support to my Mom. Please accept this book on the life and legacy of my Mom, written by Aunt Edythe. The Dream lives and the legacy continues. With Abiding Love, Bernice King.

I was pleased that my brother named the education academy after Dr. King. After all, Dr. King's SCLC was a provider of education programs throughout the South, initiatives that raised the literacy level of blacks so that they could pass literacy tests that white managers of voter registration created to prevent them from voting. I had served as SCLC education director from 1965 to 1966. During that period, I also directed a reading and job placement program in Chicago for the SCLC.

Havious also supported education abroad by raising money to build and repair schools in Africa. In addition, because children cannot learn if they are ill or hungry, he provided funds to build clinics in Haiti and Liberia and purchased Liberian land for farming in that country so that children could be better fed. In all, Havious raised more than $1 million for children, women, and poor people around the world.

I thought about Havious often during the months before his death. I recalled the days when, at age twelve, I began to work with him, delivering coal to my father's customers. I had traveled back to Michigan to spend a half day with him. I wanted to thank him for teaching me the value of hard work. My three sons also valued Uncle Havious.

I thought of my sons and their sense of social justice when I read another passage in the 1982 *The Crisis* magazine article.

> Sons: Vince (24), who has a degree in telecommunications with a minor in economics, from the University of Colorado, will receive a law degree from the University of Michigan this spring; Kurt (22), is a junior major in business/finance and Kevin, is a National Merit Scholar semi-finalist and a member of the National Honor Society, who plays varsity tennis, will enter college in the fall.

Robert L. Green with sons Vince, Kurt, and Kevin in 1981.

Writing in his school's newspaper, Vincent sympathized with the anguish of this country over Poland's crisis but wondered why there is not similar concern for blacks under the cruel and ruthless heel of the white South Africans. (Higgins 1982)

That global consciousness—an awareness beyond the traditional American focus on itself and Europe—was something my sons learned from me and also from their association with leaders such as Coretta Scott King. After the assassination of Dr. King, Coretta and her three children spent a lot of time with my family.

My boys met many Civil Rights leaders during the 1960s and 1970s—Jesse Jackson, Julian Bond, and two former heads of the Congress of Racial Equality, Floyd McKissick and James Farmer, among them. However, Coretta was their favorite visitor.

I was very happy that my family had a role in helping Coretta and her children through a trying transition period after the assassination of Dr. King. Lettie and I had three sons who were roughly the same age as three of the King children—Martin, Dexter, and Bernice. After the death of their father, the King children frequently stayed at our East Lansing, Michigan, home, swimming in our pool and playing basketball.

I took Martin and Dexter with Vince and Kurt to tennis camp in Lake Tahoe, where they received instruction from Billie Jean King. I also took all three King kids and my three sons, Kevin included, on skiing trips. Bernice was a good skier, a quick learner who was not afraid of the slopes. Bernice was the daughter that I never had.

My sons would ask Coretta about her life growing up in Alabama, one the most racially oppressive states in the South. Andrew Young, who grew up in the more genteel city of New Orleans, would sometimes talk about how he and I did not have to grow up in states such as Mississippi and Alabama, where fear-mongering was rampant and lynchings were common.

Blacks were not the only victims in those two states. I recalled arriving in Selma, Alabama, on March 10, 1965, one day after James Reeb, a white minister from Boston, had been viciously beaten with clubs by white racists for being among those supporting voting rights protests in that state. Reeb died from the injuries a day later in an Alabama hospital.

His murder capped one of the most violent and consequential episodes in the Civil Rights movement. It began on March 7 when SCLC activists led a voting rights march that was to begin in Selma and end in the state capital of Montgomery. However, when the crowd of about six hundred marchers reached the Edmund Pettus Bridge, state troopers and county posse members attacked them with billy clubs and tear gas. Many of the protesters were beaten unconscious, shocking much of the nation. It was called "Bloody Sunday."

I watched televised reports on the attack from my home in East Lansing. Dr. King had not taken part in the first Selma march, but it was reported that he was en route to that city. I knew that his close associate Andrew Young would be there. Dr. King called on ministers nationwide to join him in Selma. I could not take a leave because of my classroom responsibilities, but I decided to join the protests in Selma for two days. I contacted the Reverend John Duley, the MSU pastor and Civil Rights activist, and expressed my interest in traveling to Selma. John agreed to join me, and we obtained the funds we needed for the trip. Another East Lansing pastor, Truman Morrison, joined us.

On March 9, King led a second march from the Brown Memorial Chapel toward

Esther Gordy Edwards, Stevie Wonder, and Robert L. Green chat during a 1986 Washington, DC, gathering.

the Edmund Pettus Bridge. Again, they were met at the bridge by a mob of state troopers. However, this time, the troopers allowed the marchers to pass. Dr. King then led the marchers back to the church. Reeb was attacked that evening. While Reeb was being transported to the hospital, Dr. King held a press conference, calling the attack cowardly.

John Duley, Truman Morrison, and I arrived in Selma the day after Reeb was attacked. At that time, I did not think the Selma protests would be considered seminal because there had been racial violence in many communities in the South. The day after our arrival, the three of us took part in a little-known demonstration planned and led by Andrew Young. Andy wanted to set up a picket line at Selma's courthouse because of the unwillingness of local registrars to allow blacks to register to vote.

The courthouse was heavily guarded by police who were posted to prevent any protests at the site. Instead of marching to the courthouse down the main road, where we could be clearly seen, Andy led us via an alternative route. However, when our group of about forty arrived, police turned us away before we could create a picket line.

Reeb's death on March 11 prompted mourning and vigils in many parts of the country. President Lyndon Johnson called Reeb's widow and father to express his condolences. The violence in Selma may have expedited legislative action. I was back home in East Lansing when President Johnson referenced Reeb when he presented a draft of the Voting Rights Act to Congress at a televised special session on March 15. That same day, Dr. King eulogized Reeb at a ceremony at Brown Memorial Chapel in Selma.

By the time Dr. King organized a third march from Selma to Montgomery, he had federal support. Protected by two thousand U.S. Army soldiers and nearly as many Alabama National Guardsmen under federal control, the marchers averaged about ten miles a day along U.S. Route 80 and arrived in Montgomery on March 24. When marchers on March 25 reached the final destination, the Alabama State capitol, their ranks had swelled to about twenty-five thousand.

My sons knew about Selma. They also valued education even more after hearing stories about the Alabama of Coretta Scott King's youth during her visits to our home. Many of the schools that blacks attended in the Deep South were built by African Americans in their communities. They were usually one-room wooden structures, shelters for a classroom that included eighteen to thirty students in a wide range of grade levels.

Most teachers in these schools were graduates of historically black colleges and universities. The American Missionary Association, an Albany, New York–based Protestant abolitionist group, also recruited teachers for these schools, and the association also provided financial support for black schools in Alabama and other states in the South.

Coretta Scott was the third of four children born to Obadiah "Obie" Scott and Bernice McMurry Scott in Marion, Alabama. She was born on April 27, 1927, in her parent's home. Her paternal great-grandmother Delia Scott, a former slave, presided as midwife. Coretta's maternal grandfather, Martin, was a self-taught reader with little formal education. He helped inspire Coretta's passion for education. Though lacking formal education themselves, Coretta Scott's parents intended for all of their children to be educated. Coretta quoted her mother as having said, "My children are going to college, even if it means I only have but one dress to put on."

Coretta and her siblings attended a one-room elementary school five miles from their home and were later bused to Lincoln Normal School nine miles away. Schools closer to their home were for whites only. Coretta Scott graduated valedictorian from Lincoln Normal School in 1945 and enrolled at Antioch College in Yellow Springs, Ohio. Her older sister, Edythe, already enrolled at Antioch, was the first black student at the school. The Scott sisters both received scholarships from Antioch, part of an attempt to diversify the student body. (To be sure, blacks in Marion County valued education. The city of Perry, located in the county, has been the hometown of many black PhDs. Coretta talked frequently to my boys about the power of education.)

I helped support Coretta's effort to pick up the baton and continue Dr. King's work. In 1968, she helped establish the Martin Luther King, Jr. Center for Nonviolent Social Change in Atlanta. In January 1969, less than a year after Martin's death, she traveled to New Delhi, India, to accept the Jawaharlal Nehru Award on behalf of her husband. I recalled reading press accounts of the trip.

The awards ceremony was held at New Delhi University, where students gathered for the event. As Coretta accepted the award, the students spontaneously began to sing "We Shall Overcome." Coretta and Prime Minister Indira Gandhi joined them in the rendition, tearing up as they sang.

She also continued to support social justice movements at home. For example, in December 1970, she and Ethel Kennedy showed their support for the United Farm Workers (UFW) by traveling to California to meet with an imprisoned Cesar Chavez. Chavez had been jailed for refusing to end the Salinas Valley lettuce boycott, part of effort to obtain bargaining rights for poor and abused farm workers. She also met with Dolores Huerta, the UFW's cofounder and vice president.

During that period, the first six years after Dr. King's death, the King children joined my family on many vacations. They called us "Uncle Bob" and "Aunt Lettie." Later, during the late 1970s and the first half of the 1980s, Coretta continued speak up about issues related to education and poverty at home and continued to oppose war and the apartheid system in South Africa.

My sons also learned about the global fight for social justice from me, a son of Detroit. In school, all Detroiters learn of the proud history of the Detroit that was a major terminus and international transfer station for an Underground Railroad for enslaved people. With the help of white abolitionists and freed blacks, they escaped to the North or further north to Canada.

My sons knew that history. They also learned from their parents about how northern industrialization created an economy at loggerheads with the slavery in the agrarian South. That industrialization began in the 1800s as European immigrants provided some of the manpower. The industrial revolution was fully realized in the early 1900s in Detroit where Henry Ford had the courage and foresight to pay workers wages that would enable them to buy the cars they made—my father among them.

Regarding entrepreneurship and business, they knew that black Detroiters had created worldwide demand for black music. Berry Gordy, the founder of Motown, was—like me—the son of a man from Jones County, Georgia. My father knew the Gordy family. Berry Gordy borrowed from his family to launch the company. With my Motown connections, I brought a phenomenon named Stevie Wonder to the MSU campus, along with Esther Gordy Edwards, Berry's sister. I also had connections with Gregory Reed, a former student and prominent Detroit attorney who has represented music industry stars. Also, Greg represented Civil Rights icon Rosa Parks in her later years.

My sons also knew of Detroiters such as Congressman John Conyers, a graduate of Northwestern High School, who was a champion of social justice in South Africa and a critic of the corporations that took advantage of a very poorly paid black majority.

In 1972, I helped my sons become more globally conscious by taking them and Lettie on a two-month world tour of major cities—Paris, Rome, Jerusalem, Tel Aviv, Nairobi, Dar es Salaam (Tanzania), and Lisbon (Portugal). Thanks to the global reach of Michigan State and its many international studies programs, I had MSU-affiliated contacts in each city. They helped us understand the history and culture of each country we visited.

I was amazed at the language skills of my youngest boy, Kevin. After befriending Israeli kids during our one-month stay in that country, Kevin would speak Hebrew when he returned to us at hostels. We also met with the blacks Jews who were from the United States.

They also knew that an understanding of law and political activism were keys to civil liberties in our country. After all, my sons had attended several meetings at the home of federal judge Damon Keith, another black graduate of Detroit's Northwestern High School.

In the *United States v. Sinclair* (1971), Judge Keith famously ruled that President Nixon's attorney general, John Mitchell, was required to disclose the transcripts of illegal wiretaps that Mitchell had authorized without first obtaining a search warrant. Keith's decision was upheld by the Supreme Court. The Supreme Court's landmark decision in 1972—also known as "the Keith case"—prompted President Carter to sign the 1978 Foreign Intelligence Surveillance Act. That decision is commemorated as a "Michigan Legal Milestone" called "the Uninvited Ear."

My sons also knew that politicians dedicated to social change could make a difference. At the time *The Crisis* magazine article was published in 1982, Detroit's mayor was Coleman Young, a resourceful and energetic man who had also attended those meetings at the home of Judge Keith. Coleman had talked with my sons during frequent visits to my home. He was a courageous man who would influence my scholarship on issues related to social justice and educational equity in cities.

I had learned about the importance of education from my parents. I was pleased that my sons were learning the importance of education *and* global social justice. After all, I had been engaged in the fight for educational equity and I had helped push for an end to apartheid in South Africa and America. I began to think about that period of time because the residue of racism had not been wiped away.

CHAPTER SIX

Fighting Apartheid Abroad and at Home

Ambassador Andrew Young and I talk by phone at least two to three times a month. The conversations range from current events in the United States to foreign affairs. South Africa has been a frequent topic during a friendship that has spanned about five decades.

On an extremely hot day in September 2014, I called Andy to request a copy of *Saving Mandela*, a 2014 documentary about a 1974 trip we made together to South Africa. In 1974, Andrew Jackson Young represented part of Georgia as a member of Congress. We had made the trip to South Africa partly because the white apartheid government had given Andy the impression that he would be allowed to visit the imprisoned Nelson Mandela during our visit. He was deeply disappointed when the apartheid regime denied him access after we arrived in the country. However, during that visit, we put one hole in the apartheid wall, and we also engaged black youth leaders who would later mount a consequential rebellion against that brutal government. Mandela had died December 5, 2013, but he was still on our minds.

I had traveled to Atlanta early in 2014 for the taping of that documentary on our 1974 South African experiences. As I moved about Atlanta—the city that has touted itself as "too busy to hate"—I recalled 1965, when I lived in Atlanta while working for Dr. King as his education director. It was a very different city during those years. Hate and fearmongering were pronounced. Discrimination was rampant, and segregation was the law. This was the case in many southern states. During my stint in Atlanta with Dr. King, Lettie would observe that blacks did not shop at many stores in and around Atlanta because they did not feel welcome. This was apartheid American style.

By 1973, much had changed in Atlanta. The schools were desegregated, and Maynard Jackson was elected that year, becoming the city's first black mayor. That was also the year that Coleman Young became the first black mayor of my hometown of Detroit. In addition, it was the year that I delivered a major address to the National Alliance of Black School Educators at the Pontchartrain Hotel in Detroit—a speech that forcefully made the case that scholars who care about social justice must also be advocates and activists.

> Time and time again, I was told that one should strive to become an objective, neutral scholar. In particular, I remember one of my graduate instructors telling me, "Don't study blacks because you cannot be neutral and objective." It took me some time to understand the implications of that statement. Practically, it meant, "Let nonblack scholars study blacks."
>
> A cursory review of the literature readily supports the view that much past research on . . . poor people and minorities, has been descriptive. Furthermore, much research has failed to provide clear-cut program recommendations that would directly benefit the researched. . . . Thus, scholarly objectivity does little to alleviate problems. . . . The responsibility for positive social change lies with those of us who work in school districts and universities.

In essence, I was explaining why I had joined Dr. King in the Civil Rights crusade. We had helped end segregation in schools throughout much of the South.

Those changes were chronicled by Walter Cronkite, the famed CBS-TV news anchor. I had an opportunity to talk with him after he delivered the 1973 commencement address at Michigan State. I approached him and identified myself, noting that I headed the College of Urban Development (CUD) at MSU.

"Oh," he said. "You're a dean."

"Yes," I said, "and you're the dean of journalism."

He smiled broadly. I told him how much I admired his coverage of the Civil Rights movement and his moving reports on the assassination of Dr. King. He told me how much he and his daughter admired Coretta Scott King, and I responded by telling him that I would obtain an autographed copy of her book *My Life with Martin Luther King, Jr.* for him. Cronkite smiled again and thanked me. He began to talk about the importance of education to the process of social change and equality. He then expressed his admiration for MSU president Clifton R. Wharton Jr., the first black leader of a large, predominantly white university. Wharton was a symbol of change in America, said Cronkite.

However, in 1973, there was no sign of change in South Africa. The white minority in that country fiercely enforced apartheid, a system of legally sanctioned exploitation and segregation that enabled whites to control the government, the economy, and education.

That year, 1973, was also significant because it was the year Arthur Ashe, the great tennis player and a good friend, put the spotlight on apartheid by accepting an offer to play in a tournament in South Africa. Arthur was one of the world's most vocal opponents of apartheid. He understood the system because he had grown up poor in segregated Virginia. He did not have a tennis coach at his segregated black school. Instead, he honed his tennis skills on poorly maintained public courts in Richmond and expanded them as a student player at the University of California, Los Angeles (UCLA).

Later, as a professional tennis player, Arthur traveled the world and developed a global consciousness about injustice. Arthur and I could relate because I also believed in social justice without borders. I had spent time among poor communities in Israel and Kenya examining the impact of poverty on young people, and I shared his concern about South Africa.

Arthur had a big fan base at MSU, where global affairs are very important. Under my CUD, I hosted Arthur for several speaking engagements. He spoke at length on the horrors of apartheid. During his visits, Arthur stayed at our home. On one occasion, he played an exhibition doubles match to raise money for a local tennis program for youth. My wife, Lettie, helped organize the event.

I had always believed famous athletes and other celebrities should speak out on social justice issues, and I admired Arthur because he did so eloquently. He considered education a social justice issue, and he encouraged black youth to seek higher education. I also admired Arthur because I was a big tennis fan. My wife and three sons were also avid tennis enthusiasts and all three of my sons played the game. I had taken my family to many U.S. Open Tennis Championships, including the tournaments in 1969 and 1970.

I decided I wanted to meet Arthur when we attended the 1971 U.S. Open. At the time, my middle son, Kurt, was one of the top-ranked high school players in the state of Michigan. After Arthur completed a match in the 1971 Open, I led my family to the entrance of the open-air players' lounge to engage him.

"Arthur," I said, extending my hand. "Congratulations on a great match."

We shook hands, and I introduced myself and my family. Arthur was pleased to meet us and intrigued by my sons, who were all wearing tennis apparel. He invited us to join him in the tennis lounge, where friends and family of players were welcome. We met many of his contemporaries—Billie Jean King and Jimmy Connors among them. We were the only black visitors in the lounge.

It was the beginning of a close friendship. Over the next two years, I learned more about the South African apartheid system from Arthur, who was knowledgeable and determined to help end the system. At every opportunity, Arthur also educated the general public on the evils of apartheid. As dean of the CUD, I arranged for Arthur to return to campus to speak in 1973 a few months before he played at the South African Open in Johannesburg. Arthur explained that he had previously applied for visas to play in tennis tournaments in South Africa. The South African government, fearing that he would help rally more worldwide condemnation of apartheid, had rejected those requests.

Many South Africans of British descent opposed apartheid. Owen Williams, a white South African with political clout and a promoter of sports, was among them. He collaborated with Donald Dell, an American tennis star of the 1950s and 1960s who had become a sports agent and organized the Association of Tennis Professionals in 1972. Together, Dell and Williams convinced the apartheid government to issue Arthur a visa to compete in the South Africa Open in 1973.

Although they were concerned about Arthur, South African government leaders agreed to allow him to play because they were even more concerned about a nascent movement to isolate South Africa by excluding its athletes from all global sporting events, a campaign that also called for a boycott of all international sports competitions in that nation. The apartheid government leaders also wanted to create a facade of gradual change as they also actually quietly planned to expand oppression where it counted most—in their educational system.

In 1973, few outside of South Africa knew that the apartheid government—dominated by the Afrikaans-speaking Dutch Afrikaners—was preparing to pass a law the following year requiring all black and "colored" schools in the country's segregated educational system to provide instruction in the Afrikaans language. White schools would be allowed to continue to provide instruction in Afrikaans and

English. South Africa had been at the crossroads of fear, oppression, and freedom for many years, and in 1973 the white minority government was actually preparing to be more oppressive.

At the 1973 tournament in Johannesburg, Arthur played well, defeating white opponents en route to a finals match against his long-time nemesis, Jimmy Connors. Arthur lost a close match to Connors in the final. However, there was more tennis drama ahead.

Arthur was to play a doubles tennis championship with Tom Okker as his partner. Okker was a Dutch national, and the Netherlands was the ancestral home of white Afrikaners. However, Okker was also Jewish. Many Afrikaners supported Hitler during World War II because they agreed with his racist views and because Germany was at war with Britain, a nation they hated because it controlled South Africa at that time. Many Afrikaners also disliked Jews because many of the country's most high-profile critics of apartheid were South Africans of Jewish descent.

On the other side of this doubles championship match were Robert Maud, a South African, and Lew Hoad of Australia, another country that had racial exclusionist policies at that time. Arthur and Okker played brilliantly, defeating Maud and Hoad in four sets: 6–2, 4–6, 6–2, and 6–4.

As planned, Arthur used the opportunity to speak out against apartheid at press conferences in the country. He also met with black antiapartheid activists. However, some activists criticized Arthur for playing in the tournament because they supported the proposed international campaign to isolate South Africa.

Undaunted, Arthur decided to play in the tournament again the following year. This time, he wanted to bring American politicians and American activists to help him politicize South African apartheid in the United States. He had tried to recruit Charles Diggs, a U.S. congressman from Michigan, who was also a vocal critic of apartheid. When Diggs declined for scheduling reasons, Arthur contacted me and asked if I could help him recruit a high-profile politician to join him in South Africa. I contacted my old friend, Congressman Andrew Jackson Young.

We decided that we would help to amplify Arthur's antiapartheid messages. Andy would make an effort to visit Nelson Mandela, the imprisoned antiapartheid leader. I planned to gather information on the status of education in the country's segregated schools. I also planned to recruit black students to apply for enrollment at Michigan State, a longtime national leader in the recruitment of students from Africa and other parts of the developing world.

In addition, we developed a list of demands designed to show we could force some change and establish new precedents. I relayed our concerns and demands to Donald Dell, our intermediary to the South African government.

That government had a policy that required blacks from other countries to accept a visa stamp designating them as an honorary white to enter South Africa. We insisted on a regular visa stamp. Also, we knew that the tennis stadium—like all other venues in South Africa—was a segregated facility. We insisted that there be no segregated seating at Ellis Stadium, the site of the tennis tournament.

The South African government agreed to our conditions, and Andy and I boarded a plane to join Arthur at the tournament. En route, I turned to Andy and asked, "How do you feel about going to a racist, segregated country?"

Without missing a beat, Andy responded, referring to the Jim Crow era. "It's just like going to Alabama or Mississippi," he said.

"I felt more comfortable going to Mississippi because I knew it," I said.

"We're going to be safer in South Africa than we were in Mississippi because of our notoriety and because the South African government is responsible for our safety," Andy said.

However, the South African government, we both realized, was the organized instrument of terror suppressing the aspirations of the black majority in that country. The same had been true of the state and local governments in the South in the United States a decade previous.

It was then that I recalled that Dr. King had frequently compared the situation of black South Africans to the status of African Americans in the American South. He did so frequently at Sunday services at his church in Atlanta, sermons that drew standing-room-only crowds that included many visiting Europeans. In fact, one of the first times I heard an informative presentation about the evils of South African apartheid was at a packed Sunday service led by Dr. King. I was sitting in the second pew between Coretta Scott King and my wife, Lettie, at the Ebenezer Baptist Church in Atlanta. In addition to commenting on the brutality of the apartheid government, Dr. King talked about the caste-based inferior education system that was forced on blacks in South Africa and the United States.

As we landed in Johannesburg on November 21, 1974, I then thought of a man that Dr. King admired, a man he emulated, the man who had established nonviolent resistance as a successful strategy against oppression, a man who spent more than twenty years as a lawyer and human rights activist in South Africa: Mohandas Gandhi.

We were welcomed at the airport by a contingent of government and

Tennis great Arthur Ashe (*left*), Robert L. Green, and Congressman Andrew Young gather on a court in South Africa in 1974. With the help of Young and Green, Ashe pressured the South African government to desegregate its Ellis Tennis Stadium for the first time in the country's history in advance of his participation in a South African tennis tournament.

tournament officials. We were driven to our accommodations at a five-star hotel normally reserved for whites. In the hotel, I noticed a couple of black guests, diplomats from other African countries who had been admitted with "honorary white" visa stamps. Andy, Arthur, and I had successfully challenged that aspect of apartheid. Or had we?

I went back to my room and looked more closely at my passport. Yes, there was a regular visa stamp. However, when I looked more closely there was also an "honorary white" stamp on the back of my passport. I was upset. The South African government had tricked us. However, I was not concerned that they would renege on the promise of a desegregated stadium because I was sure they did not want to prompt Arthur to withdraw from the tournament, which was receiving national and international coverage.

Shortly after we checked in, a group of six blacks from the nearby black township of Soweto—all of them quietly antiapartheid—visited us at the hotel. I was surprised that the hotel had allowed them in and assumed that we were receiving special privileges regarding access. Members of the group wanted to know whether our visit was political or sports-related. I told them it was both.

I was eager to visit black communities on the outskirts of Johannesburg. Arthur, who had visited the black townships the previous year, arranged for a guide. During the first couple of days before the tournament, Andy and I visited Soweto, a township that provided cheap labor to Johannesburg, a city reserved for whites.

En route, I saw hundreds of men, women, and teens carrying burlap bags and various other kinds of sacks walking the long distance from Soweto to jobs in Johannesburg. Our guide explained that they were carrying their work implements—tools, cleaning supplies, and gardening equipment. There were also flat-bed trucks overloaded with other blacks on their way to Johannesburg.

When we arrived in Soweto township, the guide introduced us to a contingent of about ten residents. There were a few college graduates, a couple who were attending college, a few teenagers, and a black journalist. We responded to their questions and noted our opposition to apartheid.

They asked for our thoughts on major American corporate involvement in the apartheid system. I was aware of that involvement and knew that three of the top five investors—General Motors, Ford, and a computer giant then called Burroughs—were companies based in metropolitan Detroit, my hometown. I expressed my opposition to the American corporate presence in South Africa, noting that they were benefitting from labor exploitation of blacks.

As we continued to discuss the apartheid system, they noted that the South African government had, in that year, banned all instruction in English in black schools and were forcing students to receive instruction in the Dutch-based language of Afrikaans. White schools, they noted, were allowed to continue instruction in Afrikaans and English, an international language of commerce. I was not aware of this language instruction mandate. It was clear that the students were outraged about this, and I immediately understood their fury.

I told them that the Afrikaans instruction requirement was a political move designed to oppress them further and restrict their acquisition of knowledge. As the conversation on the Afrikaans issue continued, I began to realize that this issue could be a seed of a rebellion. I had seen these seeds germinate and sprout among students in the United States. I thought of the students who engaged in Civil Rights protests in Farmville, Virginia. I thought of similar student rebellions in Alabama and South Carolina. In fact, students around the world had been protesting against war and racism since the 1960s. Also, protests against the Vietnam War had been occurring at Michigan State and other American universities as recently as the early 1970s.

With the black South African students tagging along, Andy and I began to visit homes in Soweto. Many of these homes were one-room tin shacks with no electricity and no plumbing. During these visits, I compared their situation to that of blacks in the Jim Crow South. In many ways, the situations were similar. Blacks in the Jim Crow South and in South Africa were terrorized by brutal governments and by individual white racists. However, only the poorest blacks in the American South, a minority, lived without plumbing and electricity.

All of our hosts in Soweto were courteous and glad to see us. They were also curious about the United States. Like so many other Africans I had met, they were perplexed when they learned there was significant discrimination against blacks in the United States because the Voice of America radio broadcasts and representatives of the U.S. Agency for International Development portrayed America as the land of freedom and opportunity.

The tournament began the following day, and I was anxious to see tennis at a desegregated stadium in South Africa. As I took my seat in a section normally reserved for government officials, I looked around and noticed that there were no segregation marker signs anywhere. I had noticed during our prior South African visit that segregation signs were ubiquitous—even more prevalent than in the Jim Crow South. This was the first time the apartheid government had ever integrated a sporting event, a precedent that would generate much coverage in the national and international press.

In the first round, Arthur played well. I also noted that the crowd, which was overwhelmingly white, cheered Arthur as well as his white opponent. It was clear that when presented with a contest where merit was decisive, even white Afrikaners—fanatic sports fans—could overlook their racial bias.

When I felt the urge, I walked to a newly desegregated stadium restroom. I stood in front of a urinal next to a white man. When he saw me, he abruptly pulled away from the urinal, wetting himself. I turned to him and noticed his faced had reddened. "You damn Kaffir!" he shouted, using the Afrikaans term for "nigger." He then rushed out of the restroom without washing his hands. After my years in the American South, I was not surprised. I was even more determined to make a difference during this visit.

On my second trip to Soweto, I began to assiduously identify blacks to recruit to become students at Michigan State. I recruited about ten students—among them Sydwell Matlala, who would become a medical school student at Michigan State, and Milliswa Sobukwe, the daughter of Robert Sobukwe, one of the leaders of Mandela's African National Congress. She would obtain a BA and an MA at MSU. Some of these students returned to South Africa and became leaders in education and medicine. Among them was Zach Chuenyane, a doctoral student who later became a dean at a major educational institution in South Africa.

Other students I recruited later became major South African business leaders. I also met Harry Mashabela, a black journalist and prominent antiapartheid activist. I arranged for him to visit and give a few lectures at Michigan State. He wrote a widely read book called *A People on the Boil: Reflections on Soweto* (1987). Arthur Ashe and Andy raised money to pay the airfare of the students I recruited, and the CUD provided ten scholarships.

I also had experiences with members of South Africa's "colored" communities. The apartheid system was not as simple as black and white as it was in America, where there was no distinction between visibly mixed-race people and their darker-skinned brethren. In South Africa's hyperstratified racial system, mixed-race "colored" people and East Indians had more rights than blacks. In South Africa, nonwhites were segregated into separate urban townships—some for coloreds and some for blacks. Other blacks were forced to live in resource-poor "Bantustan" reserves in rural areas of the country.

My first extensive stay in a colored community was in the township of El Dorado. It was clear to me that the so-called coloreds were also opposed to apartheid. I talked to students and to activists in a session that included Andy and Arthur. It was my birthday. Our hosts then shocked the three of us by turning our meeting into a party for me. They brought out two cakes and other refreshments.

Emboldened and empowered, Andy and Arthur took a private plane to Cape Town hoping to meet with Nelson Mandela in his Robben Island prison cell. When they arrived, authorities refused to allow a meeting. I remained in Johannesburg to meet with more students and activists in Soweto. I also gave an interview to a reporter for the *Rand Daily Mail*. He produced a major feature on me, focusing on my work in education, Civil Rights, and my views on apartheid.

As I boarded a plane on November 27 to return to the United States, I was full of emotion. I was happy to be heading back to East Lansing in time to have Thanksgiving dinner with my family. I was elated that I had recruited black South African students to come to Michigan State to learn in a multiracial setting.

On the other hand, I was upset about the obvious parallels between the Jim Crow South and South Africa, and I was very disturbed that American corporations were major investors and major operators in South Africa's exploitative economy. As the plane lifted off for Frankfurt, Germany, my connection to a plane back to the States, I was determined to support the movement to get universities to divest financial holdings from companies that did business in South Africa.

When I returned to the States, I began to focus more on the fact that education in South Africa and the United States were both separate but unequal systems. After the Supreme Court came to the same conclusion in the *Brown v. Board* case in 1954, the NAACP and other supporters of equality helped end legally sanctioned school segregation in the South. Ironically, the last bastions of school segregation in the mid-1970s were in the North.

As I prepared to resume my role as the NAACP's court expert on school deseg- regation in 1975, I reflected on my work in the landmark court case to desegregate schools in my native Detroit. It was *Milliken v. Bradley*, a school desegregation court case based on a 1970 complaint filed by the NAACP. In that case, I testified as an expert witness in the liability phase and the remedy phase after a federal judge in 1974 concluded that there was illegal segregation in the Detroit Public Schools (DPS).

On behalf of the NAACP legal team in the remedy phase, I recommended busing to end the segregation and offered to help create a curricula and training programs to help teachers become effective in integrated school rooms. The NAACP presented my findings and plans to the court and they were accepted.

The court subsequently concluded that white flight to suburbs had circum- vented city-wide segregation and ordered cross-county school busing. Again, I was called in to create educational components for this desegregation phase. Unfortunately, the Supreme Court later overturned that ruling in a 5–4 decision, declaring that outlying school districts were not obligated to desegregate across county lines unless it could be proven that those lines were drawn with racist intent.

I was very prepared to serve as an expert witness in the Detroit cases. After all, as a native son of Detroit and the son of black immigrants from the South, I understood the history of school segregation in the Motor City. As an expert witness for the NAACP in the cases, I had also been informed of aspects of systematic discrimination in the Detroit School District.

During the first *Milliken v. Bradley* case, I testified about discrimination that affected students, teachers, and administrators. For example, we knew how the DPS discriminated against black applicants for positions as principals and assistant principals because a disgruntled white DPS secretary had disclosed to the NAACP that the district kept a coded list on the race of the applicants. The names of white applicants would be listed in elite type face, and black applicants would be listed in pica type.

We also presented evidence of school segregation during the first phase of the case. DPS transportation officials kept track of the changing racial composition of neighborhood blocks in the city. When blacks moved into an all-white block, it would trigger white flight. Professor Wilbur Brookover, a noted MSU sociologist, had determined that when neighborhoods in northern cities became 30 percent black, white flight would accelerate. It was a tipping point.

Operating on this same knowledge, when a Detroit block became 20–30 percent black, DPS transportation officials would bus "the Negroes" on that block to predominantly black schools. We knew this because the judge on the case ordered the DPS to give us access to records related to transportation. I led my team of graduate students in an investigation that uncovered this ruse.

The team also conducted course enrollment analyses by racial composition in Detroit schools to identify any variance in the strength of academic curricula. That included a review of the textbooks by level of difficulty and an examination of the range of classes offered such as advanced foreign language studies and advanced math and sciences courses. We found that the curricula offerings in black schools were not as challenging as those in white schools. The variance was comparable to the race-based differences in southern school districts during Jim Crow.

After the judge ruled in our in favor, the remedy phase began, and I had a key role in that as well. For example, we recommended that the district come up with a plan to ensure there was fair and equitable representation of blacks as teachers and principals in all schools. Also, we recommended that the district come up with a busing plan to desegregate the schools. In addition, we recommended that the district present a plan to eliminate disparities in curricula.

We didn't trust the DPS to resolve these problems on their own. We recommended that the district be required to hire outside consultants to help develop compliance plans. This was supported by the court. (Our team did a similar study in Kalamazoo, Michigan, a short time later, under the direction of Noel Fox, a federal judge.)

I recalled explaining how Detroit was a microcosmic model for creative discrimination and sophisticated segregation throughout the North in my 1973 speech to the National Association of Black School Educators in the city's Pontchartrain Hotel.

Yvonne Rogers, Iris Cox, Coretta Scott King, and Lettie Green attend a fundraiser for Detroit mayoral candidate Coleman Young in 1973.

Between 1940 and 1960, the black population of the South increased 1.4 million. Due to migration during this period, the black population of the North increased 4.6 million. However northern school officials failed to place black migrants into schools white children attended. Instead, they routed them into schools where black northerners had historically been contained. Data indicates that black youngsters were bused past all-white schools in Detroit twenty years ago to maintain and perpetuate racial segregation in the schools. The people who bused those children twenty years ago are arguing against busing for racial balance today. . . .

In the Detroit case, *Milliken v. Bradley*, Judge Roth indicted all levels of government and public policy making for failing to live up to the ideals of a democratic society. He cited the school board's role in promoting school segregation through policies and practices that deliberately built on—rather than negated—segregated housing patterns.

I then recalled the central point I made in that 1973 speech: "I now see," I told the convention, "that northern school officials have been doing a much more effective job of maintaining school segregation than southern school officials."

Following the South Africa trip, the next major school-related court battle—
Evans v. Buchanan in Delaware in 1975—also involved metropolitan desegregation.
The Supreme Court's 1974 *Milliken v. Bradley* ruling seemed to put strict restrictions
on metropolitan desegregation. However, the plaintiffs in *Evans v. Buchanan*, who
represented black students in Wilmington, contended that the governments in
Delaware had taken actions to segregate the school systems. The court agreed
and ordered that the Wilmington school district be combined with ten suburban
districts, which required some busing.

The Delaware case was a major desegregation crossroads because some local
residents made it a national issue. A group called the Positive Action Committee
(PAC) was formed to reverse the court desegregation ruling. Jeffrey A. Raffel
described the battle lines in a 1980 book titled *The Politics of School Desegregation:
The Metropolitan Remedy in Delaware*.

> As the desegregation case dragged on, PAC increasingly turned its attention to
> the national scene. Leaders of PAC were instrumental in forming the National
> Association for Neighborhood Schools (NANS) in August 1976. Jim Venema served
> as NANS chairman. Early on, PAC leaders were in contact with anti-busing activists
> in Boston, Louisville, and other cities. As the Delaware case progressed, PAC officials
> sought more actively to form a national coalition against busing. From the start
> Jim Venema described the PAC cause as part of a war that would be won or lost on
> the battlefield of Delaware. (Raffel 1980, 185)

With support from PAC, this desegregation ruling was also appealed. However,
this time, the Supreme Court declined to hear the case, allowing the ruling to stand.
Again, I was the court-ordered expert assigned to develop curricula and training to
help the newly integrated schools. In September 1978, busing commenced. It was
the first sustained court-ordered desegregation across school district lines.

I had already made an impact as an activist and as an educator. At this point
in my career, I also began to develop a reputation as a scholar on urban education
issues. One of my early major books, *School Desegregation: Making it Work*, was
important because it was published in 1976 during a fierce national debate about
busing. William Raspberry, a black columnist for the *Washington Post*, was a vocal
critic of busing. His argument: black students did not need to be bused to white
schools to achieve academically.

I had always argued that the Supreme Court had actually ruled that there were inequities in the education of whites and blacks in their *Brown v. Board* decision and that, for the most part, schools in African American communities did not have the resources in books, school facilities, and teacher quality available at schools in higher-income white communities. Dr. King had favored desegregation and so did my close friend Andy Young.

President Gerald Ford had raised the intensity of the debate by pushing for legislation that would limit the ability of judges to issue rulings requiring school desegregation. Ford was trying to turn desegregation into a political issue when he said the following: "It is the overextension of court control that has transformed a simple judicial tool, busing, into a cause of widespread controversy and slowed our progress toward the total elimination of segregation" (Ford 1976).

This, however, is not an accurate view of contemporary history. Significant desegregation in this country has always been achieved in a climate of widespread controversy. Unrest has been the very yeast of racial progress. When Rosa Parks refused to move to the back of the bus, it was controversial; when white and black students conducted sit-ins at segregated Atlanta restaurants, it was controversial. Martin Luther King, Jr.'s confrontation with "Bull" Connor in Selma was controversial.

The book included contributions from a judge, lawyer, school district superintendent, and Gary Orfield, a Harvard scholar who would become a lifelong friend. It also included contributions from four MSU doctoral students who had helped me in my school desegregation work for the NAACP.

The publication was also significant because it was based on papers delivered at a conference at Michigan State. MSU president Clifton R. Wharton Jr. made the conference possible by helping me obtain a grant from the Rockefeller Foundation. Lastly, I was proud of this book because it was published by MSU's CUD, the school I led as dean.

My work as a scholar-activist was honored by the Martin Luther King Jr. Center for Nonviolent Social Change when it awarded me the 1976 Human Relations Award. At that time, I was also supportive of student-activists who were advocating that MSU divest itself of investments in companies that operated in South Africa.

On June 16, 1976, the seeds of rebellion that were germinating during my 1974 visit to South Africa suddenly sprouted. The Soweto Uprising was a series of student-led protests in South Africa that began on that morning. An estimated twenty thousand students from numerous Sowetan schools hit the streets to protest the imposition of Afrikaans as the language of instruction in black schools. By some estimates, as many as seven hundred people were killed when police unleashed dogs and fired on unarmed youths.

In the aftermath of the Soweto massacre, the campus divestment movement picked up steam. In 1978, Michigan State, Columbia University, and the University of Wisconsin–Madison became the first major American schools to divest holdings in companies operating in South Africa. MSU action was prompted by a coalition of students and faculty who understood the connection between Western investment in South Africa and the maintenance of apartheid.

The Southern Africa Liberation Committee (SALC)—a group of MSU faculty, students, and community residents—emerged in 1972 from the East Lansing Peace Education Center, which was affiliated with the Methodist Church. Led by Patricia Beeman and her husband, MSU tennis coach Frank Beeman, the SALC became a pioneer in the movement to isolate the racist South African regime. The SALC made its first mark in 1976, when it convinced the City of East Lansing to pass the Selective Purchasing Resolution, which prohibited the city from buying goods and services from companies with operations in South Africa.

It was important because the ban included U.S. companies with operations in South Africa. Three of the biggest foreign investors in South Africa were Michigan-based companies: General Motors, Ford Motor Company, and Burroughs, a computer company now known as Unisys. East Lansing was the first city to take this step.

In the wake of its success, the SALC then took aim at MSU and its $30 million endowment. The goal was to convince the MSU Board of Trustees to sell off all stocks and bonds issued by companies with operations in South Africa. The SALC began this effort by launching a campaign to inform the university community of the evils of apartheid. Every week, the SALC hosted events such as speeches by antiapartheid activists or films about South Africa. I was among the speakers because I had been to South Africa and seen the horrors of its racial exploitation. Some of the documentaries were obtained from MSU's prestigious African Studies Center, led by Alfred Opubor, a dynamic Nigerian who had obtained a PhD in communications at State, the first African to obtain such a degree.

Alfred was the other mentor of my consulting associate George White, who I also mentored as a student. I knew Alfred. He would later return to the continent and become an internationally recognized leader in theory and practice as it relates to the communications factor in African development. Alfred, like virtually all black Africans, was very much opposed to the South African regime.

Raising the awareness of the situation in South Africa was important because MSU's trustees are elected in statewide votes and had to be responsive to the public. The SALC used events such as films and speeches as a fulcrum by providing postage-paid postcards to those who attended the gatherings. The SALC would then convince their guests to write notes to MSU trustees about the need to disassociate with companies doing business in the apartheid state.

Also, each trustee was sent a personal invitation to attend each SALC event. In addition, the SALC sent a representative to each board meeting to raise issues related to South Africa. For one meeting, the SALC prepared official-looking MSU-green folders with twenty pages of information on apartheid and content on the feasibility of divestment.

The SALC needed allies on the board of trustees. I was among those who talked to Trustees Blanche Martin and Aubrey Radcliffe, two African Americans who had been involved in the U.S. Civil Rights movement. Dr. Martin, a dentist, was a Democrat, and Radcliffe, an educator, was a Republican. I knew them both very well.

During this period, I received a few calls from some of my progressive white friends who wanted me to know that some of their conservative associates had told them that the divestment campaign was dangerous because it could lead to black majority rule in South Africa and that South African blacks were better off under white control.

The campaign grew. The SALC began to build campus coalitions. It sought and obtained prodivestment resolutions from the Associated Students of MSU and MSU's Council of Graduate Students. Also, black student organizations weighed in by demanding divestment. The board of trustees responded to the pressure by appointing a panel of faculty members to study the financial impact of the proposed divestiture. If any trustees hoped that this step might show that divestment would be too costly, they were disappointed when the panel concluded that any negative impacts would be negligible.

With no financial downside and the student body and faculty demanding action, the trustees appeared to have no reason not to divest. However, we were concerned that some of the corporate giants we were targeting would put private pressure on the trustees. It was also possible that some of the trustees owned stock in the targeted companies and would vote against divestment because a successful campaign at MSU might create momentum for a nationwide movement. Such a movement could damage the stock values of targeted companies.

However, our fears were allayed in the fall of 1978 when Trustee Radcliffe made a motion to divest from all companies with subsidiaries in South Africa. The board voted in favor of the motion.

We had done it! The divestment was national news. Our strategy would become a template for campus-based antiapartheid activists nationwide. The movement would also spread to municipalities and state governments. These economic sanctions would later become a major factor in the demise of the apartheid state.

Between January 1979 and January 1980, Michigan State sold $8.5 million of stock in thirteen companies. The transactions actually made money for the university and diversified its portfolio. However, MSU did see a decline in corporate donations from some of the targeted companies in subsequent years.

Aubrey Radcliffe may have been the only individual to suffer consequences. The state Republican Party did not approve of his action and did not allow him to run for reelection as a trustee. I respected him for the courage of his convictions. For those of us dedicated to ending apartheid, the fight was not over. Many MSU activists advised leaders at other universities on how to organize divestment campaigns.

While lending support to the divestment movement, I was completing my next significant book, *The Urban Challenge: Poverty and Race*, published in 1977 by Follett Publishing Company, the first company to introduce black characters into elementary school readers.

The self-esteem black children can glean from seeing themselves represented in books is important. However, poverty is also an important factor in academic achievement. In my mind's eye, I saw eighty young Latino and black students who lined up for a free breakfast at the Matt Kelly Elementary School in Las Vegas in 2014. Most of these kids live in poverty. It reinforced a basic truth—you can't learn if you're hungry. These kids are a just few years away from being infants, and we know why babies cry—because their diapers need to be changed or because they are hungry. In these moments, very young human beings are in crisis. Their cries are calls for help, and infants cannot be tranquil and focused until those needs are met. Similarly, very young children can be stressed and disoriented by hunger.

The Urban Challenge established these poverty-related facts on the ground at a crucial time. The urban riots of the 1960s were a warning sign. The publisher made the stakes clear in notes on the back of the book: "The effects of poverty and race are threatening American cities, presenting challenges as important as any facing Americans today."

On the front of the book were quotes from Andrew Young and Coretta Scott King. Coretta's quote offered the following:

Robert L. Green recruited South African students with full MSU scholarships: Sydwell Matlala, Zach Chuenyane, Andrew Young, Mamazane Zulu, Robert L. Green, and another student in 1975.

Dr. Green fully understands the effect that poverty and race have upon our cities and their people. From his research and his experience he outlines ways we can meet the challenges and help our cities achieve a better life for all. No one is better to write this timely and hopeful book.

Andy Young offered this:

As a child of urban America, Robert L. Green is a different kind of social scientist. He speaks from within and brings a high level of documentation to the insights he shares. His book breaks through the fear barrier and makes urban life an opportunity for America rather than a problem.

Fear was a natural reaction to racism and violence. Dr. King had taught us that if the emotion was controlled, activists could make a difference. It was a choice, a crossroads—fear or freedom.

As a scholar, I sought to generate change by identifying in *The Urban Challenge* the link between poverty and race. I expanded on the insights of other scholars who had made this connection. Consider, for example, this passage on economic development that contrasted American urban policy with the Marshall Plan, which revived postwar Europe.

> In Europe we provided the kind of help that allowed nations not only to change the countryside cosmetically, but to build an economy the people could control themselves. In the United States, however, we have chosen to keep our cities dependent on benevolent handouts—much like colonies. Author William Tabb has drawn a number of parallels between the colony and the ghetto, where we maintain our highest concentration of human misery. He noted that income is low, birthrates are high and little money is saved because labor is generally underemployed. Goods and services are imported, there is occupation by outside police forces and the area is dependent on outside economic powers for capital. . . .
>
> The ghetto has not been allowed to pick itself up, as Europe was able to do, for the ghetto has been stripped of the necessary prerequisites of development. "Economics," economist E. F. Schumacher said, "does not start with goods, it starts with people and their education, organization and discipline."
>
> These deficiencies have been carefully orchestrated through the years. Education has been separate and unequal. . . . Our city schools are not producing, and this nonproducing industry is being allowed to proceed to turn out citizens who cannot function. (Green 1977, 38)

The Urban Challenge also examined how the educational system perpetuates self-doubt among blacks and racism in the broader society.

> Traditional curricula relate almost exclusively to white, middle-income experience. This fosters strong doubts and anxieties among poor and minority persons about their own cultures and backgrounds.
>
> Some educators have attempted to rectify this bias by introducing courses or units in minority history and culture. . . . Although black history, added to "standard" American history, can give children information about black America, biased white-oriented history continues to be taught. Black children can still perceive themselves as afterthoughts, while white children can still develop superior attitudes about their culture. . . . The entire curricula must be reworked in a way that gives respect to children from all backgrounds and gives proper perspective to all racial and ethnic groups. (Green 1977, 215)

The book was successful because it was widely reviewed in many academic journals and by leading journalists—Chicago-based columnist Vernon Jarrett among them. Ultimately, the book was a success because more than eighty universities included it in the curricula of classes, enabling me to connect with hundreds of thousands of young adults. As a result of the book, I received even more respect on campus as a scholar. However, I was still an activist, and I began to spend more time advising South African divestment activists on other campuses.

MSU's divestment did indeed trigger a chain reaction, as dozens of universities followed suit. Also, more cities began to follow the lead of East Lansing by creating antiapartheid purchasing policies. Later, following the lead of the state of Michigan, other states began to divest their holdings in companies with major operations in South Africa.

In the wake of our victory in the MSU divestment campaign, I became involved in a spate of school desegregation cases throughout the North. In many school districts, there was strong resistance to busing as a strategy to end desegregation. After the 1976 *Reed v. Rhodes* case in Cleveland, I saw large crowds of whites at desegregated school sites screaming epithets at black children as they arrived on buses.

After the 1979 *Armstrong v. Board of School Directors* ruling in Milwaukee, educators at one school tried to circumvent integration by placing the black students in separate classes and even established segregated restrooms and segregated water fountains. As the court-assigned manager of education planning, I was shocked and angry. I brought this to the attention of Thomas Atkins, general counsel for the NAACP and the lead attorney in the *Armstrong* case. He, in turn, alerted the counsel for the Milwaukee school board and the situation was quickly corrected.

However, I witnessed some of the greatest resistance in Chicago after a federal court issued a series of desegregation rulings between 1977 and 1980. Whites stormed school board meetings, demanding a rejection of the desegregation plan. They gathered in large numbers at desegregated school sites with signs and organized chants. Police had to force their way through crowds of spitting, name-calling protesters to clear a path for black children to enter schools. These were some of the biggest protests since 1974, when the governor of Massachusetts was forced to call in the National Guard to quell antibusing mobs in Boston.

Although not as nearly as violent, the protests against school desegregation in Chicago reminded me of the white counterdemonstration against Dr. King's march against housing segregation in that city on August 5, 1966. On that date, Dr.

King stepped out of the car that had ferried him to the Marquette Park / Gage Park area on Chicago's Southwest Side to lead a march of about seven hundred people. Thousands of taunting, jeering whites had gathered. One placard read: "King would look good with a knife in his back."

As Dr. King marched, someone hurled a stone, striking him on the head. Stunned, he fell to one knee and remained there for several seconds. When he rose, aides surrounded him to protect him from the rocks, bottles, and firecrackers that rained down on him and the other marchers. About thirty people were injured, and more might have been harmed if the police had not stopped the assault. After the incident, Dr. King said, "I have seen many demonstrations in the South, but I have never seen anything so hostile and so hateful as I've seen here today" (Levy 2015, 63).

I was horrified by that incident. It was clear that many financially upwardly mobile blacks wanted access to better housing and better schools in middle-class Chicago neighborhoods. After the attack on Dr. King, another equally shocking incident occurred. However, this one was private and has never been disclosed previously.

We did not expect the violent attack on our open-housing campaign, and we did not expect the more sophisticated attempt to seduce us that followed. Andy Young and I were in a motel suite in Chicago during Dr. King's open-housing campaign. Without warning, a middle-aged man with a briefcase knocked on the door. We welcomed him in.

"Gentlemen," he said, "we would like to make a contribution to Dr. King for his Civil Rights work." He unclasped the latches on his briefcase, revealing large stacks of one hundred–dollar bills wrapped with bank-prepared paper strips in the middle. This appeared to be a bribe attempt. I was astonished and didn't know what to say. Andy did. In Chicago's summer heat, there was a bit of sweat on his brow but cool resolve in his voice. "We cannot," he said, "accept any contribution of this type in this city because we are involved in a campaign against housing discrimination, and we don't accept money in this fashion when we are involved in a campaign."

The courier looked at Andy and me. Sheepishly, he looked down at the briefcase, closed it, and walked briskly out of the suite without giving us a second look. When I closed the door after he stepped out, I more fully understood just how far the supporters of American apartheid would go to preserve a system of separate but unequal in the North. I thought about that incident in Chicago with Andrew Young when Jimmy Carter in 1977 appointed Andy to serve as U.S. ambassador to the United Nations. I was very pleased for Andy and considered it a proud moment in American history. To some degree, at least for a while, the appointment muted those abroad who had criticized the United States for condoning discrimination and segregation. However, this was not a symbolic appointment because Andy was already very involved in important unofficial diplomacy before his appointment.

Andy, a brilliant negotiator and bridge-builder, successfully encouraged the business community in Birmingham, Alabama, to embrace change in the wake of the 1956 bus boycott, which ended segregation in that city's public transportation. Representing antiapartheid white South African business leaders, diamond mine mogul Harry Oppenheimer contacted Andy in 1976 and asked him to speak to these captains of commerce.

Shortly before Andy was appointed UN ambassador, he made a trip to South Africa and stayed at Oppenheimer's home, where they discussed strategies for organizing an antiapartheid campaign that would be supported by businesses in that country.

After his appointment to the United Nations, Andy's first destination was South Africa, where he gave notice that apartheid would be a front-burner issue for the Carter administration. A short time later, he flew to Nigeria and met with that country's head of state, Olusegun Obasanjo. This was a bridge-building visit. During the presidency of Gerald Ford, Carter's predecessor, relations between the United States and Nigeria had become so strained that the Nigerian government refused to let a plane carrying then secretary of state Henry Kissinger land in their country.

Some of the schism between Nigeria and the United States related to perceived American support for the apartheid government in South Africa. Andy gave the United States some credibility on social justice issues. After all, he spent most of his life in opposition to discrimination and segregation.

Regarding my role in school desegregation, Chicago was one of the last major court cases. Throughout the 1970s, I served as an expert witness in the liability phase of twenty-three school desegregation cases. In some cases, after testifying on the damages, I assisted districts in developing court-sanctioned remedies. As the pace of litigation slowed, I began to focus more broadly on urban policy. As a member of the Urban Policy Working Group at the U.S. Department of Housing and Urban Development (HUD) in 1979, I advised the federal government on ways to improve urban life.

It was also in 1979—August 14 to be precise—that Jimmy Carter removed Andy from his post at the United Nations. It was a shock because earlier that year, Andy played a leading role in advancing a settlement that would end the white minority government in Rhodesia, then under siege by two black liberation armies—one led by Robert Mugabe and the other by Joshua Nkomo. In a bid to end the war and control the transition to democracy in a way that would preserve white political influence, Rhodesian prime minister Ian Smith in March 1978 reached an agreement to create an interim government led by an executive council that included himself and three black Rhodesians—religious leader Bishop Abel Muzorewa among them.

Andy publicly denounced the deal and voted with other members of the UN Security Council to condemn any "internal agreement" that did not provide a democracy that included all factions. Mugabe and Nkomo also opposed the deal and promised to fight on. Under the guidance of Smith's executive council, a new constitution was drafted and approved in January 1979 in a nearly whites-only referendum. A short time later, an election staged by Smith's executive council brought Bishop Muzorewa to power as head of the United African National Council, leading to the short-lived government of Zimbabwe Rhodesia.

Andy refused to accept the election results, calling the process "neofascist," an opposition ratified by additional UN Security Council votes. Without international legitimacy, Muzorewa's regime agreed to all-party talks that would include Mugabe and Nkomo to reach an agreement for forming a new government. Those talks, held from September through the first half of December, would lead to a fairer nationwide vote, elections that put Mugabe's party into power in 1980. However, Andy was no longer in office when the all-party talks began. The events that led to his departure began when he learned in July 1979 that an upcoming report by the UN Division for Palestinian Rights called for the creation of a Palestinian state.

Andy wanted to delay the report because the Carter administration was occupied with other issues at the time and would need time to develop strategies and policies regarding Palestinian statehood. He met with the UN representatives of several Arab countries to try to convince them the report should be delayed. They agreed in principle, but insisted that the Palestine Liberation Organization (PLO) also had to agree.

To get Palestinian agreement for a delay, Andy on July 20, 1979, met with Zehdi Terzi, the UN representative of the PLO, at the apartment of the UN ambassador from Kuwait. On August 10, news of this meeting became public when Israeli intelligence leaked its illegally acquired transcript of the meeting to Israeli prime minister Menachem Begin and then through his office to *Newsweek* magazine. The meeting was controversial because the United States had promised Israel that it

Future Detroit mayor Dennis Archer, then mayor Coleman Young, Jim Sharp, Andrew Young, and Robert L. Green gather at a 1974 political event.

would not meet directly with the PLO until the PLO recognized Israel's right to exist. Carter removed Andy from his post.

I was aghast because I believed then, as I do now, that factions in disputes should always talk. Too often, when they don't talk, there is war. To me and millions of other Americans, Andy was now even more of a hero because—motivated by a desire to see peace between the Israelis and Palestinians—he had tried to make a difference.

I knew university students would value lectures by Ambassador Young. We quickly made arrangements for him to serve as a visiting professor at Michigan State. In September 1979, I arranged for him to give classroom presentations as a visiting professor. He helped conduct a seminar called "World Conflict and Development." The class was extremely popular, and Andy's presence on campus only added to MSU's academic prestige.

Meanwhile, I continued to add to the scholarship on urban studies. My next major book on desegregation, a 1981 anthology titled *Discrimination and the Welfare of Urban Minorities*, was significant because it was inspired by Coleman Young, Detroit's first black mayor, and because it influenced other African American mayors and the growing contingent of blacks in the U.S. House of Representatives. Young prompted me to write it after he relayed many examples of discrimination in metropolitan Detroit during long conversations I had with him.

The book documented discrimination in housing, employment, and education and provided proposals for addressing bias. Geographers, psychologists, a historian, an urban planner, and a labor economist contributed chapters. It was also widely used in university courses.

Proposed solutions to these issues were welcomed and hailed because there was still hope that realistic, socially conscious Republicans—with the urging of more and more elected black officials—might resist the push of some of the more regressive supporters of Ronald Reagan, the new president. America's political memory is quite short. Considering the Watergate scandal and the unnecessary extension of the Vietnam War under Richard Nixon, it's easy to forget that his administration—pushed by environmentalists and Civil Rights activists—created the Environmental Protection Agency and affirmative action in some federal contracting.

I knew George Romney, the former governor of Michigan. Romney, who sought the presidency in a contest against Nixon, lost because he acknowledged what had happened to many other Americans regarding Vietnam. He said he had been "brainwashed." Romney was also was a supporter of Civil Rights, and Nixon appointed him secretary of HUD because of his interests and awareness. Consider what Romney said in 1970, before he was appointed by Nixon to HUD: "Our nation's metropolitan areas cannot endure . . . a run-down, festering black core, surrounded by a well-to-do, indifferent white ring" (Bonastia 2006, 3).

On a separate occasion, Romney said, "the most explosive threat to our nation is the confrontation between the poor and the minority groups who are concentrated in the central cities and the middle income and the affluent who live in the surrounding and separate communities. This confrontation is divisive. It is explosive. It must be resolved" (Bonastia 2006, 3).

Although the Republican Party—the party of Abraham Lincoln and Theodore Roosevelt—could still regain its former role as a party for social justice, Christopher Bonastia noted that Romney and his more enlightened wing of the party were on the wane when he resigned as HUD chief in 1973. Consider this passage from Bonastia's book, *Knocking on the Door*: "Nevertheless, he [Romney] was correct in pointing to the destructive effects of racial and economic isolation, effects that continue to accrue today" (2006, 3).

Discrimination and the Welfare of Urban Minorities was my last book during my first stint at MSU. I was offered and accepted the position of president at the University of the District of Columbia (UDC), a post I assumed in September 1983. As I packed, I thought about my most important legacy at MSU—the students I had helped. I thought of former students who were on track to become leaders in commerce. For example, I thought of Wanda Herndon, an MSU communications major. (She would later climb the ladder at Starbucks and became senior vice president of global communications at the company.) I also thought about MSU education major Ingrid Saunders Jones. (At Coca-Cola, she would become senior vice president of global connections and chair of the Coca-Cola Foundation.)

I thought of Herb Washington, a track-and-field star at Michigan State. (Later, Herb would build one of the nation's largest McDonald's restaurant chains and founded, in 2005, the Youngstown, Ohio, Steelhounds, a minor league hockey team.) I also thought of former students who assisted me in my scholarship and legal work on segregation, poverty, and discrimination, Spartans whom I thought might become academic leaders. Cassandra Simmons was among them. (She would later become dean of the Harvard School of Public Health.) Another Harvard University administrator, Brenda White, came to mind because she was also one of my former MSU students. Also on my mind were three other formers students: Patricia Hebert, who became an administrator for the state's education department; urban planner Jill Hirt; and Bradley Carl. (Bradley later would become a professor at the University of Wisconsin.) In addition, I thought of Frances S. Thomas, an older student who was Coretta Scott King's high school teacher in Marion, Alabama, many years before she became a contributor to some of my books.

Staff and faculty associates also came to mind—among them, John Schweitzer, one of the professors at the Center for Urban Affairs (CUA). (John would remain at MSU as an urban affairs professor and later assist me in my school district consulting work.) I also thought of former student Richard Thomas, an MSU history professor and author, and Maxie Jackson, my colleague at the CUA and the CUD. (He would become assistant dean of graduate education programs at Michigan State.)

Three fellow psychologists came to mind: Robert Morgan, James Weathers, and Lou Hofman. Hofman was a researcher and evaluator for my 1964 report on the public school shut-down in Prince Edward County, Virginia. Morgan was a psychology professor at a number of universities. Morgan was an outstanding student and was active in demonstrations against housing discrimination when I sought to buy a home in East Lansing. Also, Morgan was appointed to the East Lansing human relations commission when it was formed in the aftermath of my housing discrimination fight. Weathers was a senior executive for the president of a Detroit community college at the time of my departure from MSU. (James would later serve for a decade as a senior mayoral aide in Detroit and subsequently become chief operating officer for a consulting firm.)

Moreover, I thought of former student George White, a correspondent for *U.S. News & World Report* at that time. He would later closely cover the South African divestment movement for the *Detroit Free Press* and move on to the *Los Angeles Times*, where he would help the paper win two Pulitzer Prizes and produce exposés of sweatshop slavery, stories that helped prompt major reforms in the apparel and retail industries. As a communications consultant, education analyst, and journalist, George has been helping me with many of my publishing and consulting projects.

In addition, I thought of faculty members who had worked closely with me on books—among them, geographer Joe T. Darden, sociologist Thomas Tenbrunsel, and educational psychologist Robert Griffore.

When my departure was announced, the *State News*, the MSU student newspaper, made the following comments in an opinion page section devoted to me.

As Robert Green, outgoing dean of MSU's Urban Affairs Programs, leaves for Washington D.C. . . . we'd like to express our congratulations and best wishes for his future success.

MSU has been undeniably fortunate to have had so strong a minority voice and so conscientious an urban affairs expert. The magnitude of Dr. Green's success is reflected by the fact that he has been sought by several national universities for their presidential positions, mentioned for numerous top government posts and recognized as a national authority on black and urban affairs. . . . This community should be sorry indeed for losing its first black dean and a true conscience of the University. (1983)

I had accepted the post at UDC because I wanted to make a difference in an urban setting. I felt strongly that a student in the nation's capital deserved a high-quality university education. This move—like the title of one of my books—was "the urban challenge."

Less than a year after assuming the post, I joined the steady flow of people who were voluntarily arrested at sit-in demonstrations at the South African embassy. I did so at the behest of Randall Robinson, who led nationwide protests against apartheid. He knew about my work with Dr. King, and he knew I had been to South Africa.

At the embassy, I was part of a crowd of about seventy demonstrators. Most of the protesters remained outside the designated trespass line that the police had established to ward off demonstrators. However, I was among ten demonstrators standing inside the trespass line. About ten police officers, part of a special federal unit, stood between us and the embassy. The commanding officer loudly and clearly told us to move back or be arrested.

I thought about Jim Crow in the South, segregation in the North, and oppression in South Africa. I told the officer, "Sir, we are here to protest the brutality of the South African government and especially their brutal treatment of black children who only want a good education." Moments later the ten of us were arrested. I had never been arrested before. As an officer placed me in handcuffs, I was certain that this was a cause worth arrest. I was certain that UDC's board of trustees and students would support my action—and they did.

Early in my tenure as president, I realized the university was experiencing a maelstrom of academic politics. Two other universities were being consolidated within UDC and there were fights and intrigue over who should get a variety of faculty positions. My goal was to improve the curricula. I did the best I could under the circumstances and left the university in August 1985.

I was buoyed the same year when Plenum Press published *Metropolitan Desegregation*, an anthology I edited with major support from Frances S. Thomas. The book was important because it thoroughly reviewed the historic cross-district desegregation of Delaware schools. It included chapters on a wide range of topics, among them: the legal issues, the impact of desegregation on academic achievement, and changes in community attitudes about desegregation.

It was during my tenure in DC that I began to conduct major research on the connection between expectations and academic achievement. For example, I wrote "Expectations: A Driving Force in Human Behavior," a research paper I presented to participants at a Memphis Public Schools conference on March 2, 1984. My research on expectations was a bridge to my transition from university president to academic consultant for major public school districts, where I could apply my experience and my growing expertise on expectations to help students at underserved schools close the achievement gap.

I moved to Okemos, Michigan, established Robert L. Green & Associates, and obtained consulting contracts from the public school districts in Detroit, Portland, and Memphis in 1986. In Memphis, I was joined by Coretta Scott King who gave inspirational talks to teachers and administrators. I also brought in a number of scholars—Harvard's Gary Orfield and Ronald Edmonds, founder of the effective schools philosophy and movement, among them—professors who helped me provide training that raised the expectations of public school faculty as it related to academic achievement.

In 1986, Nolan Ellison, president of Cuyahoga Community College in Cleveland—a man I had mentored during his student years at MSU—asked me to join him at the college and expand its research capacity. I joined him in July and created and directed the Joint Center for Applied Research and Urban Education, a post I would hold for ten years. I also served as a visiting professor at the School of Applied Social Sciences at Cleveland's Case Western Reserve University. These positions afforded me an opportunity to expand my research, continue my consulting, and produce new reports for major institutions.

In this new phase, a crossroads in my personal life, I also had the freedom to choose to continue to expand my support for campaigns for social justice and educational equity abroad and at home. For example, I was extremely supportive of Coretta Scott King and her successful campaign to obtain funding for the

At a 1984 Washington, DC, gathering for the government enactment of the Martin Luther King Jr. holiday: (*front*) Yolanda King; Christine Farris; Lettie Green; Coretta Scott King; Andrew Young; Andrea Young, daughter of Andrew; and (*back*) Robert L. Green.

establishment of the Martin Luther King Jr. Center for Nonviolent Social Change, a memorial, museum, and education institution in Atlanta.

Coretta is a historic figure not yet fully recognized for her courage and foresight. She was a part of historic protests in favor of nonviolence and a pacifist approach to change as a college student at Antioch College in Ohio before she met her husband. Also—in a demonstration with famed pediatrician Benjamin Spock—Coretta took a stand against the Vietnam War before Dr. King took an official position.

Mrs. King, the widow, was universally loved and admired by Americans—the poor and the powerful, and people across the political spectrum. For example, I arranged for her to meet with Detroit auto industrialist Henry Ford II, and he gave her several million dollars to help build the King Center.

I also recalled when I escorted her to Ronald Reagan's 1985 inaugural ball after his reelection. My wife, Lettie, could not join us because she was in Kenya gathering information on hunger and poverty as part of a delegation that included Betty Shabazz, widow of Malcolm X, and Donna Shalala, who was then chancellor of the

University of Wisconsin and would later become secretary of Health and Human Services under Bill Clinton.

Mrs. King and I were seated at a table at the inaugural. President Reagan noticed us, rose from his own table, walked over, and greeted us. "Thank you for coming," he said to Coretta. "You're very welcome," she said." I'm glad to be here. I hope to communicate with you later." I thanked Reagan for his support of the King Center. He smiled. "I will continue to support it," he said.

Coretta was tireless in her efforts to make the date of Dr. King's birth a national holiday, a campaign vigorously championed by U.S. representative John Conyers, a Detroiter. That dream was realized when Martin Luther King Jr. Day was celebrated as a national holiday for the first time in 1986. That same year, Coretta traveled to South Africa to meet with Winnie Mandela, Nelson's activist wife.

January 1987 was a seminal month and year because Mrs. King demonstrated wisdom as a leader of the King Center and courage as an activist. The activism related to a legal case, *Forsyth County, Georgia, v. The Nationalist Movement* (1992), which would eventually reach the Supreme Court, involving the government of Forsyth County, Georgia, and white nationalists. The county government had set high fees for white racists seeking permits to march and gather in public places because of the high cost of providing a police presence.

On January 17, 1987, a group of ninety Civil Rights demonstrators in a march against "fear and intimidation" in Forsyth County was met by as many as three hundred counterprotesters, including members of the Ku Klux Klan and members of a white nationalist group that advocated the expulsion of all nonwhites from the United States. Eight counterprotesters were arrested on charges of carrying concealed weapons and trespassing.

In response, Coretta led the Mobilization Against Fear and Intimidation in Forsyth County the following weekend on January 24. About twenty thousand people rallied in support—among them other Civil Rights leaders, U.S. senators, and other elected government officials. They were met again by many counterprotesters; however, the white nationalists were vastly outnumbered on that day.

My wife, Lettie, one of Coretta's best friends, attended that mobilization and marched with her. When she returned, she told me she was not afraid and that she was glad to participate in the push-back against fear in Georgia.

Remarkably, on January 16, just one day before the initial Mobilization against Fear, Coretta also continued to build coalitions for social justice at home and abroad through the King Center. Like Dr. King, Andrew Young, and me, she believed blacks should build stronger coalitions with Latinos. King Center activities in January 1987 were important because—in the wake of the first King Day holiday and racial tensions in Georgia—the media was more interested in the center's annual awards event.

At a January 16 press conference, Coretta said she would continue to lobby on behalf of the poor and called for tighter sanctions on the apartheid government in South Africa. The King Center then bestowed the Social Responsibility Award to Cesar Chavez, who accepted it on behalf of the United Farm Workers (UFW).

This was the kind of multiracial, multiethnic solidarity I had seen during the final year of Dr. King's life. I was in Atlanta visiting with Dr. King in January 1968 as he was planning his Poor People's March, which would be his final campaign. During the stay, I saw activists of all races and ethnic groups—blacks, whites, Native Americans, and Latinos. Realizing that Latinos were a rapidly growing poor population, Dr. King very much wanted the UFW and its leaders—Cesar Chavez and Dolores Huerta—to support the march. A month later, the UFW endorsed the campaign and sent representatives to help with the planning.

At the time of the King Center event in 1987, few knew that Coretta had developed a very close friendship with Dolores Huerta. Also, many were not aware of Huerta's strong feelings about the state of education in the nation. I appreciated Huerta because she understood there was a connection between poverty and academic underachievement.

Huerta was born on April 10, 1930, in a small mining town in the mountains of northern New Mexico. Her father, Juan Fernández, a miner and farm worker, was a union activist who ran for political office and won a seat in the New Mexico legislature in 1938. Huerta spent most of her childhood and early adult life in Stockton, California, where she and her two brothers moved with their mother, following the divorce of her parents.

Her mother's entrepreneurial spirit and independence were among the reasons Huerta became a feminist. Huerta's mother, Alicia, was a compassionate woman who offered rooms at affordable rates in her seventy-room hotel, which she acquired after years of hard work. Alicia welcomed low-wage workers in the hotel and waived the fee when they were too poor to pay. The Stockton of Huerta's youth was a diverse agricultural community that included African Americans and people of Mexican, Filipino, Japanese, and Chinese descent.

After graduating from college, Huerta took a position as a public school teacher. However, she quit shortly after taking the job because she had been distraught at the sight of impoverished children and the indifference of teachers and administrators. "Of her resignation, she said, 'I quit because I couldn't stand seeing kids come to class hungry and needing shoes. I thought I could do more by organizing farm workers than by trying to teach hungry children'" (National Women's History Museum).

In 1955 Huerta officially began her career as an activist by helping to found the Stockton Chapter of the Community Service Organization (CSO), which fought for economic improvements for Latinos. The CSO battled segregation and police brutality, led voter registration drives, and pushed for improved public services. In 1960 she helped found the Agricultural Worker's Association. It was through her work at these organizations that Huerta met fellow activist and labor leader Cesar Chavez.

In 1962 Huerta and Chavez founded the National Farm Workers Association, the predecessor to the UFW, formed in 1965. The 1965 Delano (California) Grape Strike was a significant campaign. Huerta helped to organize the strike of over five thousand grape workers and a boycott of a major wine company. As a result, the UFW obtained a three-year contract for the workers. Subsequently, she fought against the use of harmful pesticides and for unemployment and healthcare benefits for agricultural workers.

In 1973, Huerta led a consumer boycott and lobbying efforts that prompted the state government to enact the California Agricultural Labor Relations Act of 1975, which allowed farm workers to form unions and bargain for better wages and working conditions. As vice president of UFW, she worked diligently throughout the 1970s and 1980s as a lobbyist to improve workers' legislative representation.

Huerta also spoke out about the impact of poverty and "miseducation" of Latino youth. She called for more parental and community involvement in schools. As a defender of workers who had been exploited, she was also an ardent opponent of the South African government and its system of worker exploitation and legalized discrimination in education and other aspects of life.

South Africa's apartheid system was coming to an end. As international pressure mounted, South Africa's new president F. W. de Klerk began to negotiate with the imprisoned Nelson Mandela about steps to end apartheid. In his opening address to parliament in February 1990, De Klerk announced that he would repeal discriminatory laws and lift the thirty-year ban on leading antiapartheid groups such as Mandela's African National Congress, the Pan Africanist Congress, the South African Communist Party, and the United Democratic Front. De Klerk also declared that press freedoms would be restored and the death penalty would be suspended. In addition, he made his first public commitment to release Mandela and other political prisoners.

On February 11, 1990, Mandela was released after twenty-seven years of confinement. On that day Lettie and I were guests at the Atlanta home of Andrew and Jean Young. We watched coverage of his release on television, cheering loudly.

The following year, 1991, the W. K. Kellogg Foundation launched an initiative to empower black communities to address a range of problems. The foundation consulted with thirty-four individuals with firsthand knowledge of the issues facing certain African American men and boys. It requested ideas and proposals from scholars, editors, ministers, and community leaders—specifically, social change practitioners actively engaged in making a difference for young men in their respective communities.

It was called the National Task Force on African-American Men and Boys, and my good friend Andrew Young was named chairman. When all the information was gathered, I was appointed to a six-person team that wrote the report.

We were working on the report when, in 1992, riots erupted in Los Angeles in the aftermath of not guilty verdicts in the police beating of motorist Rodney King. George White, who joined the (MSU) *State News* as a freshman with my assistance, was a reporter for the *Los Angeles Times* when the riots occurred. He was among a group of *Times* reporters that the paper cited as key contributors to the reporting that enabled the paper to win the 1993 Pulitzer Prize for Spot Coverage.

Another Spartan, Walter C. Farrell Jr., produced an impressive scholarly take on the Los Angeles riot. He coauthored "Structural Violence as an Inducement to African American and Hispanic Participation in the Los Angeles Civil Disturbance of 1992," a study published by the *Journal of Human Behavior in the Social Environment*. Walter worked for me when he was a doctoral student in urban-social geography at MSU. He was one my best researcher-writers. (He is now a professor of social work and a fellow in the Center for Urban and Regional Studies at the University of North Carolina at Chapel Hill.)

As I toiled on this and other Kellogg Foundation grants, the honorable Mandela ran as a presidential candidate in South Africa and was elected in 1994. I was very proud of him and his leadership and determination during twenty-seven years in jail. I thought about how at MSU students and faculty had helped lead the economic divestment movement that had helped pressure the South African government. However, I also realized that the economic disparities in the country would not vanish soon—that whites would continue to dominate the economy.

I also thought about the South African students I had enrolled at Michigan State. I realized that I had made a difference—that many of these students would also make a difference in the new South Africa. I also realized that with black political control, education for blacks in South Africa would improve and produce generations of educated people who would eventually gain more control of the economy and help transform the lives of the vast majority in that country.

Andrew Young and I talked about the prospects for South Africa's future. We were both buoyed by Mandela's election. We talked about how Mandela was a King-like figure. Proof of that, Andy and I agreed, was the Truth and Reconciliation Commission that Mandela authorized, which enabled victims of gross human rights violations to give statements about their experiences. White perpetrators of violence and oppression also gave testimony and requested and obtained amnesty from both civil and criminal prosecution.

Like Dr. King and Gandhi, Mandela was more interested in forgiveness than retribution—to ensure a less violent, less divided, and more cohesive society.

While working with Andy on the African American task force initiative I also worked on Kellogg Foundation projects that were focused more directly on education. For example, I helped produce two major studies for the Kellogg Foundation in 1995: "African-American Males: The Ongoing Struggle for Equality and Access" and "Grassroots Civic Leadership in Enhancing the Status of African-American Men and Boys." Kellogg Foundation administrator Bobby Austin supervised these research and writing initiatives. These were important efforts to understand and address the factors responsible for poor academic achievement.

Working with Andrew Young and the writing team, I helped produce the African American task force report. Published in 1996, it was called "Repairing the Breach: Key Ways to Support Family Life, Reclaim Our Streets, and Rebuild Civil Society in America's Communities." In the preface, titled "Public Ideas and Public Work," Andy wrote:

> The Task Force has provided information and ideas which organizations and individuals can use to begin transforming communities—and thereby assist boys and their families. We want to create long-term structures for sustained intervention for boys in trouble. We must have systemic change, in which many ideas are brought together, so that crime and violence are reduced and social life is made whole. We each have a part to play. (Young and Austin 1996)

Lettie Green and Coretta Scott King meet with Robert L. Green at the University of the District of Columbia, Washington, DC, in 1984.

We also cited the stakeholders, noting that goals "can be accomplished by the cooperative activities of civic, social, religious, professional, business, governmental, and philanthropic organizations" (Young and Austin 1996).

As for means, we proposed "to empower individuals to take control of their lives and communities through the development and use of effective leadership skills." We also said that we could create this "common good" by encouraging "entrepreneurship, economic development [and] educational reform." Dolores Huerta promoted the education of students, especially from migrant families, and encouraged their parents to participate in their education. "How parent involvement is carried out has much to do with student age and grade level, size of school, community need, and the nature and amount of communication, using strategies that stress personal contact, creating inviting learning environments, initiating opportunities for parent interaction, providing opportunities for formal and informal involvement at school and at home, and building on the Mexican American culture, values and experiences." (Young and Austin 1996).

While I worked on the Kellogg Foundation report, there was an unusual voluntary school desegregation initiative. Voters in Tennessee in 1995 approved a referendum that consolidated Chattanooga public schools, which were 62 percent black, with outlying Hamilton County schools, which were 95 percent white. They did so primarily for financial reasons. Still, it was voluntary desegregation and there was a good bit of fear before the vote. I recalled an *Education Week* article published just before schools opened under a consolidation plan.

> The word on everyone's lips here is fear.
>
> That's not the usual sentiment in this river city of 155,000 souls. Farsighted civic leaders have cleaned up downtown, rebuilt substandard housing, and dedicated the $45 million freshwater Tennessee Aquarium on the banks of the snaking Tennessee River. Chattanooga, once a dirty, declining industrial town, has been reborn over the past 20 years.
>
> The city is justifiably puffed up over its accomplishments. But its hardest task has just begun. This time, Chattanoogans are wrestling with something more important—and more fragile—than its buildings. They are talking about their children. And it's making them uneasy.
>
> Last fall, after years of declining enrollments and mounting expenses, city residents voted to give up their school system and consolidate with the Hamilton County schools. In Tennessee, state law requires counties, not cities, to furnish education. Similar votes have merged the Knoxville and Nashville school systems into their surrounding counties. . . .
>
> "The city has no history of overt racial hostility," says George A. Key Sr., a past president of the Chattanooga branch of the N.A.A.C.P. and a member of the steering committee.
>
> Key, who grew up in and later helped lead the city's oldest black Baptist church, recalls that 40 years ago Martin Luther King Jr.'s name came up as the church was searching for a new pastor. The church elders picked someone else. And that's a good thing, Key believes, since blacks and whites lived in relative peace. "The Lord knew that the climate was not quite right in Chattanooga for the things Martin Luther King was going to be doing," Key says. "He never would have gotten off the ground with his program, had he come into Chattanooga." (Bradley 1995)

I considered Key's statement with a mix of anger and amusement. It sometimes amazes me how selective the human memory can be—especially when it comes to race. Willie Ricks, a Chattanooga native, was a young colleague with Dr. King, me, Andy Young, and many other brave activists during our perilous March against Fear in Mississippi.

In January 1960, Ricks led high school students from Chattanooga's Howard High School to a sit-in at a segregated Woolworth diner in downtown Chattanooga. The protests spread to four other stores in Chattanooga. Three years before Bull Connor ordered the Birmingham police to unleash their city's fire hoses on peaceful students, the Chattanooga police viciously attacked peaceful black protesters with fire hoses on Market and Cherry Streets.

In August of 1960, after months of organized action, black students had successfully desegregated seven department stores in downtown Chattanooga. Similar stand-ins were performed in movie theaters, and within a short period many of Chattanooga's theaters and hotels were desegregated. In addition, about seventy additional restaurants and the city's buses and trains were desegregated.

Due to his notoriety in the community, Ricks was contacted by the Southern Christian Leadership Conference (SCLC) to register voters in Chattanooga in 1961. The next year Ricks joined the Student Nonviolent Coordinating Committee (SNCC) and took part in the 1966 March against Fear as an SNCC member.

I told students and other faculty members about Willie Ricks when I returned from my one year of work with SCLC, which included the March against Fear, to teach and serve as an administrator at Michigan State in the fall of 1966. Now, after my years in DC and Ohio, I was about to return to Michigan State again—this time, after a fourteen-year absence.

I returned in September 1997 to join the David Walker (research) Institute at MSU. Faculty organized a major reception to welcome me back. I was very happy to be back. I was pleased to see Dr. Thomas Gunnings and Dr. Gloria Smith, who had worked with Provost Lou Anna Simon, David Walker Institute director George Rowan, and MSU president M. Peter McPherson to arrange my return. Provost Simon wanted to increase black student enrollment at MSU and helped arrange one of my studies on academic issues in the Detroit public school system.

My responsibilities included writing and research on issues that affected the quality of life for urban residents. I also supervised undergraduate, master's, and PhD students in social sciences. I was overwhelmed by the growth of a campus that was already very large when I left it. Many students sought me out to ask me about the student activism on campus in the 1960s and 1970s, including activists such as LaMarr Thomas. Many also asked me to relay stories about my experiences with Dr.

King. Twice a year—the date of Dr. King's birth and the date of his death—I was deluged with requests to speak at events honoring the great man.

There were also former students whom I continue to work with today. For example, Bradley Carl began to work with me on public school reform when he won an MSU Robert L. Green Fellowship as a doctoral student. Many were surprised because Bradley is white, which dispelled the notion that the fellowship in my name was for black students only.

Later, in 1998, I wrote *Ownership, Responsibility and Accountability for Student Achievement*, a book published by Alpine Guild, Inc. This book, based on work I conducted for the San Francisco United School District, began to advance my theories about classroom standards and expectations. One passage cites the importance of teacher attitudes:

> Teachers need to believe in the ability of children to learn and children must be made to believe that they can learn. Teachers must take responsibility for teaching and the learning of the child. . . . Everyone should hold high expectations for student success.

Obviously, academic achievement is impossible if students drop out of school or are forced out of school for disciplinary reasons. The dropout, expulsion, and suspension rates for black students were high in San Francisco. In the book, we set the following as objectives for the school district:

- Reducing the placement of African American students in special education classes
- Reducing suspensions and expulsions
- Reducing dropout rates for African American students

The reference to the disproportionate rates of suspensions and expulsions as it relates to students of color was prescient. In 2001, the No Child Left Behind Act was passed under President George W. Bush. This set of policies included a "zero tolerance" standard that would later create a crisis in disproportionate punishment for students of color nationwide.

I continued to expand my expertise on achievement in urban school settings by taking on major consulting projects. I coauthored "Academic Achievement Study of High and Low Achieving Public Housing Students in the San Francisco Unified

School District." I followed that up in 2002 by producing "A Summary of Detroit Public School Teachers' Perceptions of Student Achievement."

Reflecting on my scholarship at the time, it was clear that I had made the case that education is the key to overcoming poverty. I was also beginning to build the case that high expectations were a key to academic achievement. As an author, I had written books that influenced public policy-makers and established my reputation as a leading expert on urban education issues.

I was proud of my career arcs. For example, after winning the Distinguished Achievement Award for Excellence in Educational Journalism, an honor bestowed by the Educational Press Association of America in 1974, I maintained a high-profile position in the public affairs arena by producing dozens of monographs, articles, reviews, and studies on education issues for newspapers, magazines, and leading academic journals.

Also, I had left global imprints. After my experiences learning about disadvantaged communities in Israel, Kenya, and South Africa, President Jimmy Carter appointed me vice cochairman of the National Commission on the International Year of the Child in 1979 at the behest of Jean C. Young, wife of Ambassador Andrew Young. Marion Wright Edelman, head of the Children's Defense Fund, and actress Marlo Thomas were among the members of the commission. After that, I spent time in Jamaica and Ghana examining issues related to poverty, education, and urban development.

When the commission made its recommendations regarding juvenile justice, health, education, and nutrition, we were guided by an international human rights charter based on the 1959 UN Declaration of the Rights of the Child:

> Whereas the United Nations has, in the Universal Declaration of Human Rights, proclaimed that everyone is entitled to all the rights and freedoms set forth, without distinction of any kind, such as race, colour, sex, language, religion, political or other opinion, national or social origin, property, birth or other status.
>
> Whereas the child, by reason of his or her physical and mental immaturity, needs special safeguards and care, including appropriate legal protection, before as well as after birth.

Those rights were not guaranteed in the United States. However, I had helped the country move closer to those ideals. I had provided services to the Head Start education program for poor children and their parents after it was launched in the

1960s. Also, as an activist-scholar I helped school districts throughout the nation desegregate to provide access to better educational resources to African American and Latino students.

However, as I observed school districts throughout the nation ending desegregation efforts, it was also clear that I had been wrong about the staying power of busing as a means to integrate schools. Professor James Coleman, a University of Chicago sociologist, had written reports predicting that busing would accelerate white flight from metropolitan urban areas. In a *Harvard Educational Review* article in May 1976, Harvard Professor Thomas F. Pettigrew and I disagreed with Coleman's conclusions.

Coleman was right about white flight. As citywide busing occurred, more and more whites fled cities across America. Also, black parents had begun to reject busing because it was their children who were being bused—not whites. As originally conceived, busing was to be a two-way system. In practice, as applied by school districts, it was a one-way system.

With waning public support, the courts began to relax judicial supervision of school districts during the 1990s in favor of voluntary efforts to achieve racial balance. In the early 1990s, the Supreme Court ruled in three cases coming from Oklahoma City, Kansas City, and DeKalb County, Georgia, that federal judges could ease their supervision of school districts once legally enforced segregation had been eliminated to the extent practicable. With these decisions, the high court opened the door for school districts throughout the country to end judicial supervision once they had achieved unitary status, which meant a school district had done enough to eliminate segregation to be released from to court-ordered mandates.

UCLA sociologist Gary Orfield, a good friend who formerly directed the Harvard Project on School Desegregation, lamented this trend in his 1996 book *Dismantling Desegregation*, explaining that the intent of busing and other integration efforts had been falsely framed by opponents.

A segregated African American or Latino school, we show, usually enrolls a large percentage of economically disadvantaged students. This concentrated poverty devastates schools; students are literally cut off from routes that lead to job and college opportunities. These students often lack family connections, money and networks that allow movement into the mainstream economy.

A recently modish dig at integrationists says: "Black kids don't need white

On April 18, 2001, during her last visit and address at MSU, Coretta Scott King and Robert L. Green confer.

kids to learn." But that phrase misses the effective property of desegregation. The policy works not when paternalistic whites "help" minorities but when it provides avenues toward opportunity. The currently stratified opportunity structure denies economically disadvantaged minorities to middle-class schools, and to the world beyond them. (Orfield and Eaton 1997, xv)

Then, in 2002, the Supreme Court upheld a lower court decision in *Belk v. Charlotte-Mecklenburg Board of Education*, ruling that the school system had achieved desegregation status and that busing was no longer necessary. This paved the way for more busing-related reversals.

Meanwhile, many blacks and Latinos were also pushing for an end to busing in favor of promised improvements in their local schools. In many cities, school districts provided additional resources to the poorest schools as part of court-arranged agreements to end busing programs. Parents of color wanted better local schools. My next mission was to help them make those improvements.

I received some personal honors in 2002. It was the year I was awarded the Gandhi-King-Ikeda Award for Human Rights and Peace Initiatives by Morehouse College, the alma mater of Dr. King. It was also the year I was honored as a distinguished alumnus and dean and professor emeritus at Michigan State.

Wanda Herndon was among those who wrote letters in favor of my selection as distinguished alumnus. Like many of my former students, Wanda was very successful. When she wrote the letter of recommendation, she was senior vice president of global communications for Starbucks—a post she held from 1995 to 2006. Wanda was one of my coauthors on a paper called "Beyond Race, Sex and Social Class," published in a scholarly journal called *Perspectives on Education* in March 1977.

In 2002 my next book, *Expectations: How Teacher Expectations Can Increase Student Achievement*, was published. It was the culmination of my research and classroom experience on academic standards as a professor and education consultant. The thesis was made clear early in the book:

> Research in both classical psychology and educational psychology has long shown that the expectations that others have for us affect the way in which we view ourselves, especially those who act as important influences in our lives. The way we view ourselves, in turn, affects our own expectations for ourselves. Finally, the expectations we hold for ourselves impact our performance, and as a result, influence the nature and quality of the lives we live. . . .
>
> In studying the issue of expectations extensively, Harvard University scholar Ronald Furguson concluded that despite the incomplete nature of the research, the evidence suggests that teachers' perceptions, expectations and behaviors probably do help to sustain, and perhaps even to expand, the test score gap between white and African American students. (Green 2002a, 19)

The book explored important related topics: how teacher expectations are formed and why and how expectations matter, among them. One of the most important sections provided details on what effective teachers do.

> Effective teachers not only have high expectations, but also set clear standards of attainable academic and behavioral performance and hold students to them.

Students must know precisely what is expected of them and why it is expected, and believe they can meet those expectations. As much as possible, they should be empowered and have played a part in setting those standards. Students should see standards upheld and know specific consequences related to each standard. Standards should be consistent and equally applied to all students; but teachers are reasonable in enforcement when conditions become modified. Good behavior should receive positive reinforcement. (Green 2002a, 41)

The book would become a manual for raising academic performance in America's major urban school districts, which were now becoming largely black and brown.

A short time later, in 2003, Lou Anna Simon was appointed Michigan State's interim president from May of that year until May 2004, replacing M. Peter McPherson, who was serving as an advisor to President George W. Bush on the reconstruction of Iraq following the toppling of Sadam Hussein's government.

I had known her since her days as a graduate student at State and had following her steady rise from associate provost to provost to vice president for academic affairs, the post she held until her appointment as interim president. I was among those who encouraged the MSU Board of Trustees to remove the interim status and elect her president. For example, I expressed my support for her in conversations with MSU trustee Joel Ferguson, one of my former students. Joel is a very successful businessman and a force in local and national Democratic Party politics. When the trustees elected Lou Anna Simon president in 2004, I was very confident that my beloved Michigan State was in the right hands—and I was right.

At that point, my book on expectations and academic achievement was still selling well partly because much of that book related to children and youth of color who were becoming the dominant population in major public school districts. Many school districts needed professional development to address these students' needs. Could I make a difference as a full-time consultant?

CHAPTER SEVEN

Legacy of Fear

W e don't see the signs of seasons such as autumn in the water-engineered oasis of Las Vegas. The dawn of the fall season in this city is somewhat uncomfortable for us older Nevadans who have spent most of our lives in northern climes, where the end of summer is signaled by the sudden emergence of grand-looking gold and red leaves poised to drop by winter.

No, we track the seasons by calendar in the consistently hot and dry Southwest, and the arrival of September 2014 meant that I would be even busier trying to help Vegas-area students via my role as a consultant for the Clark County School District (CCSD). After decades on the national stage and on international platforms as an advocate for educational equity and social justice, I was now engaged where it counted most—providing leadership on a local level to help enable educational institutions become the social "leveler" they proposed to be.

It was clear that the activist legacy of Dr. King had shown that the national government—through direct, nonviolent local action—could be moved to try to set things right as it related to Civil Rights. Increasingly, people of good will are realizing that education is also a Civil Rights issue and that they have to become activists in that arena to generate change.

I have welcomed the involvement of major philanthropic forces such as the

Bill & Melinda Gates Foundation and the foundation that represents Eli Broad—a prominent MSU graduate—in their efforts to improve our schools with national initiatives on education leadership and policy. However, I believe that corporate and philanthropic leaders can do more by providing more assistance directly to poor urban school districts that can help us find more models for academic success. As I considered these issues, my thoughts turned to an event involving another MSU graduate who had come to the same conclusion.

It was a large and festive gathering—a reception on October 27, 2012, for an exceptional man at a fine Las Vegas home. As we waited for the guest of honor, I thought of Coretta Scott King because a biography on her, *Desert Rose*, had just been published.

While waiting, I also had time to chat with some of the one hundred people who attended the event, held at the home of U.S. congressman Steven Horsford and his wife, Sonya, a scholar and education activist. Suddenly, there was a commotion. Many of the assembled were rushing to the front door. The honored guest had arrived. Looming over a crowd of admirers, he flashed his famous smile. Earvin "Magic" Johnson, a man I had mentored during his student years at Michigan State, had arrived.

I was eager to talk to Magic because I wanted to congratulate him on his recent decision to dedicate much of his time to addressing the dropout problem and the career readiness of students at underserved schools. I was aware that under a partnership with EdisonLearning, a major operator of charter schools within public school districts, Earvin had begun to open Bridgescape charter schools in major urban communities to help close the achievement gap.

Before venturing into education, Earvin Johnson engineered a spectacular career as an entrepreneur by creating a chain of Starbucks and TGIF franchises and by opening movie theaters in underserved communities. He also obtained an ownership percentage in the Los Angeles Lakers, the team that he led to five National Basketball Association championships. Suddenly, in 2011, he sold all of his properties. There was much speculation about his motives. It all became clear later that year when it was announced that he had organized a team of extremely rich investors who bought the Los Angeles Dodgers.

I've known Earvin since his preteen years when I coached a junior high school–level football team that included my sons Kurt and Vince against a team that included Magic. I recall the first time I saw him on the football field. I gawked because he was so much taller than the other boys. Before the game commenced,

Yolanda King, Dexter King, Kurt Green, Bernice King, and Kevin Green gather after the funeral of Coretta Scott King on February 7, 2006.

I walked over to the opposing coach and asked for credentials regarding Magic's age. I confirmed that he was age-eligible. Earvin was as good on the football field as he was on the basketball court.

After a spectacular run as leader of a state championship team at Lansing, Michigan's Everett High, where he was bused under a desegregation order, Earvin accepted a scholarship to attend Michigan State. During those years, I mentored him, and my wife and I also developed a good relationship with his mother, Christine. She was a well-respected member of the support staff at an East Lansing middle school.

I recalled that, in 1978, the sports agent Donald Dell wanted to represent Magic. Arthur Ashe was one of Donald's clients. Arthur and Donald both admired Magic and wanted to meet him. I arranged a meeting at my home. However, Magic later selected someone else to represent him when he decided to turn pro after MSU won the 1979 National Collegiate Athletic Association championship.

Magic joined the Los Angeles Lakers. During the Lakers years, Lettie and I maintained our contact and friendship with his mother, and I kept track of Earvin's pursuits in sports and, later, in business.

With his height advantage, Earvin spotted me and pushed forward to greet me. We hugged. "It's great to see you," we both said. When it was time to make remarks, Magic began by acknowledging me and my wife. "I'm very happy to see Dr. and Mrs. Robert Green," Magic told the gathering. "Dr. Green was my mentor and my dean at Michigan State University. He helped me become a man." As the reception ended, Magic asked me to accompany him to his car. At the car, he gave me his cell phone number and suggested that he and I should discuss how I could help him expand his education projects.

Magic is an example of the unknown potential of every student. After all, he was known as an exceptional athlete, but he also had exceptionally high expectations for himself beyond athletics. As a consultant working to help public school teachers, I have often cited the unknown potential of all students and asked the following question: "How many of you can pick out the students who will have the brightest future?" The teachers would uniformly say that they can't make such designations with certainty. I then respond with the following: "So treat them all as stars because they all have great potential."

I thought about Magic and my consulting work as I drove from the offices of the CCSD, a client, to my Las Vegas home. I had moved from Michigan to Las Vegas in 2005 after retiring from MSU as a dean emeritus and distinguished alumnus in 2004. However, I had not retired from my work as an education consultant. On the contrary, I was now working full time as a consultant, serving the public school districts in Dallas, Chattanooga, and Clark County, which includes Las Vegas.

I was proud of Magic because he had formed a business partnership to address the achievement gap and the school dropout problem. These were the issues I had been addressing in my consulting work. When I arrived at home, I went to my office and began to reflect on that work.

I recall briefly putting aside some of my work after Coretta Scott King died on January 30, 2006. Lettie and I had lost a close and precious friend. In her death, she received the credit she had not previously been given for her leadership. I continued to stay closely in touch with her children. In my mind, the sons and daughters of Coretta and Martin were like family to me.

After moving to Las Vegas, I found myself working in schools with predominantly white teaching staffs and predominantly black and brown student bodies. Fear had led to the resegregation of schools in major cities because that was an

Earvin "Magic" Johnson converses with his mentor, Robert L. Green, at a fundraiser for U.S. representative Steven Horsford in Las Vegas in 2012.

emotion that drove the campaigns to end busing designed to end school segregation. White parents feared the presence of black and brown students in their schools, and black and brown parents feared for the safety of their children bused to faraway schools. In many urban school districts, courts had ended busing in exchange for programs designed to enhance education in underserved schools. Several districts asked me to help provide consulting to improve those schools.

Fear was also rampant inside those schools. In a small percentage of cases, teachers were afraid of some of their black and brown male students. More often, they were afraid that some of the more disruptive students might impede their ability to educate a majority in the classroom. Others were afraid that they simply could not manage disruptive students. It was fear of failure.

This fear of failure on the part of some teachers and administrators prompted some strange and horrifying practices. In some schools in Chattanooga, for example, administrators encouraged some disruptive high school students to sign a form stating that they were voluntarily dropping out of school. When I learned of this, I complained to Superintendent Jim Scales and he helped bring an end to the practice.

To help teachers and administrators overcome their fears, I needed to learn more about disruptive students and students who were dropout risks because of failing grades. After all, although I was PhD in educational psychology and a noted writer on educational policies and practice, I had never taught in the public schools.

In 2007, I received a contract from Chattanooga school superintendent Jim Scales to help facilitate the academic achievement of students. I organized focus groups involving Chattanooga's so-called at-risk Howard High School. It was the same school that produced the students—Willie Ricks, my young comrade in the Mississippi March against Fear, among them—who initiated and led the protests that helped end segregation in restaurants, stores, and movie theaters in Chattanooga in the 1960s. Those activists—children leading us again—had taught Chattanoogans to reject fear and stand up for justice.

Now, Howard's current students were about to teach me something. Working with focus groups in very interactive sessions—alienated students on the path to failure, kids who were after-school drug dealers, students who were moderately successful academically, and the high achievers with high standards—I learned that my theories and published works on the power of expectations were correct. For example, one Howard student, a senior who had been admitted to Morehouse College, told me that some students had teased him about the size of his book bag.

"That's OK," he said. "My haters have been my motivators."

However, I also learned that many of their teachers did not know how to raise their students' expectations. In addition, I was able to confirm again that poverty and hunger were even greater factors in the lack of progress of the academically distressed and disruptive students than I had previously thought.

Some of the low achievers had part-time, after-school jobs to help bring income to their families. Also, some of the jaded and more disruptive students had become involved in the drug trade and criminal activity—initially, to generate income and find alternatives to traditional achievement and acceptance. Others were distracted by hunger because their families could not adequately feed them.

This had a profound impact on me and my consulting. In Dallas and in Las Vegas, I began to lead training sessions for teachers to help them spot the socioeconomic factors in academic underachievement. As a result, for example, more teachers and administrators began to keep a food pantry in schools for daily nourishment, and some schools even began to distribute food on Fridays and the day before longer holiday breaks to help some of the students through more extended periods.

I also learned more about expectations and achievement from another focus

DESERT ROSE

Bernice King, daughter of Martin and Coretta, wrote a message to Robert L. Green and Lettie on a page of a copy of *Desert Rose*, a biography on her mother.

group—this one involving seventeen African American boys in a Dallas middle school in 2010. I asked them to identify the best teacher in their school. They all agreed on the identity of the best teacher. I then visited the school principal, who agreed with their selection. Finally, I visited the classroom of this teacher, who taught math. She had high expectations for all of her students and demonstrated it by, for example, giving them a second or third opportunity to provide a correct answer. She actively and continuingly praised all her students for good work, including the underachievers. This confirmed and strengthened my belief in the power of high expectations.

Subsequently, in Dallas, I launched training programs for teachers that taught them the value of expectations and techniques for establishing high standards in the classroom, techniques that were verified as effective by an independent assessor, MSU professor John Schweitzer, a noted evaluator of urban education initiatives. As I heard these stories involving innovation in the application of training principles, my thinking evolved and I concluded that—collectively—teachers and administrators could learn more from each other than they could from me alone.

With survey-design engineering and encouragement from George White, who has expertise on education policy and digital knowledge-sharing studies, we proceeded. With George engaged, I embarked in 2012 on a bold new knowledge-sharing experiment in Nevada's CCSD. It was a project that helped principals at schools in some of Las Vegas's poorest communities identify the early warning signs of potential dropouts and determine ways to address those indicators. We relayed a list of eighteen major indicators, along with a digital survey that requested their input on best-practice responses to those indicators, to the principals.

These best-practice responses were provided by elementary school principals at selected West Las Vegas schools, administrators who are on the front lines of the battle for academic achievement in Clark County. Many of these schools have some of the poorest and most segregated student populations and have been the most academically challenged in the district.

By supporting this study, the CCSD has created a new approach to engendering academic achievement in its most challenged region. It acknowledges that, collectively, nine school principals know more than any individual principal. This report advances the notion that knowledge sharing is an effective way to address urban education issues. It is an approach supported by the Carnegie Foundation for the Advancement of Teaching.

The early warning signs and the nine principals' responses to those indicators can be grouped into the following categories: academic performance, student and parent participation and involvement, home and neighborhood environment, difficult behavior and discipline, dangerous and negative motivators, poverty, grade failure, and expectations. The principals created initiatives and practices, based on these data, that have engaged parents, addressed high-impact factors such as poverty and hunger, created school-wide standards of behavior, helped students become knowledge-sharing leaders for their younger peers, and raised academic expectations.

The project was a success because we received many creative proposed responses to early warning signs and included them in *Early Warning Signs of Potential*

Left: Granddaughter Kara Green, eldest daughter of Vince and his former wife, Sherry Brown. *Right:* Granddaughter Taylor Green, youngest daughter of Vince and his former wife, Sherry Brown.

Dropouts: What Can Be Done, a 2012 report that was published by the CCSD. The local chapter of the NAACP helped disseminate the results and informed parents by posting our knowledge-sharing report on their website.

Dropouts don't account for all student absences. In Las Vegas and in cities nationwide, the vast majority of students suspended, expelled, or placed in disciplinary classes or schools are African American and Latino boys, and there has been a dramatic increase in such punishment. This was largely due to the "zero tolerance" clauses included in the No Child Left Behind (NCLB) education "reforms" ushered in by the administration of George W. Bush.

At the request of CCSD's superintendent, I—with the help of George White— began to conduct research on alternatives to traditional discipline. I served as cochair of a CCSD committee that was tasked to conduct the research. In a November 1, 2012, memo from me and the assistant, alternative approaches to traditional discipline were referenced.

A number of school districts have recently adopted programs developed by national consultants on alternatives to traditional public school discipline. The Oakland

Left: Grandson Gibson Green, son of Kurt and Gina Eckstine. *Right:* Granddaughter Danielle Green, daughter of Kevin and his former wife, Lynn Sutherland.

(California) Unified School District is an interesting example because it has been implementing three major student behavior adjustment programs. One of each of these three programs has been adopted by a number of other school districts.

For example, a program called Restorative Justice has shown some promise. It is a community-based, therapeutic process that addresses youth violence by helping perpetrators understand the roots of their anger and understand how they have done others harm. In 2008, a pilot Restorative Justice program at Oakland's Cole Middle School resulted in an 87 percent drop in the suspension rate. After the adoption of the program in three other OUSD middle schools in 2008–2010, there were statistically significant declines in suspension.

In 2010–11, the Oakland Unified School District (OUSD) expanded the program to ten more schools and is considering an additional expansion. OUSD's work merits attention because Restorative Justice has been implemented in schools with large Latino and African American student populations.

There is a crisis in education as it relates to African American males—high expulsion and dropout rates and poor academic performance as a group. For those reasons, I gladly accepted an invitation in early spring to produce a "solutions"

Granddaughter Kayla Green, daughter of Kevin and his former wife, Lynn Sutherland.

paper on black male education for an initiative sponsored by the U.S. Department of Education and the Council of the Great City Schools (CGCS), a Washington, DC–based organization that represents the nation's largest school districts.

The Department of Education and CGCS commissioned about a dozen scholars—all of them research leaders on urban education—to produce these solutions briefs. All of us had distinguished ourselves in some field of research relevant to the needs of black male students. In my case, they wanted a paper that explains how and why high expectations can raise the academic achievement of black boys and African American teens.

The call for papers noted that completed submissions would be circulated and discussed at the inaugural National Summit on Educational Excellence and Opportunity for African-American Males later that year. Members of Congress, foundation leaders, public school administrators, scholars, and U.S. Department of Education secretary Arne Duncan would participate. The request for papers also noted that the submissions would be edited and that Houghton Mifflin Harcourt would publish them as an anthology.

After reviewing the request, I immediately contacted my consulting associate George White because he was very familiar with my research on expectations and because I recalled that he had edited and written a major solutions-oriented report, published in 2006, on the challenges facing young men of color. (At the time, George was assistant director of the UCLA Center for Communications and Community, an institute that engaged nonprofits and the media on issues related to education, health, and neighborhood development in six cities.)

George's report on young men of color had been funded through the Joint Center for Political and Economic Studies, a Washington, DC–based think tank that conducts research on public policy issues of special concern to African Americans. The Joint Center had set up a commission on young men of color headed by former Congressman Ronald Dellums.

The Dellums Commission was an impressive group that included legislators, educators, judges, and heads of civic organizations—all of them experts on specific challenges facing young African Americans, Latinos, and Native Americans. This group then commissioned a large group of scholars, elected officials, physicians, and legal experts to produce more than forty papers that proposed solutions to health challenges, high incarceration rates, joblessness, and poor academic achievement.

George read each paper, selected the best recommendations, and produced a report published as a booklet titled *A Way Out: Creating Partners for Our Nation's Prosperity by Expanding Life Paths of Young Men of Color*. The report was prescient. For example, it examined the so-called education reform law called NCLB, enacted in 2001 at the behest of the Bush administration. Anticipating the expulsion and arrest of many more young men of color for misbehavior in school, the report called for the elimination of NCLB's "zero tolerance" policy (White and McGhee 2006).

George was also perfectly suited to help me with the paper for the summit on black male education because he is a great researcher and writer. In addition, I recruited my youngest son, Kevin K. Green, a vision engineer with a PhD and experience as a public school teacher, to help with the research.

Working on the paper, the three of us updated my previous work on expectations, made new connections between high standards and achievement, and advanced my work by producing brief reports on schools that have created cultures of academic success in populations that are largely black and brown. Among those cited are Chicago's Urban Prep charter school, the Kermit R. Booker Sr. Elementary School in Las Vegas (under Principal Beverly Mathis), the Excellence Boys Charter School in Brooklyn, the Eagle Academy schools in New York, Eleanor Roosevelt High School in Maryland's Prince George's County, Madison, Wisconsin's Sherman Middle School, and the Piney Woods school in Mississippi.

In our research we learned that many of the better performing schools in black

All eight daughters of Rev. Havious V. Green have advanced degrees: *(front row)* June C. Green-Rivers (PhD, education, and MDiv, Counseling), Janet Hobson (PhD, chemical engineering), Chiarina Owens (PhD, clinical psychology), and LaClaire Bouknight (MD, internal medicine); *(back row)* Valeria Jackson (PhD, linguistics), Constance Price (PhD, violin performance), Hazel Young (MD, radiology), and Carmen Green-Lee (MD, Pediatrics).

communities had a multicultural approach, one that included African history and/
or African American studies. One of the champions of multicultural education,
James Banks, is one of my former students. James is founder and director of the
Center for Multicultural Education at the University of Washington, Seattle. James,
who obtained his MA and PhD at Michigan State, was president of the National
Council for the Social Studies in 1982 and president of the American Educational
Research Association from 1997 to 1998.

As we wrapped up work on the black male student summit report, we inserted
the following near the end:

> Raising the expectations of students and teachers is a first step toward promoting
> Black male academic achievement. As noted in this report, my experience and
> research indicates that parents, too, must be engaged and that school administrators
> must be champions of equity and achievement. Other contributors will offer
> additional solutions. However, in the end we must take the additional step of
> raising the consciousness of the public so that local resources are brought to bear
> on reforming our schools to create the high expectations that will raise achievement
> at all levels of public education. (Green, White, and Green 2012, 39)

That passage referenced "other contributors" of papers for the national summit.
Our papers were due soon, but—before the deadline—a few scholars expressed
concern about participating in the summit because it was scheduled a little more
than a month before the November presidential election.

This was of concern to a few of the contributors because the summit would
be the first major initiative on behalf of black males under Barack Obama. Some
of the scholars wanted the summit to be delayed until after the election because
they believed Obama would be criticized by the right for sanctioning the event and
that such criticism could cost him the election. These concerns were expressed in
a series of emails circulated among the contributors.

George, Kevin, and I disagreed with their position. We knew the history of
change in this country—it comes from the bottom up. Leftists pushed Franklin
Delano Roosevelt, which led to the New Deal. Dr. King and other activists pushed
President Kennedy and President Johnson, which led to Civil Rights laws. Generally,
however, blacks were reluctant to push Obama. Now, even as he was ushering in
an initiative that could help address an issue of importance to blacks, some were
so dutiful to Obama that they were more concerned about the possibility of a

conservative backlash against an initiative for black students than the president, himself.

Most of the contributors did not see the summit as a threat to Obama, and some of us believed that it *should* be held before the election because the need to address problems in black male academic achievement could become better known nationally if it became a campaign issue. To us, it was a winning issue. We prevailed. The summit would be held August 27.

George and Kevin were already in DC when Lettie and I arrived the day before the summit. Our first stop was a visit to the King Memorial, unveiled on October 16, 2011. I had planned to attend a huge gathering for an unveiling on August 28, 2011, but it was postponed because of threatening weather brought by Hurricane Irene. I did not attend the much smaller October unveiling. I was deeply moved when I finally visited the memorial on August 26, 2012.

"First class," I thought. "America has finally valued one of its greatest champions."

At a reception that night sponsored by the CGCS, I saw many friends and associates—CGCS executive Michael Casserly among them. I introduced George and Kevin to many notables in the room.

The following day, hundreds of scholars, legislators, nonprofit leaders, and leading public school educators walked through the doors of the Lyndon Baines Johnson Department of Education Building. Early in his adult life, Johnson was a teacher in hardscrabble West Texas. In this heavily Latino school district, he saw poverty up close and developed his faith in education to eradicate it. Johnson himself had escaped poverty. He once quipped, "If it weren't for education, I'd still be looking at the southern end of a northbound mule" (Zigler and Muenchow, 26). Johnson's belief in the power of education was translated to policy action when, as president, he ushered in the Head Start early education program during the heady days of the War on Poverty.

The summit activities, organized by Council of Great Cities Schools administrator Sharon Lewis, began. I was one of a few of the "solutions" authors to speak on stage during the one-day event. I began my remarks by thanking my coauthors, George and Kevin. On stage comments were made by a range of summit participants—among them, U.S. representative Danny Davis, a leading advocate for youth development programs, and Education Secretary Arne Duncan, a very tall and lithe man who had previously served as school superintendent in Obama's hometown of Chicago.

The summit's closing remarks were delivered by Freeman Hrabowski, president of the University of Maryland–Baltimore County. Obama had recently appointed him chair of the President's Advisory Commission on Educational Excellence for African Americans, a group that would rally support for some of the summit's recommendations.

Hrabowski talked about his arrest as a boy participating in SCLC's Children's Campaign. That story prompted my memories of working with activist black children in Farmville, Virginia, who protested the racially motivated closure of their schools. Hrabowski's account had also triggered my memories of working with college students during the Memphis to Mississippi March against Fear.

That night we dined at a very full table that included Alfred Tatum, a University of Illinois–Chicago professor who is a leader in research on black youth literacy. Alfred had also produced a solutions paper for the summit.

All the papers were edited by staffers at the CGCS. When the scholars approved the edits, the content in December 2012 was converted into the anthology titled *A Call for Change*. One excerpt from the chapter that my team had produced as I prepared for a trip to Detroit in February 2013 was very relevant to the situation in my hometown. "Expectations are important," the sections says, "but schools must also have the resources to create the conditions to enable students to reach high standards. Public funding is important" (Green, White, and Green 2012, 37). The Education Trust, which promotes academic achievement, framed the challenge as follows:

Research and common sense tell us that schools need more resources to help the low-income students and students of color . . . But at the federal, state, and local levels, we actually spend less on the schools serving the highest concentrations of these students. . . .

In many states, school districts that serve the highest concentrations of low-income and minority students receive less in state and local funding per pupil than districts serving affluent and white students. Nationally, the districts that serve the largest concentrations of students of color receive an average of $1,100 less per student in state and local funds. . . . What's more, even in some states that drive money to high-poverty districts, those dollars may not actually get to the highest poverty schools within the district because of differences in how teachers are paid. Simply put, the highest paid teachers generally are not teaching in the schools where they're most needed.

Closing these funding gaps is critical if we are to live up to our national ideal of providing all children with equal opportunities to become educated citizens. (Education Trust 2009)

Left: Kurt Green, a financial and music industry consultant. *Right:* Yvonne Morris, administrative assistant to Dean Robert Green.

Detroit, unfortunately, is the poster city for the relationship between poverty and poor academic performance. I was preparing for a trip to the Motor City on February 14, 2013, because I had agreed to join Andy Young on a one-day series of Black History Month talks in Detroit and other parts of Michigan on February 15.

I had contacted George White in Los Angeles. George, who is also a Detroit native, agreed to join me on Ambassador Young's speaking tour. (My eldest son Vince, a Lansing attorney, also joined us during the tour.) On the flight from Las Vegas to Detroit, I began to think about the rise and dramatic decline of the Motor City and its school system. Citing low academic performance, the state of Michigan wrested control of fifteen Detroit schools from local control in the fall of 2012. The state still controlled those schools at the time of our February 2013 Detroit visit. The decline of Detroit schools coincided with the steep drop in property tax revenues as the population declined.

Detroit reached its population peak of 1.8 million in the 1950s. By the 2010 census, the city had about 700,000 residents, a population loss of 61 percent. Those declines were due to white flight to suburbs and the loss of local jobs in a diminishing auto industry that sought revival by moving more and more of its production to low-wage states and even lower-wage sites abroad—further reducing employment opportunities in Detroit.

Detroit rose and fell with the automobile industry. In 1900, before the advent of the automobile, Detroit was a small regional manufacturing center. Over the following decades, the growth of the automobile industry, including affiliated activities such as parts production, became the dominant form of manufacturing. For example, Ford Motor Company in 1917 began to construct the River Rouge Complex. When it was completed in 1927, it was largest integrated factory in the world.

The workers for Ford, General Motors, and Chrysler—the Big Three—came from far-flung lands. Nearby Canada was an early source of manpower. Workers also came from Italy, Hungary, and Poland. However, concerned about the flow of Europeans to America in the years following the end of World War I, the U.S. government adopted the Immigration Act of 1924, which limited the number of new immigrants.

In response, the auto industry—with Ford leading the way—began to hire African Americans in significant numbers. High wages in the industry lured blacks, but the exodus from the South was also prompted by a postwar agricultural slump and continuing Jim Crow practices. At the same time, large numbers of southern whites also migrated to "Detroit City" for industry jobs. I wrote about this combustible mix in my 1977 book, *The Urban Challenge: Poverty and Race.*

> The influx of blacks and white from the South, both pursuing the same goals of housing and employment, brought an accompanying ingredient of resentment and hostility. White southerners found the competitive, integrated work settings alien to their accustomed life-styles; their fear and hatred kindled similar feelings on the part of blacks. [World War II] production plants added to Detroit's growth and development, but the city was plagued by racial discrimination, division and conflict. The destructive race riot of June, 1943 exposed the strong undercurrent of antipathy that prevailed beneath the city's bustling industrial atmosphere.

With the high wages and benefits that the United Automobile Workers (UAW) obtained, autoworkers built and bought homes. Other major cities are dense landscapes with many apartment buildings, but Detroit became a huge sprawl dominated by single-family housing—the most per capita than any other metropolis.

Blacks did not have equal opportunities to build or buy homes. Banks and federal lending institutions considered blacks and the communities where they lived "risky." In contrast, the auto industry also gave rise to a very large and well-compensated white-collar class—managers, engineers, attorneys, and advertising executives.

This upper class moved to outlying neighborhoods and, further, to wealthy suburbs such as Grosse Pointe and Bloomfield Hills. Oakland County, north of the city, became a popular place for high-paid professionals. This movement was facilitated by the construction of freeways, making Detroit much more like Los Angeles than cities in the Midwest and East.

By 1960, "white flight" and housing discrimination resulted in a Detroit with a black inner city surrounded by white outer sections and suburbs. There were very few blacks in the suburbs. Real estate agents would not sell to them, and whites in those communities were generally hostile to blacks. However, more prosperous blacks began to move outward in the early 1960s—first to middle-class neighborhoods in northwest Detroit and subsequently into more affordable suburbs in the 1970s. This was the beginning of Detroit's decline. Many of those left behind were poor or very dependent on auto industry assembly-line jobs.

But assembly-line jobs began to diminish in the 1970s and 1980s as the industry suffered setbacks. The Organization of the Petroleum Exporting Countries was formed, and these oil exporters began to push up the cost of gasoline, which hurt car sales. Also, Detroit's auto industry began to lose sales to Japanese and German automakers. In a bid to be more competitive, Detroit's Big Three began to step up its relocation of manufacturing and assembly plants to low-wage states and abroad. As a result, unemployment in the city rose rapidly. This was not a cyclical rise. Detroit was spiraling downward. By the 1990s and the early 2000s, much of the city's huge housing stock was abandoned and had become a haven for the criminal gang activity and drug dealing that emerged during the spiral.

Also, early in the 2000s, General Motors (GM) was making money from its car finance wing, but those profits were offset by huge losses from its manufacturing operations. The situation in Detroit might have become even more desperate if not for the Obama administration's 2009 financial bailout of GM.

With the backing of the UAW and support from most of the public, GM's lobbyists in Washington, DC, helped craft the bailout terms. I then thought of a GM executive who was executive director of the company's government activities from 1997 to 1999—Sandra Bulger, formerly one of my students at MSU. Prior to assuming that post, Sandra was assistant general tax counsel and general director of federal tax audits for GM, another important position. After decades with GM, Sandra left in 2007 to pursue venture capital and entrepreneurship opportunities. There is certainly a need for more African American entrepreneurs.

Despite the survival of GM, Detroit's fiscal situation had worsened. The city had entered into an April 2012 agreement with the state of Michigan, providing the state more fiscal oversight of Detroit in exchange for financial assistance. Still, the city's financial situation was dire. To be sure, when I landed at Detroit's airport for Andy Young's speaking tour, I had returned to a city that was a shell of its previous incarnations.

Andy's speaking tour was organized by Bishop Ira Combs Jr., one of my former students and pastor of the Jackson, Michigan–based Greater Bible Way Temple of the Apostolic Faith. Bishop Combs had previously worked with Ambassador Young on corporate social responsibility issues. George White, the other member of our team, had known Andy because of his association with me.

Bishop Combs, a Republican, had a great relationship with the governor of Michigan and an association with business leaders in the state—black and white. Bishop Combs, like the rest of the speaking tour team, had a great interest in economic development. For that reason, our first stop was a chat about local development issues during a visit with an aide to Governor Rick Snyder at the governor's Detroit office.

Our next stop was a hall in Detroit's St. Regis Hotel, a room reserved by the Michigan Black Chamber of Commerce, our host. A crowd of about three hundred welcomed us. At the podium, Bishop Combs introduced Ambassador Young by providing context on the topic of Andy's speech, telling the audience that the construction of a second bridge from Detroit to Windsor (Canada) had the potential to "create opportunities for all." At that time, a second bridge was in the design and planning phase.

Andrew knew a good bit about transportation infrastructure, a good bit about economic development and the connection between the two. Regarding economic development, as two-term mayor of Atlanta in the 1980s, he had turned to international markets and other investors to help attract $70 billion in investment. Under Andy's watch about 1,100 new Atlanta businesses were created. Regarding transportation infrastructure, as a congressman who represented a district that includes Atlanta in the 1970s, he helped city leaders obtain the backing necessary for a major expansion of what was then called Hartsfield Airport, the largest passenger terminal in the world. Work on that project was completed in September 1980.

Andy continued to support airport improvement after he was elected mayor of Atlanta in 1981, the first of two successful terms. He told the audience that he obtained $300 million in tax-exempt bond financing for the airport to supplement millions that his predecessor—former mayor Maynard Jackson—had obtained to launch the project. Speaking without notes, Andy told the assembled crowd that the airport was generating $31 billion a year in revenue by 1990. Many black-owned companies participated in the project, which created sixty thousand jobs, he said. With expanded capacity, the facility—now known as Hartsfield Jackson Airport—has become a major transportation hub that has also attracted foreign investors. The level of foreign investment, said Ambassador Young, has "transformed Atlanta," noting that it is now an "international city."

At that point, I thought about Atlanta's most important corporate citizen—Coca-Cola—and Ingrid Saunders Jones, one of my students at MSU. Ingrid had served Coca-Cola for thirty years by the time she retired on June 1, 2013, from her post as senior vice president for Global Community Connections and chair of the Coca-Cola Foundation, which has awarded more than $500 million to thousands of community organizations worldwide.

During her three-decade career at Coca-Cola, Ingrid expanded the company's philanthropic reach. She inherited a U.S.-focused operation and transformed it into a global force that now includes water stewardship, health projects, recycling, and education programs abroad. To be sure, to Ingrid, education was a social justice issue.

A team helped me further explore that social justice issue in a 2010 report called *The American Dilemma and Challenge: Save Our Children.* The report included research by Robert Mount, director of assessment at the Dallas Independent School District; my son Kevin, a former educator and vision engineer; and Bradley Carl, associate director of an education research center at the University of Wisconsin. (Bradley is one of my former students.)

Ambassador Young, who knows Ingrid, then pivoted on his remarks about foreign investment and economic development, telling the audience that some of the most promising business opportunities are in Africa, a continent that has seven of the ten fastest growing economies in the world.

At the current pace of economic growth—by 2025—the largest middle class in the world will be in Africa. Things are happening in the world, and they all reflect on us as people of color and the connections we have that we don't know we have. . . .

> We have got to find our place in the global economy. The problem that we face
> is that all politics is local. . . . The problem is that doesn't make any sense because
> all the decisions that matter are global. You need a global economic vision to make
> politics work.

With the right leadership, he said, Detroit could be a leader in facilitating investment in Africa, international partnerships that could create jobs in the Motor City.

Our next stop was a very different venue. It was the home of far too many black men from Detroit and other cities in Michigan—Jackson State Prison. Thousands of black men were incarcerated in Jackson, located in mid-Michigan, largely because their schools failed. This was a major terminus in the school-to-prison pipeline. However, Andy was taking a message of hope to all the inmates at the sprawling facility that is more formally known as the Southern Michigan Correctional Facility.

It was a bitterly cold day, and members of the speaking tour team were dressed accordingly in heavy coats. We were welcomed and credentialed by prison staff members in a building where new prisoners were processed for incarceration. Escorted by prison guards, we left that structure and crossed a courtyard to a much larger building. Inside, we now felt warmth for first time—some of it body heat from about six hundred inmates in the building's convening hall. Ambassador Young, who was warmly welcomed by the capacity crowd, talked about forgiveness and redemption.

"You don't forgive to let the other guy off the hook," he said. "You forgive to get the monkey off your back. There is nothing worse than holding a grudge." He then referenced Malcolm X, noting that the human rights activist transformed himself after a stint in prison. "We have the power to do anything," he said. "God wants us to believe. If you can conceive it and believe it, you can achieve it." It was a stirring speech and nourishment for the spirit for men who, if released, would have difficulty finding jobs and respect.

Ironically, our next stop was the nearby Spring Arbor University. Before a packed house at a university auditorium, Ambassador Young recounted some episodes from his years in the Civil Rights movement and provided some insight on Dr. King. For example, he noted that Dr. King lived with frequent death threats but showed no fear and frequently told fellow activists to be courageous because "fear paralyzes." He added, "Dr. King used humor to help his top aides cope with the situations. He used to say, 'Don't worry about me. They may shoot at me and get you.' He would then begin to preach a mock eulogy he would deliver at your funeral. You would think that he was Eddie Murphy. He was a very funny man."

I thought about Spring Arbor University, the terminus for some of the more fortunate in the school-to-college pipeline, when I learned that the MSU Black Alumni Association was organizing events to honor my work, celebrate my eightieth birthday, and raise money for MSU's Robert L. Green Fund, donations to the university in my name. On October 11, 2013, about 250 Robert L. Green Fund donors paid a fundraising fee for a dinner in my honor at a Lansing hotel the night before MSU's homecoming game. Two of my nephews, Amos Hewitt, a human resources consultant, and Keith Way, a telecommunications executive, were among those most involved in organizing the fundraiser and birthday salute.

The Spartans won the homecoming game convincingly. (I cannot avoid noting that this midseason victory was one step in the Spartans' march to Pasadena and a 2014 Rose Bowl championship. Before that midseason game, George White, cracking wise, told me that game-day chants of "Go Green—Go White" were not necessarily designed to encourage the two of us.) Achievements in sports had always brought the MSU community together. Therefore, a crowd of about five hundred—all contributors to my MSU scholarship funds—was in a festive mood for a banquet and second-day salute in my honor on October 12, 2013. The MSU Black Alumni Association dubbed it the "80th Birthday Celebration & Scholarship Fundraiser." I was truly honored.

Lettie and my three sons—Vince, Kurt, and Kevin—and many of my relatives, including my brother, Havious, attended the event. The organizers of the event were students, staff, and faculty I had most closely engaged at MSU for fifty years. Most of them returned for the celebration—among them, former Coca-Cola executive Ingrid Saunders Jones, former athlete and current restaurant-chain owner Herb Washington, former aides Maxie Jackson and Eric Winston, Pastor John Duley, Bishop Combs, Detroit attorney Gregory Reed, and journalist/scholar George White. I was pleased to see so many successful former students, achievers in so many fields. It made me feel great. I didn't feel like an eighty-year-old. I felt like a college dean in my forties.

The gathering reminded me of an event at Morehouse College many years ago. Dr. King, a Morehouse alum, was speaking at a packed event on campus. I was sitting next to Morehouse College president Benjamin Mays, when he told me how great it felt to see Martin and so many other former students who were making a difference in our society.

At one point during my birthday celebration, Bernice King, daughter of Martin and Coretta, joined us via a video message. During her comments, she proudly noted that I considered her the daughter that I never had. Also, officially, MSU president Lou Anna Simon sent a written message of congratulations, a note I value.

In addition, U.S. senator Carl Levin sent an official message of congratulations. When I received his letter, it transported me back to my earliest days at MSU. That was when—with then attorney Carl Levin—I successfully challenged housing discrimination in East Lansing. It was also the period when I championed integrated readers for primary school students and completed a Justice Department mission to document the impact of the segregationist shutdowns of public schools in Farmville, Virginia.

However, for me, this was not a "Goodbye, Mr. Chips" ending. I had projects to work on, the energy to lead, and great people—Spartans among them—willing to help me. My goals—and the goals of millions of fair-minded Americans—had always been to help this country become a place that truly supports social justice and educational equity. That has been the destination. However, by 2014, the crossroads choices were not as clear because the challenges facing public schools relate to national education policy as well as school practices. In my mind, the celebration in my honor was encouragement to further address those issues.

CHAPTER EIGHT

The Future of Education

Harry Potter, Clifford the Big Red Dog, the Hunger Games, the Magic School Bus, Goosebumps—these are some of the beloved characters and story series associated with Scholastic Inc., a publishing giant. Scholastic has been delivering outstanding books for children for more than ninety years. However, Scholastic is also a leader in providing books and resources to help educators improve their craft. More than half of the teachers in the United States have an active account with Scholastic, accessing free online teaching sources such as lesson plans and buying professional development books.

I thought of Scholastic on a hot day in October 2014 because I was now a member of Scholastic's family of authors and I had just made arrangements to have the company send some additional copies to the coauthors of my Scholastic book—consulting associate George White, former student Bradley Carl, now a University of Wisconsin professor, and my son Kevin Green, a former educator who is now a vision engineer and education software designer. Together, we produced *Expect the Most—Provide the Best*, a book Scholastic had published earlier that year. The book expanded on my research on the classroom connection between high expectations and achievement. The expectations factor is explained at the beginning of chapter 4, "Effective Teachers: Their Characteristics, Skills, and Practices."

High expectations are an essential factor in student achievement. Effective teachers create high standards and develop strategies that help ensure that students embrace those expectations. The best teachers are committed to their continual professional development, understanding that it enhances their ability to raise expectations and achievement. Effective teachers understand the power of expectations, summarized below:

- Expectations that others have for us affect the way we view ourselves.
- The way we view ourselves affects our own expectations for ourselves.
- The expectations we hold for ourselves impact our performance and influence the nature and the quality of the lives we live. (Green, White, and Green 2014, 48)

The book also cited the evolving role of school administrators, identified best practices in parental engagement, and explained how technology and innovation are changing schools—the future of education.

However, if the future of education is to be bright in our poorer school districts, better instruction and improvements in administrative practices are not enough. There must be an increase in resources, and national and community leaders must be more directly involved in schools.

President Barack Obama displayed his awareness of this need in February 2014 when he announced the launch of the "My Brother's Keeper" program, an initiative designed get foundations, business leaders, and community leaders to provide more support for young men and boys of color. (My former student, business leader Magic Johnson is among those Obama recruited to help lead this initiative.) Male Latino and African American students are in need because their academic performance has consistently fallen well short of girls and young women of color and has been significantly behind those of white students.

The initiative is part of a dual push to improve the education and life prospects of young Latinos and African Americans. Just one month before the announcement of "My Brother's Keeper," Obama announced the names of leaders from a spectrum of sectors who would join University of Maryland–Baltimore County president Freeman Hrabowski on a White House commission for the president's Initiative on Educational Excellence for African Americans. The commission was formed to conduct studies, identify best practices, and advise the president and the secretary of education on strategies for improving the academic performance of black students. This initiative was spawned partly as a result of the August 2012

Robert L. Green's 1977 book, *The Urban Challenge: Poverty and Race*, explored the many factors in academic achievement.

black male education summit that George, Kevin, and I attended as providers of a "solutions brief."

I also serve as chairman of the state (Nevada) and county's (Clark) "My Brother's Keeper" program, which calls for leadership and involvement on both the state and the local level. In that capacity, I began to work with Tiffany Tyler, who serves as the lead program administrator for the county's "My Brother's Keeper" program. For example, I was a supporter of the "Vegas Reads" literacy initiative. It included an "Each One, Read One" campaign to encourage adults in the county to support literacy by reading more to their young children at home and by volunteering to help teachers by reading to boys and girls in school.

The Clark County program is designed primarily to help black, Latino, and Native American children from prekindergarten through the fifth grade. The program organized community events on literacy and recruited volunteers for after-school mentoring.

More black male mentors are needed in Las Vegas and in all the nation's major urban school districts. Considering that so many black students are from single-parent homes headed by mothers, black youth need more positive black male role models.

I thought of Willie Brown, former San Francisco mayor and my former classmate at San Francisco State College because he has been very active as a mentor and has encouraged others to advise and encourage young men of color. Willie, who migrated from a small town in Texas to San Francisco, was admitted to San Francisco State on a probationary basis and then excelled in classes and, later, in politics.

We talked about the old days at San Francisco State College when I visited San Francisco on February 11, 2014, for a celebration of the renaming of part of the Bay Bridge in Willie's honor. We also discussed our third schoolmate, Louis Davis. When Louis graduated from San Francisco State, he went to medical school and over the decades delivered more than five thousand babies.

In her *Philadelphia Daily News* article "The Sinking of Sankofa," Stephanie Farr focused on a Philadelphia mentorship program for at-risk boys of color. Farr talked to Kenyatta McKinney, a black volunteer mentor in the program. The article said McKinney asked each boy enrolled into the program to name a male model in their life. "A lot of them would say their mother," McKinney told the reporter. "Sixty percent could not come up with a positive male role model" (Farr 2014).

However, the effectiveness of mentors, more community volunteers, and more support from foundations and business leaders can only be maximized if we have more enlightened national education policies. The national education reform initiative known as No Child Left Behind (NCLB) has failed. Ushered in by the Bush administration with bipartisan support in 2001, NCLB failed partly because it encouraged simplistic and short-sighted policies such as "zero tolerance" on discipline issues. The result is that students of color—primarily Latino and black males—have been suspended, expelled, or placed in special discipline classes or schools in alarming numbers.

This disproportionality even extended to prekindergarten. In March of 2014, the U.S. Department of Education released the results of a study from the 2011–12 school year. It said black children represented 18 percent of all the students enrolled in pre-K but accounted for 48 percent of the children receiving more than one out-of-school suspension. This finding prompted U.S. attorney general Eric Holder to speak up on the issue in a press release. "This critical report," the release said, "shows that racial disparities in school discipline policies are not only well-documented among older students, but actually begin during preschool. Every [discipline] data point represents a life impacted and a future potentially diverted or derailed. This Administration is moving aggressively to disrupt the school-to-prison pipeline in order to ensure that all of our young people have equal educational opportunities" (U.S. Department of Education 2014).

This is a major problem. I know that higher standards lead to improved academic achievement. However, you can't raise the expectations of a student if he or she is not in school. Students who are expelled or suspended are more likely to drop out of school, and the dropout rates of students of color are already a national scandal. In addition, dropouts are much more likely to be arrested and imprisoned. This is the "school-to-prison pipeline" that Michelle Alexander documents in her book *The New Jim Crow* (2012).

I had been addressing the problem of disproportionate discipline as cochair of a committee formed by the superintendent of CCSD in 2012, the same year that the Clark County Black Caucus, a nonpartisan volunteer organization headed by Yvette Williams, honored me with a Lifetime Achievement Award in Education. With the help of George White, we developed research on creative alternatives to traditional discipline. Other school districts across the country also began to search for options, and in 2014 many school districts abandoned "zero tolerance."

The disproportionate discipline at CCSD and at most of the nation's urban school districts stems partly from the inability of many teachers to relate to male students of color. Much of the problem is cultural. The teacher doesn't understand the culture, the student tunes out, and the teacher sometimes gives up on the student instead of making the student aware of his ability to excel.

Led by Greta Peay, the director of the Equity and Diversity Education Department, CCSD has been responding to this problem by providing extensive professional development training for educators. With the support of CCSD superintendent Pat Skorkowsky, Peay expanded the program in the fall of 2014, and by the summer of 2015 the district offered diversity and cultural competence training to members of the local board and to about one thousand school administrators. In turn, those trained administrators have been providing professional development training to their teachers. The book I co-authored, *Expect the Most—Provide the Best*, is among the materials used in the training.

One of the objectives of the training is to provide the kind of quality instruction that will engage students and reduce the number of student suspensions, expulsions, and placements in behavioral schools. This trailblazing initiative by CCSD, supported strongly by school board trustee Linda Young, is important because students of color—particularly black boys—are punished in disproportionate numbers, often placing them in the school-to-prison pipeline.

In addition, to my opposition to "zero tolerance," I was also critical of NCLB because it put a premium on student testing to more effectively measure achievement levels. However, there were no national standards. The law required states to set their own standards and grade their own success. This led to vastly inflated claims of success and, in some cases, cheating scandals involving teachers and school administrators. On the other hand, a new, more promising national reform was actually created by state associations—the National Governors Association and the Council of Chief State School Officers. Together, they created the Common Core State Standards, an initiative that seeks to establish consistent and more rigorous academic expectations across the states.

More than forty states adopted and implemented the new standards in the fall of 2014. The federal government has supported the initiative by requiring states to adopt Common Core or create their own more rigorous standards to receive U.S. Department of Education funding. Common Core's high standards are consistent with the high expectations I have advocated for decades. Common Core also requires schools to emphasize critical thinking and create or adopt curriculum that prompts students to develop real-world applications for their studies and engage in group problem-solving with their peers. However, now that most of the nation's school districts have adopted the more rigorous standards of Common Core, they must also ensure that their teachers are prepared to teach to the new expectations. The future of education can be bright if school districts increase their investments in professional development training.

The need for more professional development training is referenced in *Expect the Most—Provide the Best*.

> Although the impact of expectations on student achievement is well-documented, there is ample evidence that school districts are not providing the professional development training required to counter the biases that some teachers bring to

George White, a former Robert L. Green student, is a prize-winning journalist, historian, and education consultant.

the classroom. A December 2012 research report by the Education Commission of the States concludes that expectations of many teachers continue to be influenced by factors such as race, ethnicity, and family income levels and that those biases are affecting student academic performance.

The study said negative teacher expectations account for an estimated 5 to 10% of the variance in student achievement and contribute to achievement gaps between white and minority students. (Green, White, and Green 2014, 72)

The expectations under Common Core are to be higher, but the new standards do not mandate a specific curriculum. It leaves that up to states, and some states are deferring to school districts; some school districts have provided Common Core training to teachers but are allowing classroom instructors to draw up their own teaching plans.

However, curriculum control in the hands of people who want to suppress diversity continues to be a problem. For example, in October 2013, the Tucson Unified School District voted to remove a ban on seven books from classrooms, two years after suspending a progressive Mexican-American studies curriculum made illegal by the

Arizona legislature in 2010. The vote doesn't mean that the books have to be required reading for classes, but teachers now have the option of using them. The books—all but one penned by Latino authors—were once used in classes that some Arizona conservatives falsely claimed "politicized" Mexican-American students. Legislative proponents of the ban also contended that the classes fostered ethnic resentment or treated students as members of an ethnicity rather than as individuals. The former teachers of the forbidden classes denied the allegations and cited independent research showing the courses improved student achievement and referenced a state-commissioned audit that recommended an expansion of the classes.

Also consider the developments in Jefferson County, Colorado's second-largest school district. Early in the fall of 2014, it was in the midst of a political firestorm over what should be taught in U.S. history courses, a standoff that raised broader concerns about school board members inserting their political views into curriculum and instruction matters. In response, hundreds of Jefferson County high school students walked out of classes in mid-September to protest school board member Julie Williams's proposal to set up a committee to review the advanced placement (AP) U.S. history curriculum with the goal of promoting patriotism and downplaying civil disobedience. AP courses are a benchmark for admissions at many universities. To me, this was insidious, because it would mean the diminishment or elimination of studies on the kind of social justice movements that Dr. King and others led.

Teachers were also opposed to the proposal. Many teachers called in sick or abruptly took time out by using personal days, which forced the shutdown of four schools for a few weeks. The curriculum-review proposal and protests made the district, with 85,000 students in 155 schools, the focus of a national debate about censorship and the sanitizing of American history. It prompted the College Board, which administers the AP program, to express support for the student protests. Also, a coalition of First Amendment and education groups, including the American Civil Liberties Union and the National Coalition against Censorship, publicly condemned the proposal. The Jefferson County school board finally diffused the crisis by approving an alternative curriculum review that would have input from students, educators, and community members, as well as the district's chief academic officer.

After following the accounts of the Colorado curriculum crisis, I thought of the students I met in 1974 in South Africa, black students who rebelled against a curriculum in Afrikaans, the language of their oppressors, triggering events that helped end apartheid. I also thought about the importance of AP studies. After all, under my direction in the summer of 2014, Kevin Green, John Schweitzer (a former student who now teaches at Michigan State), and George White helped the Grand Rapids (Michigan) School District comply with a federal government directive to address the district's failure to provide an adequate number of AP courses and other college prep opportunities to black students.

The future of education will be bright only when there are reforms that ensure that school districts no longer arbitrarily put students of color on noncollege academic tracks.

Reforms continued under President Obama and Arne Duncan, secretary of education, with the 2009 introduction of Race to the Top (RTT), which provided funding to spur innovation and reforms in K–12 education. Under it, any state in the United States can be awarded points and funding by establishing performance-based standards for teachers and principals, promoting charter schools, expanding the use of digital technology in the classroom, and complying with the new Common Core standards.

Throughout my fifty years of fighting for social justice and equity and excellence in education, students have made a difference—from organizing demonstrations that helped end segregation in public accommodations and schools, to pushing for an end to discrimination in collegiate sports, to providing insights to me and other education consultants. Considering that, I should not have been surprised when the most compelling critic of the high-stakes testing under NCLB and RTT was made by a high school student. *One Size Does Not Fit All: A Student's Assessment of School*, a book published in 2012, was written by seventeen-year-old Nikhil Goyal.

Goyal referenced a major problem: at that time, a student dropped out of school every nine seconds. He also noted that many students of color are alienated. In addition, he drew upon the thoughts and theories of leading thinkers such as Howard Gardner, Seth Godin, Noam Chomsky, and Diane Ravitch and raised provocative questions about education, the following among them:

- What if we tailored education to every single child?
- What if students' voices were heard and seen as human beings, not numbers on a spreadsheet?
- What if school became an incubator of innovation and a bridge between the community and the world?

To be sure, flawed national education policies and underperforming public schools have helped pave the way for the charter school movement. The movement has grown for two reasons: because many parents believe charters have smaller classrooms and more individualized instruction, and because the federal government has encouraged school districts to facilitate the creation of charters.

However, charter schools, privately run institutions that receive public funding, are not a panacea. High expectations and good instruction can be established in charter schools and regular public schools. Moreover, there are some downsides to the charter school movement. In Chicago, for example, the school board in May 2013 closed down fifty of the city's public schools, contending that they were "underutilized." There was substantial criticism of the move in the affected communities. The critics have a point. Schools are not just learning centers. They are also neighborhood centers that give residents a sense of community and a venue for connecting.

There was also some outrage when a few months later, in August 2013, Chicago Public Schools quietly posted a fifty-two-page document asking more charter schools to apply to operate in the city in the 2014–15 and 2015–16 school years. Ironically, the document also said the district wanted to open charters in eleven neighborhoods that have overcrowded schools.

Yes, there are critics of charter schools; but they are often countered by some parents who are clamoring for charters because they are fed up with poor-performing traditional schools. However, in Chicago, there is little evidence in standardized test results that charters are performing better than traditional schools, according to a 2014 report based on an examination by the *Chicago Sun-Times* and the Medill Data Project at Northwestern University. In fact, in 2013, traditional Chicago public schools had a higher percentage of elementary students who exceeded the state's test-based standards for reading and math than their counterparts in privately run charters.

Also, an October 2014 study by the University of Minnesota's Institute on Metropolitan Opportunity concluded that charter schools have been a factor in increasing segregation in Chicago schools and may have helped weaken traditional public schools. While about 20 percent of traditional public schools showed a diverse racial mix, only seven percent of Chicago's charters did, according to the report. Lauren Fitzpatrick's report, "Charter Schools Have Worsened School Segregation," on the study included the following:

> Since students self-select into the charter system, their performance should outpace children in traditional schools—but it doesn't, said Myron Orfield, who heads

Theodore Ransaw, mentored by Robert L. Green, explores the subject of teachers and cultural literacy in a column on the website of Robert L. Green & Associates.

the institute that looked at Chicago because it's home to charter champion U.S. Secretary of Education Arne Duncan.

"The question is whether charters are the best path available to find ways to better serve low-income students and students of color, given that this approach has failed to improve overall student performance by most measures, and led to less racial and ethnic diversity in the city's schools," Orfield said. (Fitzpatrick 2014)

The study also noted that Chicago charters lagged behind traditional schools in reading and math scores and graduation rates. The University of Minnesota report called for a three-year moratorium on new charters so the district can examine how its charter policy has affected all its schools.

To be sure, a review of some of the most successful schools referenced in the book that my associates and I produced, *Expect the Most—Provide the Best*, shows that some of the most effective charter schools provide rigorous curricula that include courses not offered by traditional schools—debate classes, culturally relevant history, and arts instruction among them. However, many charters are operated by "back-to-basics" purists who classify multicultural studies and arts education as frills. Consider New Orleans.

The charter school wave in New Orleans began in the wake of Hurricane Katrina in 2005. After Katrina, the Louisiana legislature restructured New Orleans public schools by placing "underperforming" schools—about two-thirds of the total in the city—under a new state recovery school district (RSD) with the intent of having RSD schools return to the control of the Orleans Parish School Board after they improved academic performance. Those two school governing bodies cannot manage the curriculum in those schools because charters are independent operators.

The vast majority of New Orleans schools are now charter operations, and most of the managers of these schools have been part of a rigorous back-to-basics education reform movement that all but eliminated music instruction in New Orleans's primary schools—an irony considering the city's status as the cradle of jazz, America's true art form.

However, many university-based studies on learning have for decades concluded that music instruction can enhance the mental development of young children. Consider this excerpt from a 1997 article by Frances Rauscher and others:

> Approximately 90% of the brain's motor control capabilities are devoted to the hands, mouth and throat. . . . Music training, specifically piano instruction, is far superior to computer instruction in dramatically enhancing children's abstract reasoning skills necessary for learning math and science. Learning music at an early age causes long-term enhancement of spatial-temporal reasoning. (Rauscher et al. 2007)

The connection between arts instruction and academic achievement, already well documented, received another research-based endorsement in 2014. The John F. Kennedy Center for the Performing Arts recently released results from a study that examined the impact of arts education on hundreds of fourth and fifth graders at thirty-two schools across five school districts in the Metro DC area. The study found that students in arts-integrated classrooms are more creative, engaged, and effective at problem solving than their counterparts who are not in arts-integrated classrooms. That is significant because the Common Core standards, which place greater emphasis on critical thinking, project-based learning, and more student teamwork, also require more classroom problem-solving.

However, unlike other education jurisdictions—where school districts can require schools to make curriculum changes such as mandating arts programs—New Orleans's dominant block of charters are independent operators that determine their own academic offerings. Still, there is a small but growing movement—pushed along by community leaders, parents, and some elected officials—to restore music instruction in New Orleans primary schools. It is being done on a school-by-school basis, but it is happening. That is hopeful news for the future of education in New Orleans.

The connection between music instruction and academic achievement has been clear to me for a long time. My oldest sibling, Havious Green, required all eight of his daughters to become proficient in piano and at least one other instrument. Flute, violin, and cello were among my nieces' second choices. Of those eight nieces, five have PhDs and three are MDs. My brother understood the music–academics connection.

There is also evidence of a connection between arts education, in general, and academic excellence in subjects related to science and math. In *Expect the Most—Provide the Best*, we document this association by citing a National Writing Project article by Robert and Michele Root-Bernstein, "Turning STEM into STREAM: Writing as an Essential Component of Science Education" (2011), that posits that reading and writing—along with the arts—helps students become more proficient in other subjects. The authors of the article note that the movement seeks to transform the STEM acronym (science, technology, engineering, and mathematics) into the STEAM acronym by adding "arts." They then suggest a further modification by advocating that a more integrative learning approach would accommodate the creation of STREAM by adding "reading."

The relationship that the National Writing Project authors make is made clear in the following passage:

> They note that science educators realize that STEM professionals have benefitted from the arts and visual thinking—e.g., recognizing and forming patterns, modeling and manipulating skills gained using pens and brushes. Next, they cite that the National Science Foundation and the National Endowment for the Arts have begun formal meetings between the agencies to figure out how to fund research on the importance of teaching at the intersections of Science and the Arts. (Green, White, and Green 2014, 92)

The future of education in America can be significantly brighter if we require music instruction and arts education in general, in all of our schools—including the many charter schools that have been emphasizing "back to basics."

Charter school advocates contend that charters can provide competition and give parents options for their children. However, in my view, based on research my consulting team revealed in our chapter in the *A Call for Change* anthology published in 2013, both charter schools and traditional public schools are successful when they stress high expectations and provide good instruction. Like traditional schools, some charter schools stress expectations and some do not. In my view, charter schools are not a panacea, and they drain financial resources from public schools.

In addition, there is a connection between academic achievement and fitness and nutrition. Children cannot learn if they are hungry. The children of families with low incomes can qualify for free breakfast or a free or reduced-cost lunch under the federal Title 1 program. However, those meals are not provided on weekends.

Observant teachers should identify the students who are most food-deprived. Some teachers address the weekend hunger problem by getting the permission of the principal to put excess food from the federally funded program into the backpacks of needy students on Fridays before they return home for the weekend. This is an informal practice that helps students who are victims of neglect or extreme poverty.

On the other hand, obesity can sometimes also be a sign of poverty because some families—particularly families that have been have been impoverished for generations—tend to consume more fattening processed food, sugar, and carbohydrates. Obesity can lead to serious health problems, and it can also be an obstacle to learning. Studies have shown that inadequate consumption of certain food groups deprives children of nutrients necessary for optimal cognitive rigor. Iron deficiency, for example, has been linked to shortened attention span and fatigue. Also, low protein consumption has been associated with low academic achievement.

Obesity is also a result of lack of exercise. Studies have shown that physical activity is a tension-releasing outlet, providing relief that makes learning easier. Children need an hour of exercise per day, according to the Centers for Disease Control and Prevention. However, many parents in poor neighborhoods do not allow their children to play or participate in sports outside because they live in high-crime neighborhoods.

Educators have not been expected to address learning barriers related to nutrition and fitness. Slowly, that is beginning to change as educators realize that it will be more difficult to raise the expectations and achievement of the children of some low-income families if these problems are not addressed. In Las Vegas, for

MSU professor John Schweitzer, a former Robert L. Green student, discusses his current work in a column on the website of Robert L. Green & Associates.

example, health and wellness consultant Lucille Young has been providing tutorials on nutrition and fitness at Matt Kelly and H.P. Fitzgerald elementary schools in low-income communities. Parents, teachers, and students have attended these sessions. Hopefully, these kinds of programs will be adopted by school districts nationwide. If necessary, states or the federal government should provide the funding. The future of education will be brighter when more students have access to nutritious food and exercise.

Teacher compensation is another key factor to improving education. President Obama's RTT education reform ties teacher compensation to the test scores of students. There ought to be a way to identify the best teachers. However, testing should not be the only factor in teacher assessment. Classroom management skills and the ability to engage parents should also be major factors. In addition, there should be funding to retrain teachers and administrators who fail to meet high standards.

The low pay of teachers is also an impediment to addressing another problem that factors into higher achievement—the lack of diversity in the teaching and administrative ranks. The vast majority of the teachers and administrators in the nation's public schools are whites who are trying to relate to and motivate students in urban school districts that are overwhelmingly young people of color. Considering the lack of training to help white educators relate to, inspire, and raise the expectations of kids of color, it is not surprising that we have made so little progress on the achievement gap.

The obstacle to a more diverse population of educators is compensation. Black and brown high school students who go to college rarely enroll in colleges of education because compensation in public schools is so low—not because they lack interest in a career in the field. However, teachers' unions need more support for their efforts to get higher salaries for their members. The salary increases will have to be substantial if public education is to attract more of the best minds in this country. However, naysayers claim that higher salaries don't necessarily generate higher student achievement outcomes. They cite the country of Finland as an example.

Finland has been garnering much acclaim for its student achievement. In spite of the fact that Finland eschews high-stakes testing, their students have consistently scored near the top on science examinations for the Programme for International Student Assessment, a test administered in more than sixty countries. When Finland's scores were combined with the high Finnish results on recent reading and math tests, that country's teens stood out as global leaders. As for the salary comparison, a recent delegation to Finland from the National Education Association determined that American and Finnish teacher salaries are roughly comparable.

However, I know the United States and Finland are not comparable for a variety of reasons. As a professional development consultant for many school districts, I already knew one of the major differences—the training and education requirements of teachers.

In Finland, only one of eight applicants to teacher education programs is accepted, and each public school teacher has a master's degree, a minimum requirement. It's a highly competitive system that selects the cream of the crop. Finnish society rewards those who cross the finishing line by placing teaching among its most esteemed professions. (I will comment more on that later.)

However, in addition to societal esteem, the most significant differences between the two countries relate to race, ethnicity, and economic inequality. This fact was underlined in this section of a Scholastic Inc. report on another American delegation visit to Finland.

What they found was somewhat surprising. Although there are certainly pieces of the Finnish educational system that can be copied over here, the three biggest reasons for the country's success are probably the hardest to replicate.

First of all, "there is a near absence of poverty," says Julie Walker, a board member of the Partnership for 21st Century Skills. Walker visited Finland, along with Sweden and Denmark, with a delegation from the Consortium of School Networking (CoSN) in late 2007. "They have socialized medicine and much more educational funding," she adds. For residents, school lunches are free, preschool is free, college is free. "Children come to school ready to learn. They come to school healthy. That's not a problem the United States has solved yet."

The second reason is all students' fluency with languages. Most students know three languages: Finnish, Swedish, and English.

"They are way ahead of the game on the language side," says the National School Boards Association's Ann Flynn, who made the trip with CoSN. "Nearly every student can communicate in English as well as in their native tongue."

Although Finnish children don't start formal schooling until the age of 7, by the end of their first year, they all know how to read and write, says Bryan Luizzi, principal of Brookfield High School in Connecticut. Luizzi visited the country this year with a Connecticut contingent from Education Connection.

The third reason is the degree of respect and trust teachers are given in Finland. Walker compared it to the status that doctors enjoy in the United States.

Flynn agreed, adding, "I was left with the most amazing sense of respect for the teaching profession. It's how they were viewed in this country 75 years ago." (D'Orio 2015)

Respect and esteem for the teaching profession—that's what this country needs again. However, there are major cultural differences in the esteem barometer when it comes to comparisons between Finland and the United States.

Finland, like much of Western Europe, has a social democracy that protects workers partly because it gives labor—including white-collar labor—much more input on national policies and national budget matters than is the case in the United States. As a result, the economic inequality in Western European countries is much less than America's.

Here are two examples of that difference: First, the district-wide layoffs or the mass firings of teachers that occur in the United States could never happen in

Finland. Second, unlike many American teachers, teachers in Finland do not have to spend some of their own salary money to buy educational materials or food for students because they don't have the huge pockets of impoverished school districts that are common in the United States.

As for social esteem, societal respect in the United States is much more closely tied to compensation than it is in Finland partly because of the protective web of social democracy in that Nordic country. In America, anyone interested in joining the teaching ranks must be ready to accept relatively (globally speaking) low job insecurity, low wages, and little societal esteem. That is why many talented American college students of all races and ethnicities do not even consider a career in K–12 education. Also, regarding the compensation issue, American charter schools are a factor in the race to the bottom because most charters are nonunion operations that pay less and/or provide less job security than the traditional schools that school districts manage under labor contracts.

Technology will be another factor in the future of education. When it comes to the future of education as it relates to technology, I have to defer to two of my coauthors of *Expect the Most—Provide the Best*—my son Kevin Green and George White. Kevin is knowledgeable on this subject because he is a vision engineer and has a company that is developing education software. George has expertise on the potential changes because he has developed Internet projects for media, educational institutions, and foundations. Kevin and George wrote the technology chapters in *Expect the Most—Provide the Best*.

Kevin and George have made it clear that future national and local education policy-makers will have to adapt to a coming digital technology revolution in learning. Digital technology has certainly disrupted the newspaper industry. The education status quo could also be disrupted by this technology. In the book, they called on educators to embrace technology because it can advance personalized learning and enable schools to better track student progress. They explain this in the following section:

> To maximize the power of knowledge-sharing in the digital age, we strongly propose that school districts should consider creating a collaborative, online data self-paced learning repository where student, class, and teacher information can be stored and accessed via the Internet by all—administrators and parents among them.
>
> Systems and software that store student performance that can be accessed widely can be used to track and improve literacy. Teachers and school administrators

Bradley Carl, a former Robert L. Green student, discusses literacy data in a personal story in *Expect the Most—Provide the Best.*

should set high standards and then give students the tools to meet those expectations. By creating a repository (tool), a school can:

- Encourage teachers to take a more active role in the development of their students at an individual and class level
- Empower students with additional learning support material
- Give teachers access to professional development resources
- Engage and inform parents. (Green, White, Green 2014, 110)

Investment in education technology will be driving the changes. Consider the following report from Good/Corps, an organization that tracks innovation that will have social impact:

2012 was a good year for ed-tech startups, something that will take on more momentum in 2013. A perfect storm is brewing for innovation to happen beyond what is currently being done with [RTT] governmental dollars. A brilliant example is Imagine K–12. Founded by former Yahoo and Google executives, and similar to the likes of Y-Combinator, the organization focuses on supporting promising ed-tech startups, getting funding and their rolodexes behind it. (Venson 2012)

Magic Johnson is providing personalized online education in many cities via his Bridgescape academies, which focus on dropout prevention and provide assistance to dropouts who want to complete their education. In addition, the growth in online higher education programs could also shift the compensation equation in K–12. Specifically, universities—in a bid to halt high and fast-rising tuitions—will be looking for ways to cut costs. Online learning will offer ways to cut nonessential faculty costs. As a result, there could be more PhDs willing to apply their skills in K–12 education if there are increases in public school compensation. If we are fortunate, the Obama administration will follow up on its proposals to encourage public school districts to adopt digital technology that will promote the kind of personalized learning that will produce graduates who can help America remain competitive in a rapidly changing global economy.

However, structural racism—an impediment to the kind of wealth building that generates more property tax revenue for poor school districts—is still with us. Consider a 2014 lawsuit that the New York state attorney general filed against Evans Bank, a major lender in that region. It alleges that the bank has been denying mortgages to blacks regardless of their credit ratings. The suit accuses Evans Bank of violating the Fair Housing Act, a federal law intended to ensure equal access to credit. Evans Bank said it has not engaged in discriminatory practices. Some news reports, citing anonymous sources close to the investigation, said some of the nation's largest banks could also be sued for redlining in the future.

There are other areas where progress has been uneven. It has been fifty years since I called on book publishers to include black characters in their primary school readers. A few companies are showing leadership in this area. Among them is the American Reading Company (ARC). ARC's commitment to equity and diversity in publishing is reflected in their numerous books on the lives and cultures of American minorities—especially Latinos and African Americans. Their books are designed to motivate administrators, teachers, parents, and especially students to pursue high academic goals.

For the most part, however, the education publishing community has not adequately addressed the need for ethnically relevant content. The Cooperative Children's Book Center at the University of Wisconsin–Madison School of Education, which compiles statistics about the race of authors and characters in children's books published each year, found that, in 2011, only 3 percent of the 3,400 books reviewed were written by or about Latinos. That is a proportion that has not

Kevin Green provides insights on math education in *Expect the Most—Provide the Best.*

changed much in a decade. Considering that a quarter of all public school students are Latino, this is not acceptable.

Responding to concerns registered by the Southern Poverty Law Center and others, the architects of the Common Core education standards are developing a more diverse supplemental book list for schools. Motoko Rich interviewed Susan Pimentel, one of the lead Common Core standards writers, for a *New York Times* article published in December 2012, "For Young Latino Readers, an Image is Missing." "We have really taken a careful look, and really think there is a problem," she told the *Times.* "We are determined to make this right" (Rich 2012).

Despite progress that I helped initiate regarding book content that black children can relate to, more needs to be done for other races and ethnicities. For example, American Indian children also need to see Native American characters in books. More broadly, white children also need diversity in their books and studies to socialize, cope, and succeed in an America that will be predominantly nonwhite in less than three decades.

Considering the problems in book publishing, structural racism, and expanding poverty, we have not progressed significantly on issues that relate to education.

The current situation is eerily comparable to the 1970s described by then Harvard scholar Thomas Pettigrew in my 1977 book, *The Urban Challenge: Poverty and Race*. He opens by referencing a black senator, a symbol of progress at that time.

> In Washington D.C., these days a citizen can visit the legislative offices of Senator Edward W. Brooke of Massachusetts or those of the members of the Black Caucus of the U.S. House of Representatives. A walk of a few minutes from the Capitol building, however, will put the visitor in the midst of some of the most wretched, degrading black slums in the nation. This striking contrast in the status of blacks in America is both sobering and meaningful, portraying dramatically where we have succeeded and where we have failed over the past generation in the struggle for human dignity.
>
> Most white Americans know of the successes of the Civil Rights Movement of the 1960s and are aware of the political leadership of Senator Brooke and the members of the Black Caucus. Many have seen for themselves the growth of the black middle class, with new patterns of education, employment, and housing. But most citizens are not adequately informed about poverty-level urban Americans, those persons of all races whose needs are still largely unaddressed in the 1970s. (Green 1977, ix)

You could substitute the name "Barack Obama" for "Senator Brooke" and it would pretty much describe the situation today. Obama is a symbol of progress, but we need to move beyond symbolism and address educational inequities.

These inequalities in America are no accident and are not a result of disparities in intellectual capacity. They are intentional and designed. It began with slavery. Slaves were punished if they tried to learn to read or write. After slavery, blacks were consigned to segregated inferior schools. Segregation as a policy has ended, but the schools blacks attend are still inferior, and school practices such as tracking large numbers of blacks away from course work that would make them college-ready persist. (The impact of tracking has been documented by many. The late Wilbur Brookover, a former Michigan State University sociologist who served with me in the College of Urban Development, was among the leaders in research on the topic.)

To be sure, African Americans are at the bottom of the economic rung because of this lack of access to quality education. That is one of conclusions in *Inequality by Design: Cracking the Bell Curve Myth*, a book written by a team of University of California, Berkeley, sociologists (Fischer et al. 1996). Consider the following passage:

To see how politics also affect which particular individuals get to the top and which fall to the bottom of our ladder (i.e. the equality of opportunity), consider these examples: The amount of schooling young Americans receive determines the jobs they get and the income they make. In turn, educational policies—what sorts of schools are provided, the way school resources are distributed (usually according to the community in which children live), teaching methods such as tracking ... strongly affect how much schooling children receive. (Fischer et al. 1996)

Indeed, if we are to bridge the achievement gap, we must have quality by design in schools in communities of color.

Courageous men and women have risked and given their lives to remove the yoke of terror and discrimination. There could be no Civil Rights Movement without action. Although the March against Fear was a seminal event, it was not just an effort to register blacks to vote. The right to an equal education was also a goal. Education can be the great leveler because knowledge can empower the subjugated to overcome fear and pursue freedom and social justice.

Both Nelson Mandela and Martin Luther King Jr. believed that education was the key to social justice. Mandela said "education is the most powerful weapon you can use to change the world." I urge parents, community leaders, and educators to come together to help students develop a passion for education and encourage them to return to their communities and fight for political, social, and economic justice. An educated community will not be a subjugated community.

It is often said that education is the new Civil Rights. That's not correct. Educational equity has been at the center of the struggle for social justice in America since the end of the Civil War. To be sure, we are still at a crossroads. We have two paths. One is an easy path of quick fixes, rhetoric based on fear of people of color, and ignorance about the factors that produce educational inequity. The other is a more challenging path that leads to freedom from injustice.

Sources

Adams, Walter. 1971. *The Test.* New York: The Macmillan Company.

Alexander, Michelle. 2012. *The New Jim Crow: Mass Incarceration in the Age of Colorblindness.* New York: New Press.

American Psychological Association. 1999. "King's challenge to the nation's social scientists." *APA Monitor,* January. Http://www.apa.org/monitor/features/king-challenge.aspx.

Bagley, Edythe Scott. 2012. *Desert Rose: The Life and Legacy of Coretta Scott King.* Tuscaloosa: University of Alabama Press.

Bonastia, Christopher. 2006. *Knocking on the Door: The Federal Government's Attempt to Desegregate the Suburbs.* Princeton, NJ: Princeton University Press.

———. 2011. *Southern Stalemate: Five Years without Public Education in Prince Edward County, Virginia.* Chicago: University of Chicago Press.

Bradley, Ann. 1995. "Tennessee Waltz." *Education Week,* October 1.

Bruns, Roger. 2006. *Martin Luther King Jr.: A Biography.* Westport, CT: Greenwood Publishing.

Carmichael, Stokely, and Ekwueme Thelwell. 2003. *Ready for Revolution: The Life and Struggles of Stokely Carmichael (Kwame Ture).* New York: Scribner.

Chicago Sun-Times and Medill Data Project. 2014. "Charter Schools Show Little Difference in School Performance." *Chicago Sun-Times,* April 7.

Council of the Great City Schools. 2012. *A Call for Change: Providing Solutions to Black Male*

Achievement. New York: Houghton Mifflin Harcourt.

D'Orio, Wayne. 2015. "Finland is #1! Finland's Education Success has the Rest of the World Looking North for Answers." Scholastic's Administrators Magazine.Http://www.scholastic.com/browse/article.jsp?id=3749880.

Education Trust. 2009. "Funding Fairness." Education Trust. Http://edtrust.org.

Farr, Stephanie. 2014. "The Sinking of Sankofa." *Philadelphia Daily News*, September 23.

Farrell, Walter C., Jr., and James H. Johnson, Jr. 2008. "Structural Violence as an Inducement to African American and Hispanic Participation in the Los Angeles Civil Disturbance of 1992." *Journal of Human Behavior in the Social Environment* 4, no. 4 (October): 337–59.

Fischer, Claude S., Michael Hout, Martín Sánchez Jankowski, Samuel R. Lucas, Ann Swidler, and Kim Voss. 1996. *Inequality by Design: Cracking the Bell Curve Myth.* Princeton, NJ: Princeton University Press.

Fitzpatrick, Lauren. 2014. "Charter Schools Have Worsened School Segregation." *Chicago Sun-Times*, October 14.

Ford, Gerald. 1976. "Special Message to the Congress Transmitting Proposed School Busing Legislation." The American Presidency Project, June 24. Http://www.presidency.ucsb.edu/ws/?pid=6150.

Goyal, Nikhil. 2012. *One Size Does Not Fit All: A Student's Assessment of School.* Roslyn Heights, NY: Alternative Education Resource Organization.

Green, Robert L. 1965. "What I Saw in the South." *CEP News.*

———. 1976. *School Desegregation: Making it Work.* East Lansing: Michigan State University.

———. 1977. *The Urban Challenge: Poverty and Race.* Chicago: Follett Publishing Company.

———. 1981. *Discrimination and the Welfare of Urban Minorities.* Springfield, IL: Thomas Books.

———. 1985. *Metropolitan Desegregation.* New York: Plenum Publishing.

———. 1998. *Ownership, Responsibility and Accountability for Student Achievement.* Oak Park, IL: Alpine Guild.

———. 2002a. *Expectations: How Teacher Expectations Can Increase Student Achievement.* Columbus: McGraw Hill SRA.

———. 2002b. "A Summary of Detroit Public School Teachers' Perceptions of Student Achievement." Detroit Public Schools.

Green, Robert L., Janet Brydon, and Wanda Herndon. 1977. "Beyond Race, Sex and Social Class." *Perspectives on Education* (March).

Green, Robert L., Bradley Carl, Kevin Green, and Robert Mount. 2010. *The American Dilemma and Challenge: Save Our Children.* Las Vegas: Robert L. Green & Associates.

Green, Robert L., George White, and Kevin K. Green. 2012. "The Expectations Factor in Black Male Achievement: Creating a Foundation for Educational Equity." In *A Call for Change:*

Providing Solutions for Black Male Achievement, by Sharon Lewis, Michael Casserly, Candace Simon, Renata Uzzell, and Moses Palacios, 21–46. New York: Houghton Mifflin Harcourt.

Green, Robert L., George White, Kevin K. Green, and Bradley Carl. 2014. *Expect the Most—Provide the Best: How High Expectations, Outstanding Instruction, and Curricular Innovations Help All Students Succeed.* New York: Scholastic Inc.

Green, Robert L., George White, and Theodore Ransaw. 2012. *Early Warning Signs of Potential Dropouts: What Can Be Done.* Las Vegas: Clark County School District.

Higgins, Chester. 1982. "For Black History Month . . . An Outstanding American Family." *The Crisis*, February.

Institute on Metropolitan Opportunity. 2014. "Charter Schools in Chicago: No Model for Education Reform." University of Minnesota Law School, October.

The Kennedy Center. 2014. "An Impact Evaluation of Arts-Integrated Instruction through the Changing Education through Arts (CETA) Program." John F. Kennedy Center for the Performing Arts.

King, Coretta Scott. 1969. *My Life with Martin Luther King, Jr.* New York: Holt, Rinehart and Winston.

King, Martin Luther, Jr. 1947. "The Purpose of Education." *The Maroon Tiger*.

———. 1967. *Where Do We Go from Here: Chaos or Community?* Boston: Beacon Press.

———. 2003. *Strength to Love.* Minneapolis: Fortress Press.

Levy, Peter B. 2015. *The Civil Rights Movement in America: From Black Nationalism to the Women's Political Council.* Santa Barbara, CA: Greenwood.

Lusane, Clarence. 2013. *The Black History of the White House.* San Francisco: City Lights Publishers.

Mashabela, Harry. 1987. *A People on the Boil: Reflections on Soweto.* Johannesburg: Skotaville Publishers.

Michener, James A. 1976. *Michener on Sport.* New York: Random House.

Muehlenbeck, Philip E. 2012. *Betting on the Africans: John F. Kennedy's Courting of African Nationalist Leaders.* New York: Oxford University Press.

National Women's History Museum. "Dolores Clara Fernandez Huerta (1930–)." Education and Resources. Https://www.nwhm.org/education-resources/biography/biographies/dolores-fernandez-huerta.

Orfield, Gary, and Susan E. Eaton. 1997. *Dismantling Desegregation: The Quiet Reversal of* Brown v. Board of Education. New York: New Press.

Pettigrew, Thomas F., and R. L. Green. 1976. "School Desegregation in Large Cities: A Critique of the Coleman 'White Flight.'" *Harvard Educational Review* 46, no. 1 (February): 1–53.

Raffel, Jeffrey A. 1980. *The Politics of School Desegregation: The Metropolitan Remedy in Delaware*. Philadelphia: Temple University Press.

Rauscher, Frances H., Gordon L. Shaw, Linda J. Levine, Eric L. Wright, Wendy R. Dennis, and Robert L. Newcomb. 1997. "Music Training Causes Long-Term Enhancement of Preschool Children's Spatial-Temporal Reasoning." *Neurological Research* 19 (February): 2–8.

Rich, Motoko. 2012. "For Young Latino Readers, an Image Is Missing." *New York Times*, December 4.

Root-Bernstein, Robert, and Michele Root-Bernstein. 2011. "Turning STEM into STREAM: Writing as an Essential Component of Science Education." National Writing Project, March 16. Http://www.nwp.org/cs/public/print/resource/3522.

Simon, Lou Anna. 2013. "Message from the President." Project 60/50, November. Http://project6050.msu.edu/about/message-from-the-president.html.

Stanton, Mary. 2011. *Freedom Walk: Mississippi or Bust*. Jackson: University of Mississippi Press.

State News (East Lansing). 1983. "Green Formally Accepts D.C. Position." July 22.

Sullivan, Neil V. 1965. *Bound for Freedom: An Educator's Adventures in Prince Edward County, Virginia*. Boston: Little, Brown & Company.

U.S. Department of Education. 2014. "Expansive Survey of America's Public Schools Reveals Troubling Racial Disparities." Press release, March 21.

Venson, Viktor. 2012. "Best of 2012: Visionaries, Organizations and Innovations Changing the Way We Learn." *Good Magazine*. Http://magazine.good.is/articles/best-of-2012-visionaries-organizations-and-innovations-changing-the-way-we-learn.

von Hoffman, Nicholas. 1966a. "The March Celebrates Flag Day at Grenada." *Washington Post*, June 15.

———. 1966b. "Rights Column, United in Fear, Voices Warning." *Washington Post*, June 21.

White, George, and Heather McGhee. 2006. *A Way Out: Creating Partners for Our Nation's Prosperity by Expanding Life Paths of Young Men of Color*. Washington, DC: Joint Center for Political and Economic Studies.

Wickham, DeWayne. 2002. "Book Fails to Strip Meaning of 'N' Word." *USA Today*, February 14.

Young, Andrew, and B. W. Austin. 1996. "Repairing the Breach: Key Ways to Support Family Life, Reclaim Our Streets, and Rebuild Civil Society in America's Communities." Dillon, CO: Alpine Guild.

Zigler, Edward and Susan Muenchow. 1992. *Head Start: The Inside Story of America's Most Successful Educational Experiment*. New York: Basic Books.

Index